Global Talent Management

This book draws on recent theoretical contributions in the area of global talent management and presents an up-to-date and critical review of the key issues which MNEs face. Beyond exploring some key overarching issues in global talent management the book discusses the key emerging issues around global talent management in key economies such as China, India, the Middle East, and Eastern Europe.

In contrast to many of the currently available texts in the area of global talent management which are descriptive and lacking theoretical rigor, this text emphasizes the critical understanding of global talent management in an organizational context. Drawing on contributions from the leading figures in the field, it will aid students, practitioners, and researchers alike in gaining a well grounded and critical overview of the key issues surrounding global talent management from a theoretical and practical perspective.

Hugh Scullion is Professor of International Management at the National University of Ireland, Galway. He has published work in journals such as *Academy of Management Journal*, *Journal of World Business*, *Human Resource Management Journal* and *International Journal of Human Resource Management*.

David G. Collings is Senior Lecturer in International Management at the National University of Ireland, Galway. He has edited five books, most recently *Human Resource Management: A critical approach*, with Geoff Wood and published by Routledge (2009).

Routledge Global Human Resource Management Series

Edited by Randall S. Schuler, Susan E. Jackson, Paul Sparrow and Michael Poole

Routledge Global Human Resource Management is an important new series that examines human resources in its global context. The series is organised into three strands: Content and issues in global human resource management (HRM); Specific HR functions in a global context; and comparative HRM. Authored by some of the world's leading authorities on HRM, each book in the series aims to give readers comprehensive, in-depth and accessible texts that combine essential theory and best practice. Topics covered include cross-border alliances, global leadership, global legal systems, HRM in Asia, Africa and the Americas, industrial relations, and global staffing.

Managing Human Resources in Cross-Border Alliances
Randall S. Schuler, Susan E. Jackson and Yadong Luo

Managing Human Resources in Africa
Edited by Ken N. Kamoche, Yaw A. Debrah, Frank M. Horwitz and Gerry Nkombo Muuka

Globalizing Human Resource Management
Paul Sparrow, Chris Brewster and Hilary Harris

Managing Human Resources in Asia-Pacific
Edited by Pawan S. Budhwar

International Human Resource Management 3rd edition
Policies and practices for the global enterprise
Dennis R. Briscoe, Randall S. Schuler and Lisbeth Claus

Managing Human Resources in Latin America
An Agenda for International Leaders
Edited by Marta M. Elvira and Anabella Davila

Global Staffing
Edited by Hugh Scullion and David G. Collings

Managing Human Resources in Europe
A thematic approach
Edited by Henrik Holt Larsen and Wolfgang Mayrhofer

Managing Human Resources in the Middle-East
Edited by Pawan S. Budhwar and Kamel Mellahi

Managing Global Legal Systems
International employment regulation and competitive advantage
Gary W. Florkowski

Global Industrial Relations
Edited by Michael J. Morley, Patrick Gunnigle and David G. Collings

Global Talent Management

Edited by
Hugh Scullion and David G. Collings

Routledge
Taylor & Francis Group

NEW YORK AND LONDON

First published 2011
by Routledge
270 Madison Avenue, New York, NY 10016

Simultaneously published in the UK
by Routledge
2 Park Square, Milton Park, Abingdon, Oxon OX14 4RN

Routledge is an imprint of the Taylor & Francis Group, an informa business

© 2011 Taylor & Francis

The right of Hugh Scullion and David Collings to be identified as the editors of this work
has been asserted by them in accordance with sections 77 and 78 of the Copyright,
Designs and Patents Act 1988.

Typeset in Times New Roman and Franklin Gothic
by Keystroke, Station Road, Codsall, Wolverhampton
Printed and bound in the United States of America on acid-free paper
by Walsworth Publishing Company, Marceline, MO

Library of Congress Cataloging in Publication Data
Global talent management / edited by Hugh Scullion and David G. Collings.
p. cm.
Includes bibliographical references.
1. International business enterprises--Personnel management. 2. International business
enterprises–Employees. I. Scullion, Hugh. II. Collings, David G.
HF5549.5.E45G627 2011
658.3–dc22
2010019641

ISBN13: 978–0–415–87170–9 (hbk)
ISBN13: 978–0–415–87171–6 (pbk)
ISBN13: 978–0–203–86568–2 (ebk)

SUSTAINABLE
FORESTRY
INITIATIVE
Certified Chain of Custody
Promoting Sustainable
Forest Management
www.sfiprogram.org

NSF-SFI-COC-C0004285
The SFI label applies to the text stock.

To Denise. Thanks for all your support
HS

To Anita and Aoife who help to keep it all in perspective.
DC

Contents

Illustrations

Figures

Tables

Contributors

Editors

David G. Collings is Senior Lecturer in International Management at the National University of Ireland, Galway. Previously he was on the faculty at the University of Sheffield Management School and Visiting Research Fellow at Strathclyde Business School. His research interests focus on management in multinational corporations with a particular emphasis on staffing, talent management and industrial relations issues. His work in these areas has been published in outlets such as the *Journal of World Business, International Journal of Human Resource Management, Human Resource Management, Human Resource Management Review* and *the International Journal of Management Reviews*. He has edited five books, most recently *Human Resource Management: A Critical Approach*, with Geoff Wood (Routledge 2009). He sits on a number of editorial boards including the *Journal of World Business* and is editor of the *Human Resource Management Journal* and *Irish Journal of Management*.

Hugh Scullion is Professor of International Management at National University of Ireland, Galway. Previously he held positions at the Business Schools in Nottingham University, Warwick University and Newcastle University. He has held Visiting Professor appointments in North America, Europe and Asia. Currently he is Visiting Professor at Poznan University of Economics and Business (Poland) and Universitat Rovira I Virgili (Spain). Professor Scullion has an international research reputation in international HRM and has published in leading journals including the *Academy of Management Journal, Journal of World Business, International Journal of Human Resource Management* and *Human Resource Management Journal*. Professor Scullion is increasingly active in the area of executive education and has acted as adviser and consultant to a number of leading multinational companies including Rolls Royce plc, Sun Microsystems, Scottish and Newcastle International, Aggreko and Telecom Malaysia. Professor Scullion also acts a convenor of network meetings of senior HR directors in Scotland and Ireland.

Authors

Abbas J. Ali is Professor of Management and Director at the School of International Management, Eberly College of Business, Indiana University of Pennsylvania. His current research interests include strategy and international management. He has published more than 145 scholarly journal articles. He has authored six books, including, *Islamic Perspectives on Management and Organization*, Edward Elgar and *Business and Management Environment in Saudi Arabia* Routledge (2008). He serves as editor of the *International Journal of Commerce and Management, Advances in Competitiveness Research* and *Competitiveness Review*.

Fang Lee Cooke is Professor of HRM and Chinese Studies at the School of Management, RMIT University, Australia. Previously, she was a chair professor at Manchester Business School, University of Manchester, UK. Her research interests are in the area of employment relations, gender studies, strategic HRM, knowledge management and innovation, outsourcing, Chinese outward FDI and employment of Chinese migrants. Fang is the author of *HRM, Work and Employment in China* (2005), and *Competition, Strategy and Management in China* (2008).

Jonathan P. Doh is the Herbert G. Rammrath Endowed Chair in International Business, founding director of the Center for Global Leadership, and Professor of Management at the Villanova School of Business. His research on international strategy and corporate responsibility has been published in *Academy of Management Review, Journal of International Business Studies, Organization Science, Strategic Management Journal*, among others. His most recent books are, with Alan Rugman, *Multinationals and Development*, (Yale University Press, 2008) and, with Michael Yaziji, *NGOs and Corporations:* (Cambridge University Press, 2009). He received his Ph.D. in strategic and international management from George Washington University.

Elaine Farndale is Assistant Professor in the Department of Labor Studies and Employment Relations at Pennsylvania State University, USA, and holds a part-time position in the Department of Human Resource Studies at Tilburg University, the Netherlands. Her specialist areas of interest include: international HRM; the power, professionalism and roles of the HR department; change management and HRM; and eHRM and new HR delivery mechanisms. Her work has been published in refereed academic journals and practitioner publications, and has been presented at international conferences.

Saskia Groen-in't-Woud is Head of Employer Branding in the Global Talent Management function of a major international building materials organization employing 90,000 people in seventy countries. Prior to this, she was in charge of employer branding for an Australian subsidiary of her current organization and also ran her own communications consulting company. Saskia has a master's degree in communications and an undergraduate business degree.

Nigel Holden is Director of the Institute of International Business at Lancashire Business School (University of Central Lancashire, UK), where he is Professor of Cross-Cultural Management. In 2008 he was described by the *International Journal of Cross Cultural Management* as having 'influenced a generation of scholars in Europe and North America with his work on knowledge management, and perhaps his alternative approach to the well trodden paths of cross-national values research'.

Susan E. Jackson is Distinguished Professor of Human Resource Management at the School of Management and Labor Relations, Rutgers University, USA. Her research interests include designing human resource management systems to support business strategies and the dynamics of effective work teams. She is the author or editor of several books on these and related topics, including *Managing Human Resources* (10th edition) (with Randall S. Schuler and Steve Werner), *Managing Knowledge for Sustainable Competitive Advantage* (with Michael Hitt and Angelo DeNisi), and *Managing Human Resources in Cross-Border Alliances* (with Randall Schuler and Yadong Luo).

Graeme Martin is Professor of Human Resource Management at the University of Glasgow. He has written or co-authored five books, numerous articles and reports on HR, strategy and technology, including two on corporate reputation management. He also holds visiting professorships and appointments at Peking University, Toulouse Business School, Macquarie University in Sydney, Ca Foscari in Venice and Blekinge Institute of Technology. Graeme also has experience of HR consulting, including employer branding and reputation management, in the UK, continental Europe and Australia.

Anthony McDonnell is a Research Fellow at the Centre for Institutional and Organisational Studies (CIOS), University of Newcastle, Australia. He is a previous Government of Ireland Irish Research Council for the Humanities and Social Sciences Scholar and Ireland Canada University Foundation Scholar, and is a chartered member of the Chartered Institute of Personnel and Development (CIPD). His primary research interests include talent management, global staffing and more generally, HRM in multinationals and call centres. His work has been published in journals that include *Human Resource Management (US), Human Relations, Journal of World Business, Human Resource Management Journal* and the *European Journal of International Management*. He also recently co-edited *Human Resource Practices in Multinational Companies in Ireland: A Contemporary Analysis* and sits on the editorial board of the *Irish Journal of Management*.

Randall S. Schuler is Distinguished Professor of Strategic International Human Resource Management at Rutgers University and a Research Professor at the Lorange Institute of Business Zurich. His research interests are global and international human resource management, strategic human resource management, the human resource management function in organizations and the interface of business strategy and human resource management tasks. He has written extensively in academic and professional journals and is the author or editor of several books on these and related topics including *International Human Resource Management* (3rd edition) (www.routledge.com/textbooks/0415338344). His other interests are in Global Talent Management, management of international joint ventures and alliances and knowledge transfer.

Deepak Somaya received his Ph.D. in Business Administration from the Walter A. Haas School at the University of California at Berkeley, and is currently an Assistant Professor in the College of Business at the University of Illinois Urbana-Champaign. In his research, he seeks to understand how companies strategize and derive competitive advantage from their knowledge assets, in particular, from their talented knowledge workers and intellectual property.

Paul Sparrow is Director of the Centre for Performance-led HR and Professor of International Human Resource Management at Lancaster University Management School. His research interests include cross-cultural and international HRM, HR strategy, cognition at work and changes in the employment relationship. He recently worked on research projects on *Globalizing HRM* for the CIPD and *International Mobility* for Brookfield GRS. He has consulted with major multinationals, public sector organisations and inter-governmental agencies. In 2009 he was voted amongst the Top 15 most influential HR thinkers by *Human Resources Magazine*. He is an editorial board member on *Human Resource Management, British Journal of Management, People Management, European Management Review, Career Development International, Cross-Cultural Management: An International Journal* and *International Journal of Cross-Cultural Management*.

Stephen A. Stumpf is Professor of Management and Fred J. Springer Chair in Business Leadership at Villanova School of Business (VSB) where he has also served as interim dean and Management department chair. Dr. Stumpf has been chief learning officer of professional development at Booz Allen Hamilton and is a frequent speaker, consultant, and facilitator on leadership and relationship building. Dr. Stumpf earned a B.S. degree in chemical engineering from Rensselaer Polytechnic Institute, an M.B.A. from the University of Rochester, and an M. Phil. and Ph.D. in organizational behavior and industrial psychology from New York University.

Ibraiz R. Tarique is an Associate Professor at the Lubin School of Business at Pace University, New York City Campus. His research interests include international human resource management, with a focus on training and development of global assignees, global talent management, and global leadership development. He has presented numerous papers at the Annual Academy of Management Meetings and his academic publications include several book chapters and articles in the *International Journal of Human Resource Management* and *Journal of World Business*.

Walter G. Tymon, Jr. is an Associate Professor of Management at the Villanova School of Business and a Faculty Associate of the Center for Global Leadership. Dr. Tymon has also served as the Management department chair at Villanova School of Business. Dr. Tymon's research interests include employee practices in emerging economies, strategic human resource management, career development, and employee engagement. Dr. Tymon earned a B.S. in Psychology from St. Joseph's University (Philadelphia), an M.B.A. from the College of William and Mary, and a Ph.D. in Business Administration from Temple University.

Vlad Vaiman is an Associate Professor of International Management and the Director of graduate programs at the Reykjavik University School of Business in Iceland. Dr. Vaiman is also a visiting professor in several top universities around the world, including Helsinki School of Economics (Finland), Danube University of Krems (Austria), ISEG (France), etc. He is a co-founder and an executive editor of the critically acknowledged *European Journal of International Management* (*EJIM*).

Ian Williamson (Ph.D., University of North Carolina at Chapel Hill) is the Helen Macpherson Smith Chair of Leadership for Social Impact at the Melbourne Business

School (Australia). He is also a Research Fellow of the Intellectual Property Research Institute of Australia (IPRIA) and an Associate Scholar of the University of Maryland Robert H. Smith School of Business (USA) and the Lorange Institute of Business Zurich (Switzerland). His research focuses on the recruitment, development, retention and the creation of value by knowledge workers. He currently serves as Director of the Asian Pacific Social Impact Leadership Centre.

Foreword

Global HRM is a series of books edited and authored by some of the best and most well-known researchers in the field of human resource management. This series is aimed at offering students and practitioners accessible, coordinated and comprehensive books in global HRM. To be used individually or together, these books cover the main bases of comparative and international HRM. Taking an expert look at an increasingly important and complex area of global business, this is a groundbreaking new series that answers a real need for serious textbooks on global HRM.

Several books in this series, **Global HRM**, are devoted to human resource management policies and practices in multinational enterprises. For example, some books focus on specific activities of global HRM policies and practices, such as global compensation, global staffing, global performance management, and global labour relations. Other books address special topics that arise in multinational enterprises across the globe, such as managing human resources in cross-border alliances, global legal regulations, global careers, and developing the HR function in multinational enterprises. In addition to books on various HRM activities and topics in multinational enterprises, several other books in the series adopt a comparative and within-region approach to understanding global human resource management. These books on comparative human resource management can adopt two major approaches. One approach is to describe the HRM policies and practices found at the local level in selected countries in several regions of the world. The second approach is to describe the HRM issues and topics that are most relevant to the companies in the countries of the region.

This book, *Global Talent Management*, co-edited by Hugh Scullion and David Collings, utilizes the multinational enterprise perspective, along with a comparative perspective. That is, it covers all aspects of global talent management (GTM) in multinational enterprises, including the challenges, drivers and strategic issues in GTM, the role of the corporate HR function, the identification of internal talent, employee turnover and employer branding. In addition, it offers in-depth country perspectives from India, the Middle East, China and Eastern Europe. Overall, the book is divided into three sections and ten chapters authored by outstanding scholars from all over the world, including the co-editors, complete with the most recent and thorough references, tables and figures. Throughout there are numerous examples of what multinational enterprises are doing in global talent management. No doubt it will be a highly valuable book for any global human resource student and scholar or any global human resource professional.

This Routledge series, **Global HRM**, is intended to serve the growing market of global scholars and professionals who are seeking a deeper and broader understanding of the role and importance of human resource management in companies as they operate throughout the world. With this in mind, all books in the series provide a thorough review of existing research and numerous examples of companies around the world.

Because a significant number of scholars and professionals throughout the world are involved in researching and practising the topics examined in this series of books, the authorship of the books and the experiences of companies cited in them reflect a vast global representation. The authors in the series bring with them exceptional knowledge of the human resource management topics they address, and in many cases the authors have been the pioneers for their topics. So we feel fortunate to have the involvement of such a distinguished group of academics in this series.

The publisher and editor also have played a major role in making this series possible. Routledge has provided its global production, marketing and reputation to make this series feasible and affordable to academics and practitioners throughout the world. In addition, Routledge has provided its own highly qualified professionals to make this series a reality. In particular we want to indicate our deep appreciation for the work of our series editors, Francesca Heslop and John Szilagyi. Together they have been very supportive of the series from the very beginning and invaluable in providing support and encouragement to us and to the many authors in the series. They, along with their staff, including Simon Whitmore, Russell George, Victoria Lincoln, Jacqueline Curthoys, Lindsie Court, and Sara Werden, have helped make the process of completing this series an enjoyable one. For everything they have done, we thank them all.

Randall S. Schuler, Rutgers University and Lorange Institute of Business Zurich
Paul Sparrow, Lancaster University
Susan E. Jackson, Rutgers University and Lorange Institute of Business Zurich
Michael Poole, Cardiff University

Part 1

The context of global talent management

Global talent management: introduction

HUGH SCULLION AND DAVID G. COLLINGS

Talent management is increasingly identified as a critical success factor in the corporate world. The topic came to prominence in the late 1990s when a group of McKinsey consultants coined the term *The War for Talent* (for a summary see Michaels, Handfield-Jones and Axelrod, 2001). The typical focus of talent management is on differentiated performance. For the McKinsey consultants this differentiation related to individual employee performance. The key focus of this approach is that all roles within the organisation should be filled with 'A performers', referred to as 'topgrading' (Smart, 1999) and it emphasizes the management of 'C players', or consistently poor performers, out of the organization (Michaels, Handfield-Jones and Axelrod, 2001). Appositely an emerging stream focuses on the differentiation of positions. The emphasis here is on the identification of key positions which have the potential to differentially impact the competitive advantage of the firm (Boudreau and Ramstad, 2007; Huselid *et al.*, 2005). The point of departure is identification of key positions rather than talented individuals *per se* (see also Collings and Mellahi, 2009).

Research suggests that interest in global talent management has increased considerably in the past decade (Scullion, Collings and Caligiuri, 2010, Farndale *et al.*, 2010). A recent report highlighted the growing interest in talent management among Chief Executive Officers (CEOs) and suggested that 70 per cent of corporate leaders spend more than 20 per cent of their time on talent management activities (Economist Intelligence Unit, 2006). Similarly, PricewaterhouseCoopers' 11th annual global survey showed that almost 90 per cent of CEOs surveyed put the 'people agenda' as one of their top priorities (Price waterhouseCoopers, 2008). Notwithstanding this, the Boston Consulting Group (2007) identified wide differences between the rhetoric and reality of talent management in practice and showed that while firms recognized the importance of talent management, they often lacked the competence required to manage it effectively. Commenting on the global financial crisis Beechler and Woodward (2009) concluded that 'talent remains a critical agenda item' for key organizational decision makers. Thus, the global recession and resultant restructuring has increased the emphasis on talent and high value employees for many firms (Guthridge *et al.*, 2008, Farndale *et al.*, 2010).

However, while practitioners' interest in the topic of talent management has grown rapidly over the last decade, surprisingly, academic research on the area has developed more slowly. This book builds on a number of recent contributions to the global talent management literature (see for example the special issue of the *Journal of World Business*, 2010 and Beechler and Woodward, 2009) and seeks to increase both our theoretical and empirical understanding of global talent management in different parts of the world.

Specifically, this book critically examines a wide range of topics within the rapidly developing field of global talent management which is a relatively new, multi-disciplinary field of enquiry, encompassing both strategic and operational aspects of the field. Four major themes run through all the chapters of the book. The first theme is the need to understand talent management in relation to the context in which it takes place. This book will seek to highlight some of the country/region specific contexts of talent management by providing comparative perspectives on talent management in India, China, the Middle East and Central and Eastern Europe. In highlighting the importance of country-specific factors on global talent management the book challenges the primarily prescriptive nature focus of the global talent management literature (Collings and Mellahi, 2009).

The second theme is the need to understand global talent management strategies and practices in relation to the changing strategies of international business firms. Research has suggested there is considerable variation in approaches to global talent management in different types of international firm and that GTM strategies and issues will vary as the firm passes through the various stages of the internationalization process (Scullion and Starkey, 2000; Farndale *et al.*, 2010). For example, global firms which have a growing need for co-ordination and integration of international activities require a greater central control over the careers and mobility of their international managers and high potentials while decentralized multinationals tend to pursue more of a multi-domestic international strategy requiring lower degrees of co-ordination and integration and tend to operate with a less centralized approach. Also, the co-ordination of transfers of managers, professionals and high potentials across borders in decentralized multinationals tends to be more problematic than in global firms due to the greater tensions between the short-term needs of the operating companies and the long-term strategic plans of the business (Scullion and Starkey, 2000).

The third theme considers the different nature of the challenges associated with the implementation of global talent management strategies and policies in a variety of different contexts. The book therefore takes an alternative approach to the prescriptive best practice approach to global talent management which is still dominant in the global talent management literature and which tends to provide best practice case studies of talent management in large well known MNCs (Scullion, *et al.*, 2010). In contrast, this book focuses on the complex problems of implementing talent management in different countries and in different types of organizations, where industry and organizational factors interact with institutional and cultural forces in shaping talent management in practice (Wright and van de Voorde, 2009).

The final theme recognizes the need to develop more comprehensive frameworks to reflect the complex set of environmental factors that affect talent management in the international context and to provide some development in the theoretical underpinning of GTM systems. This implies the need to examine more rigorously the links between the different elements of GTM systems. It has been suggested that firms increasingly seek to integrate their talent management processes closely with performance management practices, staffing practices, training and development and rewards (Scullion and Collings, 2006). However while there is much prescription about the need for integrated approaches to global talent management practices there is little rigorous research in this area, and similarly while some research suggests that leading MNCs adopt a strategic approach to talent management there is a lack of empirical evidence on how universally this approach has been developed (Mellahi and Collings, 2010; Stahl *et al.*, 2007).

We acknowledge from the outset that talent management is in its infancy in terms of development. And hence we were not overly restrictive with regard to how authors framed their respective contributions to the volume. Although we propose a definition of global talent management below, authors were permitted, and indeed in the context of the comparative chapters, encouraged, to frame their discussion of global talent management around the definition most appropriate to the context which they were considering.

This introductory chapter has four main aims. First, it seeks to review some definitions of global talent management and to consider the particular challenges of talent management in the global context. Second, it examines the main factors associated with the growing importance of global talent management. Third, it outlines the distinctive contribution of this volume which seeks to critically review important theoretical and empirical developments in the area of GTM over the last decade. The final section provides a brief summary for each of the chapters in the book to help the reader to quickly identify the main themes and issues covered in each of the chapters.

Definitions of global talent management: exploring the conceptual and intellectual boundaries of global talent management

Despite a decade of debate around the importance of talent management for success in global business, most of the literature in this field is practitioner or consultancy based (e.g. Bryan *et al.*, 2006; Guthridge *et al.*, 2008), not well grounded in research and often over-dependent on anecdotal evidence. Hence, the concept of talent management is openly criticized as lacking adequate definition and theoretical development, particularly in the global context. One of the key challenges which talent management has experienced in establishing its academic merits over the past decade has been the unresolved issue around its conceptual and intellectual boundaries (Lewis and Heckman, 2006; Collings and Mellahi, 2009; Scullion, *et al.*, 2010). As Lewis and Heckman (2006: 139) conclude there is 'a disturbing lack of clarity regarding the definition, scope and overall goals of talent management'.

In this regard Lewis and Heckman (2006) identify three key streams of thinking with regard to what talent management is. The authors aligned with the first stream appear to be largely substituting the label talent management for human resource management, often limiting their focus to particular HR practices such as recruitment, leadership development, succession planning and the like. A second stream emphasizes the development of talent pools focusing on 'projecting employee/staffing needs and managing the progression of employees through positions' (Lewis and Heckman, 2006: 140) typically building upon earlier research in the manpower planning or succession planning literatures. The third stream focuses on the management of talented people. This literature argues that all roles within the organization should be filled with 'A performers', referred to as 'topgrading'

(Smart, 1999) and emphasizes the management of 'C players', or consistently poor performers, out of the organization (Michaels *et al.*, 2001). Collings and Mellahi (2009) identify a further stream which emphasizes the identification of key positions which have the potential to differentially impact the competitive advantage of the firm (Boudreau and Ramstad, 2007; Huselid *et al.*, 2005).

The wide variation in how talent management is defined raises two key challenges which apply equally to global talent management. The first challenge is that scholars in this area need to gain clarity and build consensus regarding the meaning of global talent management from both empirical and theoretical perspectives. The second key challenge is that global talent management needs to differentiate itself from international human resource management. Global talent management can and should draw upon international human resource management (see for example Tarique and Schuler, 2010), but it must differentiate itself from international human resource management to fully establish itself as a field of study in its own right (Scullion, Collings and Caligiuri, 2010).

Global talent management has been defined in broad terms as an organization's efforts to attract, select, develop and retain key talented employees on a global scale (Stahl *et al.*, 2007). A key aspect of this definition is the focus on a key group of core employees, rather than the multinational's entire human capital pool (see also Becker, Huselid and Beatty, 2009; Boudreau and Ramstad, 2007; Collings and Mellahi, 2009). This definition emphasizes an international focus and emphasizes the role of multinational enterprises' internal systems in ensuring key strategic employees are attracted, retained and deployed to best meet the organization's strategic priorities. However, as noted above, a separate stream of literature (Boudreau and Ramstad, 2007; Collings and Mellahi, 2009; Huselid *et al.*, 2005) emphasizes the importance of the positions which these talented individual employees fill in the context of talent management systems and argues that this should be the point of departure for talent management systems.

As the field continues to develop over the coming years, the emergence of a consensus around the definition and intellectual boundaries of global talent management may be reflective of a greater stage of maturity in the field. However, it is equally important that we gain increasing understanding of differences in how talent management is defined and conducted in different national contexts. This comparative understanding will also be important as the field matures. Such an understanding should help to counteract an overly ethnocentric or Anglo-Saxon conceptualization of talent management gaining hegemonic dominance which is not reflective of practice.

Finally in the global context there is also scope for comparative studies which consider how talent management systems operate in different national contexts. For example, Doh, Stumpf and Tymon (2010) explore talent management in the Indian context, while Cooke's contribution considers the Chinese context and Vlamin and Holden consider the Central and Eastern European context. Thus, building on Scullion *et al.* (2010: 106) we define global talent management as follows:

> Global talent management includes all organizational activities for the purpose of attracting, selecting, developing, and retaining the best employees in the most strategic roles (those roles necessary to achieve organizational strategic priorities) on a global scale. Global talent management takes into account the differences in both organizations' global strategic

priorities as well as the differences across national contexts for how talent should be managed in the countries where they operate.

The above definition is a starting point which we hope will be useful to researchers in the area in building and deepening our theoretical and empirical knowledge in the area. We now consider the factors which over the last decade have driven the emergence of global talent management as a key strategic issue for managers and scholars alike.

Factors influencing the growth of global talent management

Global talent management has emerged in recent years as a key strategic issue for multinational corporations (MNCs) for several reasons. Some of these have been outlined by Scullion, Collings and Caligiuri (2010) and are developed further below.

- The effective management of human resources is increasingly being recognized as a major determinant of success or failure in international business. In this regard, there is a growing recognition both of the critical role played by globally competent managerial talent in ensuring the success of MNEs reflecting the intensification of global competition and the greater need for international learning and innovation in MNCs (Bartlett and Ghoshal, 1989). Indeed there is a growing recognition that the success of global business depends most importantly on the quality of management in the MNC (Black et al., 2000; Scullion and Starkey, 2000; Collings et al., 2007).
- However, shortages of international managers have become an increasing problem for international firms and have been a significant constraint on the implementation of global strategies (Scullion, 1994; Cohn et al., 2005; Stahl et al., 2007; Farndale et al., 2010). Indeed, shortages of managerial and professional talent have emerged as a key HR challenge facing the majority of MNCs (Bjorkman and Lervik, 2007; Scullion, 1994) and research highlights that shortages of leadership talent are a major obstacle facing many companies as they seek to operate successfully on a global scale (Scullion and Brewster, 2001; Stahl et al., 2007).
- Competition between employers for talent has shifted from the country level to the regional and global levels (Sparrow et al., 2004). There is a growing recognition that MNCs need to manage talent on a global basis to remain competitive and that talent may be located in different parts of their global operations (Ready and Conger, 2007). MNCs are facing growing difficulties in recruiting and retaining the necessary managerial talent for their global operations and increasingly MNCs compete for the same global talent pool (Stahl et al., 2007).
- Talent management issues are becoming increasingly significant in a far wider range of organizations than previously due to the rapid growth in internationalization of small and medium-sized enterprises (SME) and the emergence of 'micromultinationals' in recent years (Dimitratos et al., 2003). Research highlights the importance of developing a global mindset among the top management team, in such international SMEs and the importance of succession planning in family owned SMEs (Anderson and Boocock, 2002).
- Demographic trends also influence the nature of the talent management challenges facing organizations. Declining birthrates and increasing longevity are the key demographic trends driving a rapid shift in the age distribution of the general population and also the

supply of labour (Taylor and Napier, 2005). In addition, the baby boom generation are aging with Europe and Japan facing the most dramatic shift in population profiles and old age dependency ratios (Beechler and Woodward, 2009). Research has highlighted rapid shifts in the demographic profiles of many countries. For example, many European countries face rapidly aging populations and changing demographics and for example, countries such as US, Germany, Italy and Japan will experience a significant decline in the number of workers aged 35–44 years over the next decade (Stahl *et al.*, 2007). The US will soon have a population dominated by immigrants or second-generation young people with a non-European background. The problem of uneven gender balances is a major challenge for China as the one-child policy has resulted in more boys than girls thus altering the balance of men to women. These trends affect such issues as the types of employees that will be available to employers, and as the labour supply declines in some countries, firms may have to change their recruitment strategies (see also Tarique and Schuler, 2010).

- Another factor impacting on global talent management is that companies operating in a globalized environment increasingly face the challenge of managing highly diverse employee groups (Briscoe *et al.*, 2009). It has been argued that the level of ethnic, cultural, generational and gender diversity of individuals working within organizations is increasing (Beechler and Woodward, 2009). For example, there is increasing gender diversity with female labour force participation rates increasing significantly across the world. However, research highlights that women continue to be seriously underrepresented in senior international management positions (Linehan and Scullion, 2008), despite research which shows the performance benefits of having women in senior management positions (Jacobs, 2005).

- Global talent management is also influenced by the increasing mobility of people across geographical and cultural boundaries which results from globalization and lower barriers to immigration and emigration (Tung and Lazarova, 2007). These flows of labour are also stimulated by wide differences in levels of economic development between countries and in real wage rates. The trend towards greater mobility is higher amongst professionals and high skilled workers and migration (flows of such people are known as 'brain drain') as these talents have much larger emigration rates than for medium-skilled workers (Tung and Lazarova, 2007). The greater integration of labour markets across the world, which is largely driven by foreign direct investment, also increases global labour flow.

- Research suggests that reverse migration is becoming more significant in recent years with many countries seeking to encourage returnee immigrants due to their international management experience and networks as well as their social capital in the domestic market (Tung and Lazarova, 2006). Countries which have traditionally been exporters of skilled workers are increasingly seeking to convert 'brain drain' into talent flow by proactively encouraging reverse migration (Carr *et al.*, 2005). This offers the opportunity to both foreign-owned and indigenous firms in these economies to recruit from this pool which may have significant expertise and potential.

- One trend resulting from the current recessionary climate is corporate rationalization and downsizing, meaning that professionals and managers are increasingly trading security for flexibility and becoming less dependent on a single employer (Sparrow *et al.*, 2004). Trust between employer and employees is decreasing and the traditional social contract based on loyalty, commitment and accountability in return for job security is increasingly being replaced with one where employers see employees as free agents responsible for their own employability, learning and career development (Pink, 2001).

- Researchers have highlighted a trend where people with special talents show little loyalty to country or region, often live outside the country of their birth and are comfortable crossing cultural and geographical boundaries. It has been suggested that such people tend to relate more to other people of similar skills and talents than to a particular country regardless of setting or ethnic background (Taylor and Napier, 2005). Those forming this new global elite have been described as 'cosmopolitans' (Kanter, 1995) or 'global souls' (Iyer, 2000) and due to their global connections and worldview they have little in common with the majority of their fellow citizens. It has been argued that this trend towards more people who are comfortable crossing borders results in a 'talent divide' with a growing number of talents spanning national borders, and at the same time, a large pool of people who are denied the opportunities to be globally mobile due to discrimination, lack of access to education and career opportunities (Taylor and Napier, 2005).

- The move to knowledge-based economies is another factor impacting on global talent management. The shift from product-based to knowledge-based economies and the dominance of the service sector in developed economies has been widely reported. For example more than seven in ten of all jobs in the EU are reported to be in the service sector, and service economies shift investment towards intangible and human assets. Consequently there is a growing need by companies to hire high-value workers in more complex roles which requires higher levels of cognitive ability. The retention and motivation of these knowledge workers is a key talent management challenge for many organizations (Johnson *et al.*, 2005; Beechler and Woodward, 2009).

- The growth of the emerging markets has resulted in an increasing demand for a distinctive type of managerial talent which can operate effectively in these culturally complex and geographically distant markets (Li and Scullion, 2006; Scullion, Collings and Gunnigle, 2007). And while the demographics are more favourable in countries like India and China, the inability of these countries to produce graduates of the quality needed by multinational companies has resulted in acute skill shortages in key areas (Farrell *et al.*, 2005; Farrell and Grant, 2007; Farndale *et al.*, 2010). Despite the growth of unemployment in recent years in these countries due to the global recession, the evidence suggests there is still a scarcity of high-level knowledge talent in these countries and that the demand for such talent remains high (Teagarden *et al.*, 2008; Lane and Pollner, 2008; Li and Scullion, 2010). The retention of knowledge workers and managers in the emerging markets is a major challenge for MNCs with annual turnover rates of 45 per cent reported in key sectors of the economy in India (Bhatnagar, 2007). There is also growing recognition that the preparedness of top talent to move to the new strategic emerging markets cannot be guaranteed. Due to the intense competition for scarce highly skilled leaders in these markets, these leaders are able to be more selective in the assignments they choose to accept, and often prefer to avoid locations seen as high risk (Farndale *et al.*, 2010; Yeung *et al.*, 2008).

- While talent is becoming more mobile, which means companies compete internationally for the best employees (Sparrow *et al.*, 2004; Farndale *et al.*, 2010), there is also emerging a growing technological divide with many countries, particularly those in Africa and South America falling behind in developing the labour market skills in the new technologies that permit participation in the global economy. Singer (2002) argues that technological change increases inequality between highly skilled workers, who can make use of the new technologies, and unskilled workers who may be made redundant due to the new technologies.

Notwithstanding the aforementioned trends which point towards the significance of global talent management in the multinational company, it is apparent that while the rhetoric of maximizing the talent of individual employees as a unique source of competitive advantage for MNCs has been central to the discourse surrounding strategic HRM in recent years, the extent to which organizations effectively manage their human talent – especially on a global scale – often fails to live up to this hype (Cohn *et al.*, 2005; Scullion and Collings, 2006). Research has suggested that MNCs are frequently unable to identify who their most talented employees are and where they are located around the world (Collings, Scullion and Morley, 2007). Thus this text is intended to contribute to the development of our understanding of global talent management and to facilitate our understanding of the potential contribution of global talent management to organizational performance. In doing so, this book brings together a number of contributions by leading researchers on different aspects of global talent management from different cultural contexts around the world. New empirical and theoretical insights into global talent management are explored in the different contexts of Europe, Asia and North America. The emerging markets of India and China are given particular attention due to their strategic importance, their distinctive cultures affecting talent management in those countries and the dearth of research about them.

The distinctive contribution of the book

The book is based on leading edge research which goes beyond the prescriptive approaches which dominate writing on global talent management. In each chapter, GTM is subjected to rigorous critical analysis from a recognized expert in the field. It also seeks to be fairly comprehensive through covering a wide range of themes in GTM and incorporating both strategic and operational issues. The book also seeks to offer an integrated approach across a wide range of topics and themes and to provide a coherent overview of the field of GTM. A key distinctive feature of the book is the global perspective which comes from our contributors who are leading specialists in Europe, Asia, the Middle East and North America. The chapters on India, China, the Middle East and the CEE countries reflect the growing importance of emerging markets and the distinctive nature of the talent management challenges organizations face in these markets.

A common theme of all chapters in this book is the recognition that global talent management has emerged as a critical element of strategic human resource management in the multinational enterprise. The chapters highlight a number of emerging topics which we hope will inform and shape the arena of global talent management research over the next decade and the book seeks to provide a platform for researchers to develop our theoretical and empirical understanding and knowledge of global talent management in the future. The study of global talent management is still a relatively new area of research, and as the emergence of new topics suggests, it is a dynamic and continually evolving area. The chapters in this book offer access to leading edge research on global talent management and we view the book as contributing to the emerging conceptual and empirical foundations of this increasingly important area of study, but perhaps the book's main contribution will not be to provide definite answers to questions raised but rather to open up a more sophisticated and more informed research agenda in global talent management which guides future research directions in this area. A key challenge, however, is to locate the areas of current discussion and debate about global talent management within the wider context of the current economic crises and to develop a more informed and critical research agenda in global talent management in this context.

It is envisaged that this book will be useful to advanced undergraduate students in business and management seeking to develop their understanding of the international dimensions of HRM and talent management. The book should appeal, in particular, to Masters students majoring in international business, international management and HRM as well as MBA students. While the latter may not find ready-made solutions for ready-made problems, the book offers frameworks which will allow them to better understand the nature of GTM in relation to different organizational and geographic contexts.

The organization of the book

The book is divided into three parts and seeks to develop an integrative approach. Taken together we think the three parts presents a coherent and fairly comprehensive approach to the field of global talent management. Our readers will be the judge.

Part 1 The context of global talent management

In contrast to several other chapters of the book, where considerable attention is paid to the operational aspects of GTM, Part 1 focuses more on the strategic aspects. The central theme in the current chapter and Chapter 2 is that global talent management should be linked to the strategy and corporate culture of the firm. The focus of the GTM agenda is likely to shift over time as a firm passes through the various stages of the internationalization process.

Following the introduction, the second chapter by Schuler, Jackson and Tarique examines some critical challenges in global talent management and the drivers of those challenges. The chapter focuses on the strategic HR issues associated with GTM and examines some important developments in the area of GTM research, identifying the key variables which determine GTM approaches. Finally the chapter seeks to inform the work of senior HR professionals who are engaging with talent management issues in the global context and also suggests some new directions for the future research in this field.

Part 2 Global talent management in practice

This part explores in depth some of the core areas of GTM practice which includes internal talent identification, employee turnover, employer branding and the role of the corporate HR function in GTM. These chapters seek to shed light on the issue of the integration of talent management practices recognizing that while there is much prescription about the need for integrated approaches to global talent management there is little rigorous research in this area. Some avenues for further study are highlighted. The differences between standardized GTM policies at parent company level and the practices which are actually implemented at subsidiary level are also highlighted and discussed.

The first chapter in this part by Sparrow, Scullion and Farndale examines the major challenges facing the corporate human resource function in multinational corporations with respect to global talent management. Global talent management is considered from the perspective of increasing global competition for talent and new forms of international mobility. The mechanisms of GTM are considered in the former, and the latter considers individual willingness to be mobile and the organizational capability needed to manage this talent. The chapter highlights how new corporate HR roles are emerging in response to the complex challenges of global talent management.

Chapter 4 by McDonnell and Collings highlights some of the key challenges in the area of the identification and evaluation of talent, one of the key areas of the talent management systems. The key focus is on leadership talent and the authors provide some good insights into both the areas where MNCs should be focusing and on the tools they may utilize to be effective in GTM. The authors point to the need for a balanced approach between the internal and external labour markets and they highlight the limitations of off-the-shelf approaches to talent management.

Chapter 5 by Somaya and Williamson argues that the problem of employee mobility and employee turnover will become more marked in the future due to a number of trends such as the increased pace of globalization, demographic shifts, changing career norms and the further development of the knowledge-based economy. The authors argue that companies must move beyond the old 'war for talent' mindset and instead develop a new more holistic approach to global talent management which takes into account human capital and the social capital implications of employee mobility. They argue that this approach will help managers adopt strategies that minimize the damage caused by employee turnover.

Chapter 6 by Graeme Martin and Saskia Groen-in't-Woud explores the links between employer branding and talent management. Their principal aim is to shed further light on our earlier attempts to combine ideas from HRM, marketing, organizational behaviour and communications to show how employer branding might work in theory and practice in multinational enterprises (MNEs). In doing so they hope to bridge a research–practice gap in this field. First, they amend and develop their previous context, content and process framework of employer branding by linking it to signalling theory and incorporating new ideas on employee engagement. Second, they illustrate different features of their revised framework drawing on a case study of employer branding in a global construction materials company. Their key arguments are illustrated through a case study.

Part 3 Global talent management: comparative perspectives

This part brings together a number of chapters by leading researchers on the nature of talent management in different areas of the world. New empirical and theoretical insights into global talent management are explored in the different contexts of Central and Eastern Europe, the Middle East and Asia. The emerging markets of India and China are given particular attention due to their rapidly growing importance, also considered are the distinctive nature of the talent management challenges faced and the lack of research in these areas. The chapters in this section explore in some depth some of the most critical current GTM issues in the context of these key developing countries and emerging markets, which gives the book a distinctive approach and offers a broader coverage than the standard focus on Europe and North America of much of the extant study. Our authors adopt a critical and research-based approach to identify and explain key trends in a number of countries and regions.

Chapter 7 by Doh, Tymon and Stumpf examines the challenges of talent management in India, one of the largest and fastest growing emerging economies in the world where economic activity has considerably outpaced the availability of skilled employees. The authors review some of the most important contributions to understanding talent management in the Indian context, including the link between talent management and firm performance. The chapter highlights the importance of intrinsic rewards as a key element of the talent management system in the Indian context and suggests that employers should more closely examine non-pecuniary mechanisms to encourage employee retention and employee satisfaction. The authors conclude by suggesting a number of areas for further research on talent management in different types of firms and different sectors in the Indian context.

Chapter 8 by Cooke discusses some of the main tensions in and challenges relating to talent management in China, a leading emerging economy, in a period of rapid economic and social transformation. The first part of the chapter examines some key talent management issues and challenges in the Chinese context and while focusing mainly on managers and professionals. The second part investigates talent management and related organizational practices by drawing on research which provides examples from a number of MNCs operating in a range of sectors in China. The chapter therefore goes considerably beyond much existing work which tends to focus on best-practice case studies of talent management of foreign MNCs operating in China. The chapter highlights some of the country-specific contexts of talent management in China, and in so doing challenges the primarily prescriptive nature of the global talent management literature.

In Chapter 9, Ali examines the development of talent management in the Middle East region, an area on which there is a dearth of previous research. Ali argues that while there has been an increasing interest in utilizing human capital in the region, talent management remains in the infancy stage of development. The particular challenges of implementing talent management systems in the Middle East context are highlighted in a situation where development issues were traditionally seen as the responsibility of state bureaucrats and politicians. The main barriers to effective talent management in the Middle East context are discussed and a number of steps to improve talent development and deployment are outlined.

Chapter 10 by Vaiman and Holden examines the emergence of talent management in the context of the complex geopolitical and socio-economic countries of Central and Eastern Europe (CEE). Talent management and HRM in CEE countries remain relatively underdeveloped in comparison to literature on these areas in Europe and North America.

The challenges of talent management are discussed in the context of transition economies which although undergoing rapid economic and social transformation are still influenced by the region's socialist legacy. The chapter discusses developments in talent management in relation to these tensions and highlights the distinctive country-specific and regional factors which influence both the perception of talent and the management of talent in the CEE countries.

References

Anderson, V. and Boocock, G. (2002) Small firms and internationalisation: learning to manage and managing to learn, *Human Resource Management Journal*, 12 (3): 5–24.

Bartlett, C.A. and Ghoshal, S. (1989) *Managing Across Borders: The Transnational Solution*, Boston: Harvard Business School Press.

Becker, B.E., Huselid, M.E. and Beatty, R.W. (2009) *The Differentiated Workforce: Transforming Talent into Strategic Impact*, Boston: Harvard Business School Press.

Beechler, S. and Woodward, I.C. (2009) The global 'war for talent', *Journal of International Management*, doi: 10.1016j.intman.2009.01.002.

Bhatnagar, J. (2007) Talent management strategy of employee engagement in Indian ITES employees: Key to retention, *Employee Relations*, 29: 640–663.

Björkman, I. and Lervik, J.E. (2007) Transferring HR practices within multinational corporations. *Human Resource Management Journal*, 17(4): 320–335.

Black, J.S., Morrison, A.J. and Gregerson, H.B. (2000) *Global Explorers: The Next Generation of Leaders*, New York: Routledge.

Boston Consulting Group (2007) *The Future of HR: Key Challenges Through 2015*, Dusseldorf: Boston Consulting Group.

Boudreau, J.W. and Ramstad, P.M. (2007) *Beyond HR: The New Science of Human Capital*, Boston, MA: Harvard Business School Press.

Boussebaa, M. and Morgan, G. (2008) Managing talent across national borders: the challenges faced by an international retail group, *Critical Perspectives on International Business*, 4 (1): 25–41.

Briscoe, D., Schuler, R., and Claus, E. (2009) *International Human Resource Management*, 3rd edition, London: Routledge.

Bryan, L.L., Joyce, C.I. and Weiss, L.M. (2006) Making a market in talent, *The McKinsey Quarterly*, 2: 99–109.

Cappelli, P. (2008). *Talent on Demand: Managing Talent in an Age of Uncertainty*, Boston: Harvard Business Press.

Carr, S.C., Inkson, K., and Thorn, K. (2005) From global careers to talent flows: reinterpreting brain drain, *Journal of World Business*, 40: 386–398.

Cohn, J.M., Khurana, R. and Reeves, L. (2005) Growing talent as if your business depended on it, *Harvard Business Review*, 83(10): 62–70.

Collings, D.G. and Mellahi, K. (2009) Strategic talent management: a review and research agenda, *Human Resource Management Review*, 19: 4, 304–313.

Collings, D.G. and Scullion, H. (2009) Global staffing, *International Journal of Human Resource Management*, 20 (6): 1249–1272.

Collings, D.G., Scullion, H. and Dowling, P.J. (2009) Global staffing: a review and thematic research agenda, *International Journal of Human Resource Management*, 20 (6):1253–1272.

Collings, D.G., Scullion, H. and Morley, M. (2007) Changing patterns of global staffing in the multinational enterprise: challenges to the conventional expatriate assignment, *Journal of World Business*, 42 (2): 198–213.

Dimitratos, P., Johnson, J., Slow, J., and Young, S. (2003) Micromultinationals: new types of firms for the global competitive landscape, *European Management Journal*, 21 (2): 164–174.

Doh, J.P., Stumpf, S.A and Tymon, Jr., W.G. (2010) Exploring talent management in India: the neglected role of intrinsic rewards, *Journal of World Business*, 45 (2): 109–121.

Economist Intelligence Unit (2006) The CEO's role in talent management: How top executives from ten countries are nurturing the leaders of tomorrow, London: *The Economist*.

Evans, P., Pucik, V. and Barsoux, J. (2002) *The Global Challenge: Frameworks for International Human Resource Management*, New York: McGraw Hill.

Farndale, E., Scullion, H. and Sparrow, P. (2010) The role of the corporate human resource function in global talent management, *Journal of World Business*, 45(2): 161–168.

Farrell, D. and Grant, A. (2007) China's looming talent shortage, *McKinsey Quarterly* 4, 70–79.

Farrell, D., Laboissiere, M. and Rosenfeld, J. (2005) Sizing the emerging local labour market, *McKinsey Quarterly*, (3): 92–103.

Gregerson, H., Morrrison, A. and Black, J.S. (1998) Developing leaders for the global frontiers, *Sloan Management Review*, Fall: 21–32.

Guthridge, M., McPherson, J.R. and Wolf, J.R. (2008) Upgrading talent, *McKinsey Quarterly*, 1–8 (December).

Huselid, M.A., Beatty, R.W. and Becker, B.E. (2005) 'A Players' or 'A Positions'? The strategic logic of workforce management, *Harvard Business Review*, December, 110–117.

Iyer, P. (2000) *The Global Soul: Jet Lag, Shopping Malls and the Search for Home*. New York: Knopf.

Jacobs, D. (2005) In search of future leaders: managing the global talent pipeline, *Ivy Business Journal Online 1* (March/April).

Johnson, B., Manyika, J. and Lee, L. (2005) The next revolution in interactions, *McKinsey Quarterly*, 4, 20–33.

Kanter, R.M. (1995) *World Class*, New York: Touchstone.

Lane, K. and Pollner, F. (2008) How to address China's talent shortage, *McKinsey Quarterly*, 3.

Lewis, R.E. and Heckman, R.J. (2006) Talent management: A critical review, *Human Resource Management Review*, 16: 139–154.

Li, S. and Scullion, H. (2006) Bridging the distance: Managing cross border knowledge holders, *Asia Pacific Journal of Management*, 23: 71–92.

Li, S. and Scullion H. (2010) Developing the local competence of expatriate managers for emerging markets: a knowledge based approach, *Journal of World Business*, 45(2): 190–196.

Linehan, M. and Scullion, H. (2008) The role of mentoring and networking in the development of the female global manager, *Journal of Business Ethics*, 18: 29–40.

McDonnell, A., Lamare, R., Gunnigle, P. and Lavelle, J. (2010) Developing tomorrow's leaders – evidence of global talent management in multinational enterprises, *Journal of World Business*, 45 (2): 150–160.

Mellahi, K. and Collings, D.G. (2010) The barriers to effective global talent management: the example of corporate élites in MNEs, *Journal of World Business*, 45(2): 143–149.

Michaels, E., Handfield-Jones, H. and Axelrod, B. (2001) *The War for Talent*. Boston: Harvard Business School Press.

Nohria, N. and Ghoshal, S. (1997) *The Differentiated Network: Organizing Multinational Corporations for Value Creation*, San Francisco: Jossey Bass.

Pink, D. (2001) *Free Agent Nation: The Future of Working for Yourself*, New York: Warner Books.

PricewaterhouseCoopers (2008) *The 11th Annual Global CEO Survey*, New York: PwC.

Ready, D.A. and Conger, J.A. (2007) Making your company a talent factory, *Harvard Business Review*, 85 (6): 68–77.

Scullion, H. (1994) Staffing policies and strategic control in British multinationals, *International Studies of Management and Organization*, 24 (3): 86–104.

Scullion, H. and Brewster, C. (2001) Managing expatriates: messages from Europe. *Journal of World Business*, 36(4): 346–365.

Scullion, H. and Collings D.G. (2006) *Global Staffing*, New York: Routledge.

Scullion, H., Collings, D.G. and Caligiuri, P. (2010) Global Talent Management, *Journal of World Business*, 45 (2): 105–108.

Scullion, H., Collings, D.G. and Gunnigle, P. (2007) International HRM in the 21st century: emerging themes and contemporary debates, *Human Resource Management Journal*, 17: 309–319.

Scullion, H. and Starkey, K. (2000) In search of the changing role of the corporate HR function in the international firm, *International Journal of Human Resource Management*, 11: 1061–1081.

Singer, P. (2002) *One World: The Ethics of Globalization*, New Haven, CT: Yale University Press.

Smart, B.D. (1999) *Topgrading: How Leading Companies Win by Hiring, Coaching, and Keeping the Best People*, Paramus, NJ: Prentice Hall Press.

Sparrow, P., Brewster, C. and Harris, H. (2004) *Globalizing Human Resource Management* London: Routledge.

Stahl, G.K., Björkman, I., Farndale, E., Morris, S.S., Paauwe, J., Stiles, P., Trevor, J. and Wright, P.M. (2007) Global talent management: How leading multinationals build and sustain their talent pipeline, *INSEAD Faculty and Research Working Papers*, 2007/24/OB.

Tarique, I. and Schuler, R.S. (2010) Global talent management: literature review, integrative framework, and suggestions for further research, *Journal of World Business*, 45(2): 122–133.

Taylor, S. and Napier, N. (2005) International HRM in the twenty-first century: crossing boundaries, building connections, in H. Scullion and M. Linehan *International Human Resource Management: a Critical Text*, London: Palgrave Macmillan.

Teagarden, M.B., Meyer, J. and Jones, D. (2008) Knowledge sharing among high-tech MNCs in China and India: Invisible barriers, best practices and next steps, *Organizational Dynamics*, 37(2): 190–202.

Tung, R. and Lazarova, M. (2006) Brain drain versus brain gain: an exploratory study of ex-host country nationals in Central and Eastern Europe, *International Journal of Human Resource Management*, 17: 1853–1872 (November).

Tung, R. and Lazarova, M. (2007) The human resource challenge to outward foreign investment aspirations from emerging countries: the case of China, *International Journal of Human Resource Management* 18 (5): 868–889.

Wright, P. and van de Voorde, K. (2009) Multi-level issues in IHRM: mean differences, explained variance, and moderated relationships, in Sparrow, P. (ed.) *Handbook of International Human Resource Management*, Chichester: John Wiley.

Yeung, A.K., Warner, M. and Rowley, C. (2008) Growth and globalization: evolution of human resource practices in Asia, *Human Resource Management*, 47: 1–13.

2 Framework for global talent management: HR actions for dealing with global talent challenges*

RANDALL S. SCHULER, SUSAN E. JACKSON
AND IBRAIZ R. TARIQUE

Introduction

Up until 2008 firms around the world were confronted with a major threat to doing business: a demand for talented employees that far surpassed the supply. This was especially acute in the developing countries that were benefiting from a strong business cycle based upon tremendous exports to the developed nations, and increased foreign direct investment from firms in developed nations wishing to take advantage of substantially lower wages. Forecasts were being made of even greater shortages to come due to forecasts for continued global economic growth virtually everywhere, but especially in the developing nations. Firms worked aggressively to retain their current employees, often providing training and development benefits to make the firm more attractive, and also to develop the talents of these workers. "Talent" became a key word in global business. Firms faced many global talent challenges including having the right number of competent employees at the right place and at the right time.

They also faced the challenge of needing to reduce the costs of operations, thus moving operations abroad, paying lower wages and then having to find competent employees to staff the facilities. All of these challenges were dealt with through "global talent management" initiatives. These were composed of various HR actions depending upon the nature of the global talent challenge. This chapter describes these global talent management initiatives. Some of our discussion reflects conditions that were present during recent economic and financial boom times (i.e., the two decades prior to 2008), when worker shortages were a primary concern. Economic expansion is likely to return eventually, so labor shortages are of continuing concern. Nevertheless, in the near term, this concern may subside somewhat. Regardless of the size of the gap between the available and desired pool of talent globally, a variety of other concerns remain as major global talent challenges.

We begin this chapter by defining more specifically what we mean by global talent challenges and global talent management. Next, we describe in some detail the major drivers of the global talent challenges facing modern multinational firms. Having set the stage by describing the broader context, we then turn to a discussion of specific HR actions that comprise a domain of activity that often is now referred to as "global talent management." Finally, after acknowledging some of the barriers that can make achieving effective global talent management difficult, we conclude with a brief summary of the potential results of effective global talent management, for it is these desired results that motivate multinational firms to continuously improve their approaches to global talent management.

Global talent challenges and global talent management

In today's rapidly moving, extremely uncertain, and highly competitive global environment, firms worldwide are encountering numerous global talent challenges. Global talent challenges arise as firms compete on a worldwide stage under dynamic conditions to ensure that they have the necessary amount of talent, at the appropriate places, at the right prices and times. Firms that successfully address these challenges are able to secure and/or create a workforce that meets the talent needs of the firm in the short term while positioning the firm to also meet their longer-term talent needs. We assume that effective global talent management requires employers to be responsive to the concerns of a global workforce and work with them as partners to achieve business objectives. (For a more complete discussion of this partnership perspective, see Jackson *et al.*, 2009.)

To successfully address global talent challenges, firms of all sizes can and must take advantage of a wide variety of human resource management (HR) actions, which include the development of human resource policies and the design and implementation of specific HR practices (see Jackson *et al.*, 2009). Conceptualized broadly, global talent management refers to the use of HR actions to ensure access to needed talent by multinational enterprises competing in a global environment; it includes HR policies and practices related to planning and forecasting, obtaining, selecting, motivating, developing, evaluating, retaining, and removing employees consistent with a firm's strategic directions while taking into account the evolving concerns of the workforce and regulatory requirements.

Major drivers of the global talent challenges

Global talent management is carried out in the context of a dynamic environment. Among the many factors that shape the specific challenges and responses of particular firms are several major drivers, which include: (a) globalization, (b) changing demographics, (c) demand for workers with needed competencies and motivation, and (d) the supply of those needed competencies and motivation. Figure 2.1 depicts the linkage between these drivers and several HR actions used to manage global talent. We describe these drivers in more detail in the following paragraphs.

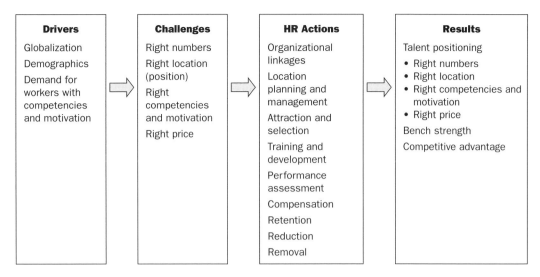

Figure 2.1 Framework for global talent challenges and management

Globalization: world trade, competition, customers, individuals

Globalization is a concept that people use when referring to many different phenomena. Of particular relevance to our discussion are: expansion of world trade, intensified competition among firms, the potential to reach many more customers around the world, and the array of individuals worldwide who now comprise a global labor market.

World trade

The value of world trade expanded from $89 billion in 1953 to more than $10 trillion in 2008. Although the contraction that occurred in 2009 may slow the rate of future expansion in the near term, the value of world trade may nevertheless reach $27 trillion by 2030. Foreign direct investment (FDI) went from $59 billion in 1982 to more than $1 trillion in 2008. The formal labor market expanded from 2 billion workers in 1990 to more than 3.5 billion in 2008. The global economy is projected to expand to $75 trillion by 2030, up from $10 trillion in 1970 and $40 trillion in 2008 (Kearney, 2008; Stephenson and Pandit, 2008). While forecasts of specific values such as these are only best estimates, most observers agree that the long-term trend is for continued expansion of world trade in the longer term. Thus, while forecasts made early in 2009 pointed to a significant slowdown in FDI and world GDP that year (*The Economist*, February 21, 2009), by the end of the same year, forecasts for 2010 were projecting a modest upturn globally.

Competition

Competition has never been this intense and so multifaceted: it is fast developing, complex, extremely widespread, but also subject to the current global economic and financial crises (*The Economist*, February 21, 2009; Zakaria, 2008; Cairns and Sliwa, 2008; IBM, 2008; Hill, 2007). Global competition has forced many firms to improve quality and strive for innovation (often based on rapidly developed and more sophisticated technology), and increasingly global competition means that enhanced quality and innovation must be achieved while also keeping costs low. Thus, small and larger firms in almost every country are being forced to adapt and quickly respond as they compete with firms worldwide to gain and sustain global competitive advantage (*The Economist*, March 14, 2009; Engardio and Weintraub, 2008; Porter, 1985; IBM, 2008; Stephenson and Pandit, 2008; Palmisano, 2007; Schuler and Tarique, 2007; Gupta and Govindarajan, 2001). Globalization requires multinational companies to seek economies of scale and scope, find and take advantage of optimal locations while anticipating future relocations, adapt to local differences, learn continuously, and transfer knowledge more effectively than their competitors (Ghemawat and Hout, 2007; Porter, 1985; Krugman, 1979; 1981; Gupta and Govindarajan, 2001). A global competitive advantage awaits those firms that succeed in meeting these challenges (Daniels, Radebaugh and Sullivan, 2007).

Customers

Customers in virtually all industries are demanding more, and often for less. The telecom industry is migrating rapidly from traditional fixed-line phone service to mobile, smart phones. Companies like BT (British Telecom) are selling "experiences" more than telephone "hardware." Customers are demanding innovation and BT is responding by focusing on services and providing a social networking capability (Werdigier, 2008). And this applies to customers the world over, with some differences reflecting unique characteristics of the countries (Zakaria, 2008). Thus for the typical company today, it is important to think and act global (IBM, 2008; Mendenhall, *et al.*, 2008; Dickmann and Baruch, 2010), which includes being where the customers are. Increasingly companies like Nokia, IBM, Tata, Caterpillar, and BT find that the growing customer base is in the BRIC countries (Brazil, Russia, India, and China) and in emerging economies throughout Asia, Latin America, and Eastern Europe. (For a greater consideration of the talent issues in some of these countries see Part 3 of the current volume.)

Individuals

Individuals have been entering into the labor market in increased numbers over the past fifteen years (Zakaria, 2008; Friedman, 2005). It has been estimated that more than 1.5 billion people have entered the global formal labor market during this time. Friedman (2005) argued that the development and spread of inexpensive technologies has flattened the world and facilitated the entry of all these workers into the workforce. One major consequence is the ability of firms to employ workers in the developing economies of the world at much lower wages than is possible in the developed economies. Weekly wages in the developed economies are equivalent to monthly and even yearly wages in developing economies (U.S. Department of Labor, 2008; Gomez-Mejia and Werner, 2008). The movement of work to an array of dispersed locations that may include both developed and developing economies is most likely to succeed: when all employees have the needed the competencies and motivations to do the work; when the work of dispersed employees is effectively coordinated; and when a firm's HR actions are consistent with the full array of relevant employment regulations in every location (Porter, 1985; Hill, 2007; World Bank,

2008; Palmisano, 2007). In addition to meeting these challenges, as multinational firms make decisions about workforce location and relocation, they also must address the challenges of developing an appropriate customer base, identifying and outmaneuvering competitors, managing transportation costs, reducing the possible consequences of political instability, protecting their intellectual property, and rights and so on (Porter, 1985; Daniels *et al.*, 2007; World Bank, 2008; Palmisano, 2007).

Demographics

Worldwide demographics are another major driver of global talent management. In North America, Western Europe, Japan and Australia, the age of retirement is being ushered in by the baby boomer generation. While this may be a relatively short-term phenomenon in North America (due to current birth and immigration rates), population shrinkage is a longer-term event in Western Europe and Japan (Strack, *et al.*, 2008). The long-term outlook is grim: by 2025 the number of people aged 15–64 is projected to fall by 7 percent in Germany, 9 percent in Italy and 14 percent in Japan (Wooldridge, 2007; *The Economist*, 2006a).

"If you take into consideration the 70 million baby boomers expected to retire over the next 15 years (in the U.S.) and only 40 million workers expected to enter the workforce in the same period, you can plainly see that a shortage of workers is imminent" (Adecco, 2008: 9). "By 2010, it is expected the U.S. will face a shortage of more than 10 million workers" (Adecco, 2008: 10). And according to Stephen Hitch, a human resource manager at Caterpillar in Peoria, Illinois: "We've got a global problem and it's only going to continue to get worse" (Coy and Ewing, 2007: 28). Of course, these pre-2008 projections are now being adjusted somewhat with more baby boomers extending their retirement dates due to significant depletions of their retirement savings as a consequence of the current economic and financial crises (Hansen, 2009a).

While the populations of many developed economies are aging and shrinking in size, the populations of developing and emerging economies are expanding and getting younger (Strack, *et al.*, 2008). Thus there are major variations in demographic characteristics by age and by region that multinational firms need to know and consider in locating and relocating their operations internationally.

Demand for workers with competencies and motivation

Although the pace of globalization has diminished greatly, new jobs are still being created that require higher levels of competencies, which are broadly defined as "basic and advanced skills, knowledge and abilities," or the "right know-how" (Daniels, *et al.*, 2007; Palmisano, 2007). For existing jobs, there is a growing need for employees who are willing to do the job under new and changing conditions that require the development of additional competencies (motivation). For skilled jobs, for example, there is a need for increased competencies to operate more sophisticated machinery, to interact with more demanding customers and to use more advanced technology to perform the functions of the traditional skilled jobs (National Commission on Adult Literacy, 2008). And it appears that these increased competencies are being associated with almost all jobs traditionally performed in multinational firms around the world today (Price and Turnbull, 2007).

In addition to the increased need for basic skills and advanced skill levels for basic entry-level, frontline and skilled jobs, there are a rising number of jobs that involve "knowledge work" and thus there is increasing demand for so-called "knowledge workers." This is true around the world, be it in China, India, Europe or North America. By one estimate, 48 million of the 137 million workers in the U.S. alone can be classified as knowledge workers. Knowledge work often requires competencies that are developed through extensive education and training. Such work is generally seen as capable of having a significant impact on the success of the company (Jackson, Hitt, and DeNisi, 2003). Knowledge workers include managers, leaders, technicians, researchers, accountants, information specialists, consultants, medical and pharmaceutical professionals. In multinational firms, such knowledge workers often work together in teams that cross cultural and geographic borders: "In the 21st century knowledge creation, integration and the leveraging of such "new" knowledge are considered the *raison d'etre* of multinational firms" (Brannen, 2008). "The growing need for talented managers in China represents by far the biggest management challenge facing multinationals and locally owned businesses alike" (Cooke; this volume; Lane and Pollner, 2008). Even if demand for managers and other knowledge workers has slowed significantly recently, the need for highly motivated and talented knowledge workers is likely to remain strong well into the future (Roach, 2009).

Just before the economic and financial crises began in 2008, the most prevalent question was: "Where are all the workers?" Although this is not the prevalent question today, it is likely to return sooner rather than later: "Whether you can hear it or not, a time bomb is ticking in C-suites worldwide. Its shock waves will resonate for decades . . . Surveys conducted by the firm I work for (Egon Zehnder International) indicate that the number of managers in the right age bracket for leadership roles will drop by 30 percent in just six years. Factor in even modest growth rates, and the average corporation will be left with half the critical talent it needs by 2015" (Fernández-Aráoz, 2009: 72).

Just as the global economy began to slow in 2008, a study conducted by the global staffing agency Manpower, found that nearly 40 percent of 37,000 companies across twenty-seven countries were finding it a challenge to hire the people they needed (Manpower, 2008a). A 2007 survey of more than 1,300 senior managers around the world found that the most significant trend expected to affect their business over the next five years was greater competition for talent worldwide (Price and Turnbull, 2007). More specifically, CEOs are searching for industry technical and particularly management skills to support geographic expansion. Many CEOs consider insufficient talent to be a significant barrier to global integration, surpassing the importance of regulatory and budgetary hurdles (IBM, 2008). In other words, most companies worldwide, regardless of size, are confronting and/or will soon confront their global challenge of talent shortage that if ignored will impact their global business strategies (Dunning, 2000; Manpower, 2008b).

This global talent challenge appears to be a concern across many countries/companies, and especially in India, China and Brazil: According to a recent survey in China "88 percent of the Chinese executives said their globalization efforts were hindered by the scarcity of people with real cross-cultural knowledge or experience managing foreign talent; ninety-three percent said that Chinese companies would not achieve their global aspirations unless they developed suitable leaders more aggressively" (Dietz, Orr and Xing, 2008). For entry-level corporate positions, there seems to be a mismatch between the skills found among graduates in many Chinese universities and the types of skills that are needed by local, regional and multinational companies (Lane and Pollner, 2008). (See also Cooke, this volume for a detailed discussion of the talent issues in China.)

The most frequently cited reasons for candidates being under-qualified include: poor English skills (which are needed to conduct international business), lack of experience working in teams, and a reluctance to assume leadership roles (Guthridge, Komm and Lawson, 2008). So while the graduation numbers of countries like India, China and Brazil are very impressive, those who are qualified to begin working in many companies are significantly less so. For example, in India, the percentage of engineering graduates deemed qualified enough to hire is estimated to be 25 percent; in China the estimated portion is 10 percent; and in Brazil it is 13 percent (Guthridge, *et al.*, 2008). Guthridge *et al.* predicted that India would face a shortage of 500,000 staff capable of doing work for multinationals (Engardino, 2007). Clearly, the skills gap is threatening the technology boom in India (Sengupta, 2006). According to Jose Sergio Gabrielli, President of Petrobras, the state-run oil company in Brazil, "The lack of availability of technical ability may be a constraint on growth, no doubt about it" (Downie, 2008: C1,5; see also Doh *et al*, this volume). The supply situation in other major countries around the world is largely the same as in India, China and Brazil.

Supply of workers with requisite competencies and motivation

In developed economies such as North America, Western Europe and Japan there is also an expected shortage of competencies. According to a report from the U.S. National Commission on Adult Literacy (2008) between 80 and 90 million American adults do not have the basic communication (also called people or "soft") skills to function well in the global economy or to earn family-sustaining wages. Alone among other advanced industrial countries, American 25 to 35 year olds are not as well educated as their parents. This same reality is also being found in Arab nations where the younger generation sees that connections rather than education are often the route to career success (Harry, 2007; See also Ali's contribution to this volume). According to the U.S. National Commission on Adult Literacy, declining educational achievement now puts the U.S. at a competitive disadvantage (2008). The lack of technical knowledge workers continues to drive companies such as Microsoft, Cisco and Wipro to plead with the U.S. Congress to expand the number of H-1B visa permits granted each year (Preston, 2008; Herbst, 2009; Wadhwa, 2009).

Today the situation related to worker "shortages" is substantially different from the pre-economic and financial crises period described above, the period of time when "global talent management" became popular (*The Economist*, February 21, 2009). By late in the year 2008, a majority of companies that had already begun to downsize were planning to continue making more cuts that year (McGregor, 2009). So, while the shortages described above are likely to return eventually, in the near term firms may find that there is a surplus of workers at all levels of competency and motivation worldwide. As the economic slowdown continues, it will result in reduced demand for goods and services worldwide, creating excess capacity in most firms and putting downward pressure on prices. The pressure for cost reduction may become intense and the use of workforce cost reduction may become irresistible (Mohn, 2009; *The Economist*, February 21, 2009). An increase in recent mergers and acquisitions to reduce capacity and costs suggests that workforce reductions are likely to continue in the next few years (*The Economist*, March 14, 2009). Competition among workers and countries is likely to result in more wage competition and more governmental support to encourage firms to bring jobs to their country.

Because these conditions will be with us for the near term, it seems appropriate to include them in our discussion and framework of global talent management (GTM). That is, we recognize that managing global talent is difficult in times of both talent shortages and talent surpluses. Because labor market conditions are always in flux, global talent management requires firms to stay focused on how the actions they take in the near term might influence their ability to adapt to changing conditions in the longer term. Furthermore, we include the talent characteristics of location and price (wage level) in our treatment of GTM. For a more complete treatment of this approach and a review of the academic GTM literature see Tarique and Schuler (2010).

Global talent challenges: summary

Thus there are several global talent challenges that firms need to manage as effectively as possible, including:

- too little talent is available now when it is needed
- too much talent is available now and it is not needed
- the needed talent is available in the wrong place (or position)
- the needed talent is available at the wrong price.

As a consequence of such conditions, firms may need to: (a) reduce/add workers and positions in their home country; (b) move to another country and establish new operations at lower cost levels; or (c) reduce/add workers even in other countries. In addition, they may need to train and develop existing staff rather than hire new staff from the outside. They may also need to improve their performance management and compensation systems to ensure that the workers they have are as productive as they can be. In some situations, firms may need to reduce and remove workers from multiple locations. In other words, there are many HR actions that can be taken by firms, both to manage through the current environment of economic and financial crises, and to position themselves for the period of recovery after the crises. Appropriate HR actions taken to address the challenges of global talent management can enable a multinational firm to gain and sustain a global competitive advantage (Lane and Pollner, 2008; Porter, 1985; Stephenson and Pandit, 2008; Palmisano, 2007).

HR actions to address global talent challenges

Due in part to the existence of many drivers of the global talent challenges, there are many possible HR actions that firms can use in their global talent management initiatives (Beechler and Woodward, 2009). Matching an accurate diagnosis of a company's talent management situation with possible HR actions is a first step in gaining and sustaining a global competitive advantage that may result from the successful implementation of the correct action. Several categories of possible HR actions that can be considered by multinational firms include:

- organizational linkages
- location planning and management
- attraction and selection
- training and development
- performance assessment
- compensation
- retention
- reduction, and
- removal.

Organizational linkages

Talent management actions can only gain and sustain a global competitive advantage if they are linked to the actions and strategies of the organization (Nag, Hambrick and Chen, 2007). Nokia decided to relocate to Cluj, Romania knowing that the labor force there was both competent and willing to work at substantially lower wages than the workforce in Bochum, Germany (Ewing, 2008). This move by Nokia fit well with their business strategy, which was to produce high quality cell phones in a highly competitive market near a new market place. The HR action reflected a tight linkage between the firm's business strategy and its global talent management strategy. This linkage was possible because Nokia gathered extensive labor market information and then used it to make an informed decision about where to (re)locate their operations. The business strategy and talent management strategy development reflected a tight reciprocal linkage (Ewing, 2008).

Location planning and management

Multinational firms such as Nokia have been rapidly expanding and (re)locating around the world (Porter, 1985; Hill, 2007; Daniels, et al., 2007; Ewing, 2008). In a period of just three years, IBM hired more than 90,000 people in Brazil, China and India (Hamm, 2008). In 2001 Accenture had 250 employees in India; by 2007 it had more than 35,000 employees there (Engardino, 2007). As a consequence of firms moving rapidly to India, India's seemingly unlimited skilled labor supply was nearly fully employed by 2008. Now, companies thinking about moving operations to India need to develop new talent management strategies in order to attract workers away from their existing employers, and then retain these same individuals (see also Doh *et al*, this volume). As the available supply of workers shrinks, decisions must be made about whether to locate elsewhere or perhaps develop training programs to train for the competencies that are needed, as Microsoft has done in China and Nokia did in Romania (Chen and Hoskin, 2007; McGregor and Hamm, 2008). When Chinese companies locate abroad, they also send many of their own employees to help ensure a supply of dependable labor at the right price (Wong, 2009).

Multinational firms that are now thinking of expanding or relocating operations confront a large number of questions that are the essence of location planning and management, including:

- Why go? Why move at all from where we are right now? Should we rather just outsource part of our existing operations, or offshore part of our existing operations?
- Where go? What locations should we move to? Have we done country assessments on the country locations on such issues as: compensation levels, workforce skills availability, employment legislation, and culture compatibility? An extensive list of items composing a "country assessments for location management decisions for IHRM" is shown in Figure 2.2.
- How go? Shall we expand our operations by ourselves? Should we outsource some of our existing operations to others? Should enter into a joint venture with a local partner? Should we use a merger or acquisition?
- When go? Do we need to go within a year? Do we have time to develop an image in a new country that will enable us to attract the best applicants (i.e., be perceived as "One of the Best Companies to Work for"?). If we enter another country, will we need to develop new ways of managing the workforce? Will we have to change our practices of recruiting and training, for example, for the local employees? Will want to create a common set of HR policies and practices for all our locations?
- How link? How do we link employees in multiple international locations with each other so as to gain efficiencies and transfer knowledge effectively?

Besides addressing these questions, multinational firms will likely need to also engage in more traditional human resource planning and forecasting, i.e., making estimates of the numbers of individuals and skills that will be needed in their various locations, using existing attrition and retirement data of the current employees in conjunction with the business plans of the firm. Of course, even traditional planning tools may benefit from modifications that take into account the fact that the past is not always a good predictor of the future, especially in these more uncertain and dynamic times (Cappelli, 2008). Under conditions of great uncertainty, scenario planning might be more prudent than the use of more traditional forecasting techniques (Courtney, 2008; Dye, Sibony and Viguerie, 2009; *The Economist*, February 28, 2009).

Attraction and selection

Today organizations are finding that they are having a much more challenging time finding workers with the competencies they need to perform a wide variety of jobs, regardless of

Topic	Content	Example Websites
General facts about country	Size, location, population, Infrastructure, country culture, customs, business etiquette, political systems, societal concerns, natural resources, educational system.	(odci.gov/cia/publications/factbook; getcustoms.com; cyborlink.com; economist.com/countries; news.bbc.co.uk/2/hi/country_profiles/default.stm; geert-hofstede.com; foreignpolicy.com; bsr.org; export.gov/marketresearch.html)
Attractiveness of country to business	Familiarity of country, government support; favorable labor conditions; economic and political stability	(economist.com; doingbusiness.org; sustainability.org; bsr.com; news.bbc.co.uk2/hi/business/5313146.stm; kpmg.com; orcworldwide.com)
Competitive-ness factors	Familiarity of country, government support; favorable labor conditions; economic and political stability	(economist.com; doingbusiness.org; sustainability.org; bsr.com; news.bbc.co.uk2/hi/business/5313146.stm; kpmg.com; orcworldwide.com)
FDI flows/ levels	Amount of foreign direct investment coming into a country by other countries and companies establishing operations or buying operations	(economist.com; census.gov/foreign-trade/balance)
Labor market	Regulations, size, competencies, ease of hiring/firing, costs, unemployment rates	(doingbusiness.org; manpower.com; adecco.com; atkearney.com; wfpma.org; pwc.com; mckinsey.com; ilo.org/public/English/employment/index.htm)
HR policies (actual/likely)	Wage levels for several job classes; talent management; human resource planning; union qualities; T&D support; safety and health	(dol.gov; ilo.org; atkearney.com; economist.com/countries; businessweek.com; ft.com; iht.com; bcg.com; mckinsey.com; jobzing.com)

Figure 2.2 Country assessments for location management decisions

© Randall S. Schuler, 2010, Rutgers University (selected websites provided to access current data on topics of interest).

worldwide location (Scullion and Collings, 2006). In essence, workers at every level are more important than ever to multinationals that hope to be competitive, both globally and locally (Guthridge, *et al.*, 2008; Huselid, Beatty and Becker, 2009). How firms navigate this challenge reflects assumptions they make about workforce management. Two philosophically distinct approaches to attracting and selecting talent are evident in the current literature: One approach assumes that some of a firm's employees are more valuable than others. Huselid *et al.* (2009) capture this approach with the use of alpha terminology, e.g., Type "A" players, Type "B" players, and Type "C" players. They also assign these same letters to the positions in the firm. For positions, "A" indicates the most significant impact on the firm's strategy and its key constituencies and positions that offer the greatest variability in performance. For players (the employees), "A" indicates those employees who perform at the highest level of performance variability. The result of this categorization is that firms then would devote the most, but certainly not all, of their resources in their global talent management efforts to "A"–"A" combinations.

In contrast to what Huselid *et al.* (2009) refer to as their "differentiated workforce approach," companies like the UK insurance company Aviva have developed a global talent management strategy that focuses on managing the "vital many" rather than risks alienating the bulk of its workforce by focusing exclusively on highfliers" (the "A"–"A" combinations) (Guthridge, *et al.*, 2008).

From the premise that all employees are equally valuable (vs. the differentiated approach in which some are treated as more important than others), flows a number of actions that help confront the talent management challenge. Rather than differentiate the workforce based on their value to the firm, the alternative approach leads a firm to create differentiated value propositions to attract and retain the full diversity of applicants and employees available in the labor market. For example, the UK retailer Tesco develops separate recruiting and selection tactics for applicants for frontline clerks depending upon whether they are straight from school, are part-time or graduates wanting full-time work. There is a separate website whose materials and language are tailored to that group (Guthridge, *et al.*, 2008). Tactics used for different groups are based on what the firm considers will be most effective and valued by the applicants, not on the firm's view that some applicants are more valuable than others.

Although we have presented these two competing philosophies as if firms must choose one or the other, this is overly simplistic. Indeed, a better approach to thinking about who is included as "talent" may be to recognize that firms vary in their degree of inclusiveness, going from including everyone (high inclusiveness) to only the top 5 percent or so (low inclusiveness).

Training and development

In locations where competencies fall short of what firms need, training and development programs can be used to improve the quality of talent available and at the same time increase a firm's appeal as an employer. In China, Microsoft uses development and recognition programs that appeal to first time programmers. Development programs include a rotation to the U.S. and recognition programs include being selected as a Silk Road Scholar (Chen and Hoskin, 2007).

Multinational firms like Microsoft and Schlumberger also offer attractive career management opportunities. Schlumberger makes it possible for engineers to achieve recognition and compensation equivalent to managers while remaining on their engineering career track (Schlumberger, 2007; 2008). Applying this more broadly, multinational firms can be expected to emphasize internal markets even more (allowing employees to move around from job to job more freely), with rapid promotion for the superstars (Wooldridge, 2007).

To address the need for leaders and managers with a global mindset that is broader than knowledge about the details of local country operations, many Chinese companies have begun sending their best managers to intensive management-training programs, such as those offered through a corporate university or business school (Dietz, *et al.*, 2008).

Performance assessment

Performance assessment is a key ingredient in successful global talent management (Varma, Budhwar and DeNisi, 2008). The performance assessment system at Novartis is central to its global talent management efforts (Siegel, 2008). At the heart of it is a system that grades employees on (a) business results (the "what") and (b) values and behaviors (the "how"). While the business results are unique to each business area, the values and behaviors (ten in all) are common across the entire firm. Combining these two performance dimensions results in a nine-box matrix for assessing employee performance. This assessment process takes place within the context of the business performance cycle, which begins with the strategic plan for the firm and cascades down to define "what" each business unit is expected to accomplish. Novartis employees receive quarterly performance feedback, participate in self-assessments, engage in development planning and career discussions. Together, these practices are aimed at improving competencies, motivating talent, determining training needs and establishing a basis for performance-based pay (Siegel, 2008).

Compensation

Compensation rates around the world reflect today's dynamic economic and competitive business conditions (U.S. Department of Labor, 2008; Gomez-Mejia and Werner, 2008). In response to multinationals locating in their countries, local companies in China and India often must pay Western-level salaries (Wooldridge, 2007; Banai and Harry, 2005). Demands for compensation increases by workers in China caused some multinationals to move and/or consider moving operations to Vietnam and Bangladesh, in addition to keeping some of their operations in China, producing what is often referred to as "China plus one strategy" (Bradsher, 2008).

The recent global economic slowdown has put more pressure on firms to move to lower wage nations, and this trend may continue as global demand contracts and industries find themselves with excess capacity. Nevertheless, as long as the supply of qualified managers is limited in emerging economy nations, firms that wish to expand into those markets will need to offer high salaries in order to secure the talent they need.

At Novartis, pay-for-performance is an important component of their global talent management effort (Siegel, 2008). Using the results of an employee's performance assessment in the nine-box performance matrix, a bonus payout is calculated that recognizes both the individual's performance and the performance of their business unit. Because the market for employees such as those in research and development is global, firms like Novartis set compensation rates at levels that reflect the global environment, even when that means paying salaries that are above the norm in some countries (Siegel, 2008). To help manage compensation costs, however, firms in this situation may locate their operations to second-tier (lower cost) cities. Another tactic is to recruit talent that is currently under-employed (e.g., engineers who are temporarily working as taxi drivers because they have lost their jobs during the economic downturn).

Retention

Retaining talent is one of the biggest talent management challenges for global accountancy firms. Historically, annual turnover rates at these firms have been between 15 and 20 percent. In these accountancy firms, a variety of factors contribute to high turnover rates among early-career employees, including long hours, pressure to study during off-hours in order to pass professional certification exams, and an "up or out" partnership model (Harry, 2008). Jim Wall, the managing director of human resources at Deloitte, estimated that every percentage-point drop in annual turnover rates equated to a savings of $400–$500 million for the firm (*The Economist*, 2007). To stem the turnover tide among early-career accountants, some firms have attempted to increase long-term commitment by providing data to employees, showing that employees who stay at least six years with their first employer are likely to earn higher pay at other firms when they do eventually leave (*The Economist*, 2007). More likely to be effective are retention strategies that include characteristics such as: (a) top management making a strong commitment that talent management is a priority for all employees; (b) assessing the efficacy of current recruiting sources; (c) expanding the list of recruiting sources; (d) sourcing talent globally; (e) constantly monitoring labor markets worldwide; (f) establishing diversity programs; (g) establishing accountability amongst managers for retention goals; and (h) rewarding managers for improving talent retention (Guthridge and Komm, 2008; Caye and Marten, 2008; Holland, 2008).

Reduction and removal

If global economic and financial conditions continue to deteriorate, unemployment will likely spread dramatically (*The Economist*, January 31, 2009; *The Economist*, March 14, 2009; Powell, 2009). The ILO estimated that more than 50 million jobs would be lost globally in 2009, and again in 2010. Because hiring usually lags behind economic recovery, low employment levels were expected to persist until at least 2012. Thus the challenge of managing under conditions of surplus talent is likely to be with us for the next few years. Accordingly, "reduction and removal" HR actions are likely to dominate the global talent management agenda of many firms.

Reduction can involve the reduction of work hours, days, overtime, pay levels, pay increases, benefits, new hires and holidays, and also the increased use of attrition, unpaid leave, assignment for local volunteer work, sabbaticals, and contract employees and outsourcing (Mirza, 2008; Boyle, 2009). From these activities firms can reduce their costs and existing employees can retain their jobs. In contrast, removal refers to the use of layoffs or other measures that result in permanent job loss (Hansen, 2009b). Firms have a great deal of choice in how they shrink their workforces, but their choices are not unlimited. For multinationals, decisions about which HR actions to use must reflect the concerns of various unions, governmental regulations, cultural norms and corporate values.

Integrated and flexible systems of HR actions for global talent management

As this brief summary of possible HR actions suggests, multinational firms must make an array of decisions about how to manage their global talent. Ideally, the HR actions they select reflect both the specific challenges facing the firm currently and consideration of future challenges that are likely to arise as economic conditions change over time. Although the recent economic downturn has slowed business globally, firms still need to hire and manage their talent in anticipation of future needs. Furthermore, the selection of particular HR actions is likely to be most effective in firms that adopt a systemic approach to global talent management. That is, HR actions need to be mutually supportive and internally consistent with each other, while also fitting firm characteristics such as top management leadership, vision, values, strategy, size, culture and industry.

In a study entitled *The War for Talent* (Michaels, *et al.*, 2001), it was found that HR professionals spent a great deal of their time formulating and managing the traditional HR policies and practices such as recruiting, selecting, training, performance appraisal and compensation. While these are important for addressing talent management challenges, their effectiveness results from being linked with the firm's strategies and directions, and this linkage was found to be lacking. "HR underperforms in companies where its capabilities, competencies, and focus are not tightly aligned with the critical business priorities" (Rawlinson, *et al.*, 2008: 23). Additionally, the study concluded that most HR professionals need to do a better job of measuring the impact of HR actions using metrics that are aligned with business strategies. Thus, for example, a firm might track the performance records of employees who have participated in global management training programs and compare them to those who have developed global skills on the job and/or compare them to people with no global exposure, using performance metrics that reflect desired strategic business outcomes such as revenue, profit targets or retention of direct reports.

Results of effective global talent management

As shown in Figure 2.1 there are several potential results likely to follow from HR actions that successfully address a firm's global talent challenges. In particular, we have argued that addressing the challenge of global talent management improves the firm's success in having the right people in the right place at the right time with the needed competencies and motivation and at the right price at all levels and all locations (positions) of the firms (Lane and Pollner, 2008; Guthridge, *et al.*, 2008). In time, these effects accumulate and deepen the firm's bench strength (or future positioning) for all positions the company, both anticipated and unanticipated, in all current and future locations around the world (Rawlinson, *et al.*, 2008).

In the short term, successful HR actions may provide a firm with a temporary advantage over competitors. In the long term, as the firm's global talent management system matures and as learning about how to manage global talent becomes embedded in organizational systems, it may be possible for the firm to establish a sustainable global competitive advantage. Sustainability of competitive advantage is never assured, because the drivers of global talent management are likely to change continually (Porter, 1985; Daniels, et al, 2007). Nevertheless, as firms gain experience and begin to develop the competencies needed for global success, they simultaneously position themselves to adapt as changing conditions require in the future. The development of such a virtuous cycle of effects seems more likely to occur in firms that take actions specifically designed to train and develop the firms' leaders and HR managers (Caye and Marten, 2008; Guthridge, *et al.*, 2008).

Barriers to global talent management

It seems apparent that multinational firms have good reason to invest considerable resources in meeting the global talent challenges they face, but success in this endeavor remains elusive. Based on the responses of more than 1,300 executives worldwide, Guthridge, *et al.* (2008) identified several barriers to the use of HR actions for global talent management. Many of these barriers to successful talent management exist for domestic firms, but they become more complex and difficult to overcome in global firms. The barriers include:

- the fact that senior managers do not spend enough time on talent management, perhaps thinking that there are other more pressing things to be concerned with;
- organizational structures, whether based on regions, products, or functions, that inhibit collaboration and the sharing of resources across boundaries;
- middle and front line managers who are not sufficiently involved in or responsible for employees' careers, perhaps because they see these activities as less important than managing the business, and/or because they require such a long-term perspective;
- managers are uncomfortable and/or unwilling to acknowledge performance differences among employees—a step that is required in order to take actions to improve performance;
- managers at all levels who are not sufficiently involved in the formulation of the firm's talent management strategy and therefore have a limited sense of ownership and understanding of actions designed to help manage the firm's global talent;
- HR departments that lack the competencies needed to address the global talent challenge effectively, and/or lack the respect of other executives whose cooperation is needed to implement appropriate HR actions.

While there are many barriers to overcome, multinational firms such as IBM, Toyota, Procter & Gamble, Novartis, ThyssenKrupp, and Schlumberger have shown that success is possible with the commitment, leadership and involvement of the top management (Farndale, Scullion and Sparrow, 2010; Takeuchi, Osono and Shimizu, 2008; Lane and Pollner, 2008; Palmisano, 2007).

Conclusion

Many of the most pressing global challenges facing global firms today are directly related to human capital challenges, and more specifically global talent challenges (Rawlinson, *et al.*, 2008; Adecco, 2008; Walker, 2007; Scott, *et al.*, 2007; Price and Turnbull, 2007;

Scullion and Collings, 2006). These global talent challenges arise due to the ever-changing characteristics of the environment. In particular, among the major drivers are: enhanced globalization, evolving demographics, the need for more competencies and motivation, and the growing shortage/surplus of needed competencies and motivation. For firms throughout the world, the changing environment—particularly during volatile economic and financial periods of boom-and-bust such as those experienced in recent years—presents both global talent challenges and an opportunity to gain a sustainable global competitive advantage (Porter, 1985; Cairns and Sliwa, 2008). In this chapter we have sought to provide a brief overview of possible HR actions that can be used to build an integrated and flexible system for global talent management, and described some of the barriers to success in this endeavor. The greatest challenge may simply be the need for firms to be relentless in their efforts to effectively manage global talent, for even when success is achieved in the near term, new HR actions will soon be required simply to stay one step ahead of competitors. For the HR profession, an immediate challenge is to develop the supply of HR talent with the competencies and motivations required to understand the drivers that create global talent management challenges, develop systems that are tailored to address a particular firm's specific global talent needs, and work in partnership with the senior management team to ensure a close linkage between HR actions programs and the strategic objectives of the firm.

Acknowledgment

* The authors wish to express thanks for preparatory comments and suggestions to Clemens Brugger, Gary Bruton, Dave Collings, Tim Devinney, Bill Guth, Wes Harry, Mike Hitt, Paul Sparrow, Mark Saxer, Hugh Scullion, Ken Smith, Rosalie Tung and Nadia Wicki. Supported by a grant from the School of Management and Labor Relations, Rutgers University.

References

Adecco (2008). *The Next Decade's Talent War*. Geneva: Adecco.

Banai, M. and Harry, W. (2005). Transnational managers : a different expatriate experience. *International Studies of Management and Organization* 34 (3): 96–120.

Beechler, S. and Woodward, I.C. (2009), Global talent management. *Journal of International Management* (in press).

Boyle, M. (2009). Cutting costs without cutting jobs. *Business Week*, March 9:55.

Bradsher, K. (2008). Investors seek Asian options to costly China. *The New York Times*, June 18: A 20.

Brannen, M.Y. (2008). What would it take for Japanese managers to be globally agile? Pressing concerns for Japanese talent management. Paper presented at the Academy of Management Annual Conference, 9–13 August, Anaheim, CA.

Cairns, G. and Sliwa, M. (2008). *A Very Short, Fairly Interesting and Reasonably Cheap Book about International Business*. London: Sage.

Cappelli, P. (2008). *Talent on Demand*. Harvard Business School: Boston.

Caye, J-M. and Marten, I. (2008). *Talent Management*. The Boston Consulting Group: Boston.

Chen, W. and Hoskin, J. (2007). Multinational corporations in China: Finding and keeping talent. *SHRM*: October:1–4.

Courtney, H. (2008). A fresh look at strategy under uncertainty: an interview. *McKinsey Quarterly*, December.

Coy, P. and Ewing, E. (2007). Where are all the workers? *Business Week*, April 9: 28–31.

Daniels, J.D., Radebaugh, L.H. and Sullivan, D.P. (2007). *International Business: Environment and Operations*. Upper Saddle River, NJ: Pearson/Prentice-Hall.

Dickmann, M. and Baruch, Y. (2010) *Global Career Management*. London: Routledge.

Dietz, M.C., Orr, G., and Xing, J. (2008). How Chinese companies can succeed abroad. *McKinsey Quarterly*, May.

Deutsch, C. (2008). At home in the world. *The New York Times*, February 14: C1, C4.

Downie, A. (2008). Wanted: skilled workers for a growing economy in Brazil. *The New York Times*: C1; 5.

Dunning, J. (2000). The eclectic paradigm as an envelope for economic and business theories of MNE activity. *International Business Review*, 9: 163–190.

Dye, R., Sibony, O. and Viguerie, S.P. (2009). Strategic planning: Three tips for 2009. *The McKinsey Quarterly*, April.

The Economist (2006a). The battle for brainpower. *The Economist*, October 5.

The Economist (2006b). The CEO's role in talent management: How top executives from ten countries are nurturing the leaders of tomorrow. *The Economist*, London: The Economist Intelligence Unit.

The Economist (2007). Accounting for good people. *The Economist*, July 21: 68–70.

The Economist (2009). Swinging the axe. *The Economist*, January 31: 69–70.

The Economist (2009). Turning their backs on the world. *The Economist*, February 21: 59–61.

The Economist (2009). Managing in a fog. *The Economist*, February 28: 67–68.

The Economist (2009). When jobs disappear. *The Economist*, March 14: 71–73.

Engardino, P. (2007). India's talent gets loads of TLC. *Business Week*, August 20 and 27: 52–53.

Engardio, P. and Weintraub, A. (2008). Outsourcing the drug industry. *Business Week*, September 15: 49–53.

Ewing, E. (2008). Nokia's new home in Romania. *Business Week*, January.

Farndale, E., Scullion, H. and Sparrow, P. (2010). The role of the corporate HR function in global talent management. *Journal of World Business*: 46, #2.

Fernández-Aráoz, C. (2009). The coming fight for executive talent. *Business Week*, December.

Friedman, T. L. (2005). *The World is Flat*. New York: Farrar, Straus and Giroux.

Ghemawat, P. and Hout, T. (2007). *Redefining Global Strategy*. Boston: Harvard Business School Press.

Gomez-Mejia, L. and Werner, S. (2008). *Global Compensation*. London: Routledge.

Gupta, A. and Govindarajan, V. (2001). Converting global presence into global competitive advantage. *Academy of Management Executive*, 15: 45–58.

Guthridge, M. and Komm, A.B. (2008). Why multinationals struggle to manage talent. *The McKinsey Quarterly*, May: 1–5.

Guthridge, M., Komm, A.B., and Lawson, E. (2008). Making talent management a strategic priority. *The McKinsey Quarterly*, January: 49–59.

Hamm, S. (2008). International isn't just IBM's first name. *Business Week*, January.

Hansen, F. (2009a). Downturn dilemma. *Workforce Management*, February 16: 29–30.

Hansen, F. (2009b). HR in the downturn. *Workforce Management*, February 16: 16.

Harry, W. (2007). Employment creation and localization: The crucial human resources issues for the GCC. *International Journal of Human Resource Management*, 18 (1): 132–146.

Harry, W. (2008). Personal communication, 1 October 2008.

Herbst, M. (2009). A narrowing window for foreign workers? *Business Week*, March 16: 50.

Huselid, M. A., Beatty, R. W. and Becker, B. (2009). *The Differentiated Workforce*. Boston: Harvard Business School Press.

Hill, C.W.L. (2007). *International Business: Competing in the Global Marketplace*, 6th edition, New York: McGraw-Hill/Irwin.

Holland, K. (2008). Working all corners in a global talent hunt. *The New York Times*, February 24: 17.

IBM (2008). *The Enterprise of the Future*. New York: IBM.

Jackson, S.E., Hitt, M.A. and DeNisi, A. (2003). *Managing Knowledge for Sustained Competitive Advantage*. San Francisco: Jossey-Bass.

Jackson, S.E., Schuler, R.S., and Werner, S. (2009). *Managing Human Resources*, 10th edition, Mason, OH: Cengage, Southwestern Publishing Company.

Kearney (2008). *Globalization 3.0*, Boston: A.T. Kearney.

Krugman, P. (1979). A model of innovation, technology transfer, and the world distribution of income. *The Journal of Political Economy*, 87 (2): 253–66.

Krugman, P. (1981). Intraindustry specialization and the gains from trade. *The Journal of Political Economy*, 89 (4): 959–73.

Lane, K. and Pollner, F. (2008). How to address China's growing talent shortage. *McKinsey Quarterly*, 3: 33–40.

McGregor, J. (2009). A pink-slip pandemic. *Business Week*, March 23 & 30: 14.

McGregor, J. and Hamm, S. (2008). Managing the global workforce. *Business Week*, January 28: 36–51.

Manpower (2008a). Borderless Workforce Survey. *Manpower White Paper*.

Manpower (2008b). Confronting the Talent Crunch. *Manpower White Paper*.

Mendenhall, M.E., Osland, J.S., Bird, A., Oddou, G.R. and Maznevski, M.L.G (2008). *Global Leadership: Research, Practice and Development*. London: Routledge.

Michaels, E., Handfield-Jones, H. and Axelrod, B. (2001). *The War for Talent*. Boston: Harvard Business School Press.

Mirza, B. (2008). Look at alternatives to layoffs, *SHRM On-line*, December 29.

Mohn, T. (2009). The long trip home. *The New York Times*, March 10: D 1,5.

Nag, R., Hambrick, D.C., and Chen, M-J. (2007). What is strategic management, really? Inductive derivation of a consensus definition of the field. *Strategic Management Journal*, 28: 935–955.

National Commission on Adult Literacy (2008). *Reach Higher America: Overcoming Crisis in the U.S. Workforce*. Washington, D.C.: National Commission on Adult Literacy, June.

Palmisano, S. (2007). The globally integrated enterprise. *Foreign Affairs*, 85, 3: 127–136.

Porter, M. (1985). *Competitive Advantage: Creating and sustaining superior performance*. New York: Free Press.

Powell, B. (2009). China's hard landing. *Fortune*, March 16: 114–120.

Preston, J. (2008). Visa application period opens for highly skilled workers. *The New York Times*, April 1, A:5.

Price, C. and Turnbull, D. (2007). The organizational challenges of global trends: A McKinsey global survey. *McKinsey Quarterly*, May.

Rawlinson, R., McFarland, and Post, L. (2008). A talent for talent. *Strategy + Business*, Autumn: 21–24.

Roach, S. (2009). Testimony before the Chinese American Committee on Economic and Security, February 17.

Schlumberger Annual Reports (2007; 2008)

Schuler, R. S. and Tarique, I. (2007). International HRM: A North America Perspective, a Thematic Update and Suggestions for Future Research. *International Journal of Human Resource Management*, May: 15–43.

Scott, V., Schultze, A., Huseby, T., and Dekhane, N. (2007). *Where Have all the Workers Gone?* Chicago: A.T. Kearney.

Scullion, H. and Collings, D. (2006). *Global Staffing Systems*, Routledge: London.

Sengupta, S. (2006). Skills gap threatens technology boom in India. *The New York Times*, October 17: A1; A6.

Siegel, J. (2008). Global talent management at Novartis. *Harvard Business School* (Case #9–708–486).

Stephenson, E. and Pandit, A. (2008). *How Companies Act on Global Trends: A McKinsey Global Survey*, Boston: McKinsey.

Strack, R., Baier, J., and Fahlander, A. (2008). Managing demographic risk, *Harvard Business Review*, February: 2–11.

Strack, R., Dyer, A., Caye, J-M., Minto, A., Leicht, M., Francoeur, F., Ang, D., Bohm, H. and McDonnell, M. (2009). Creating competitive advantage: How to address HR challenges worldwide through 2015 (BCG/World Federation of People Management Associations: Special Report).

Takeuchi, H., Osono, E., and Shimizu, N. (2008). The contradictions that drive Toyota's success. *Harvard Business Review*, June: 96–104.

Tarique, I. and Schuler, R.S. (2010). Framework and review of global talent management and suggestions for future research. *Journal of World Business*, H. Scullion and D. Collings (special guest editors), 46, #2.

U.S. Department of Labor, (2008). *International Comparisons of Hourly Compensation Costs in Manufacturing, 2006*, Washington, D.C.: Bureau of Labor Statistics.

Varma, A., Budhwar, P. and DeNisi, A. (2008). *Performance Management Systems*, London: Routledge.

Wadhwa, V. (2009). America's immigrant brain drain. *Business Week*, March 16: 68.

Walker, M. (2007). *Globalization 3.0* (*Wilson Quarterly* and reprinted by A.T. Kearney, 2008.

Werdigier, J. (2008). Retooling for a changing telecom landscape. *The New York Times*, March 8: C2.

Wong, E. (2009). China's export of labor faces growing scorn. *The New York Times*, December 21: A1–9.

Wooldridge, A. (2007) The battle for the best. *The Economist: The World in 2007*: 104.

World Bank (2008). See the six indicators the World Bank uses to describe the extent of employment regulations in countries at www.doingbusiness.org.

Zakaria, F. (2008). *The post-American world*. New York: Norton.

Part 2

Global talent management in practice

3 Global talent management: new roles for the corporate HR function?

PAUL SPARROW, HUGH SCULLION
AND ELAINE FARNDALE

Introduction

As we have seen in Part I, the issue of global talent management (GTM) is an interesting area for research and practice as competition between employers has become more generic and has shifted from the country level to the regional and global levels (Sparrow, *et al.*, 2004; Ashton and Morton, 2005). This importance placed on *global* talent, and the related supply and demand pressures, have the potential to impact on the role of human resource management (HRM) in multinational corporations (MNCs) operating at this level (Novicevic and Harvey, 2001; Scullion and Starkey, 2000). However, the role of the corporate human resource (HR) function in such organizations has until recently been neglected in the international HRM literature (Farndale, *et al.*, 2010).

When talking about global *talent* management, we define talent in terms of the key positions within an organization, rather than as the 'stars' who will fill these positions (Beechler and Woodward, 2009; Collings and Mellahi, 2009). This view of GTM means focusing on developing a global pool of people to fill these positions, as well as creating a differentiated set of HRM practices to support people filling them (Kim, *et al.*, 2003). It creates two new opportunities for the study of GTM:

1 both a top–down (management controlled approach to moving talent around the firm) and bottom–up (self-initiated, culture-driven flow of talent through key positions) perspective on the impact of GTM on the corporate HR (CHR) role;
2 an expansion of the territory that might legitimately be considered part of a GTM system into marketing-driven concerns such as market-mapping and employer branding (Sparrow, 2007).

This focus on *global* flows of talent implies new roles for the CHR function: in addition to the well known strategic roles for HR laid down by Ulrich and Brockbank (2005), the multinational context requires a more nuanced approach which considers additional international pressures (Farndale, *et al.*, 2010). We focus our discussion on four core roles for CHR derived from the extant literature (Champion of processes, Guardian of culture, Network leadership and intelligence, and Managers of internal receptivity) and explore how these roles support GTM in MNCs. These four roles are summarized in Figure 3.1, showing each role's unique activities and interconnections.

We examine the challenges faced by the CHR function in managing talent on a global basis and expand upon these emergent roles for the function. We then take an in-depth look at the importance of the context in which a firm is operating in order to understand better how these roles might play out in reality. Finally, we use these analyses to identify and discuss the key issues which still need to be addressed to advance our understanding of the theory and practice of GTM and the implications for CHR.

The corporate HR function in MNCs

Previous research suggests that HR involvement in strategic decision-making is patchy and mostly concerned with implementation rather than the formulation of strategy. In Europe the HR function remains low in influence relative to other major functions (Brewster, 1994; Farndale, 2005). However, the more rapid pace of internationalization and globalization leads to a more strategic role for HRM (Novicevic and Harvey, 2001; Scullion and Starkey, 2000). For example, in the US, some claim that the status of HR managers has increased due to the perception that their contribution to business performance has increased (Schuler, et al., 2002). An influential study concludes 'while there is some divergence of opinion, the dominant view in the international literature is that HR specialists, senior or otherwise, are not typically key players in the development of

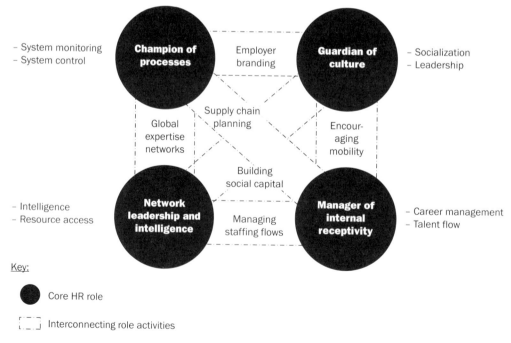

Key:

● Core HR role

⌐ ⌐ Interconnecting role activities

Figure 3.1 Corporate HR roles in global talent management

corporate strategy' (Hunt and Boxall, 1998: 770). While there have been attempts to integrate international corporate strategy and human resource strategy (see, for example: Taylor, *et al.*, 1996), the role of the corporate HR function has been relatively neglected in the literature, particularly in the context of the MNC.

Recent research has begun to shed more light on this topic (Evans, *et al.*, 2002; Farndale, *et al.*, 2010; Kelly, 2001; Sparrow, *et al.*, 2004; Sparrow, 2007). Empirical research on UK MNCs has highlighted a considerable variation in the roles of the CHR function in different types of international firms (Scullion and Starkey, 2000). In centralized/global firms the CHR function undertook a wide range of activities and the key roles were management development, succession planning, career planning, strategic staffing, top management rewards and managing the mobility of international managers. The growing need for coordination and integration of international activities required greater central control over the mobility of top managers, expatriates and high-potential staff. Strategic staffing was under central control and corporate HR played a key role in the allocation of strategic human resources – including control over the mobility of expatriates worldwide (Scullion and Starkey, 2000). In the global firms, international assignments were increasingly linked to the organizational and career development process, and the management development function became more important for developing high potential local managers and third country national staff. The practice of developing the latter two groups through developmental transfers to corporate HQ, known as inpatriation, was becoming increasingly important in these global firms (Harvey, *et al.*, 2001).

Highly decentralized firms, on the other hand, tended to pursue more of a multidomestic international strategy requiring lower degrees of co-ordination and integration, with the CHR executives concentrating on a narrower range of activities focused on management development and succession planning for senior executives. The co-ordination of transfers of managers across borders was more problematic than in the global firms due to the greater tensions between the short-term needs of the operating companies and the long-term strategic plans of the business (Scullion and Starkey, 2000). Informal controls were therefore crucial in introducing a degree of corporate control, e.g. centralized control over management development for senior managers. In this context Bartlett and Ghoshal (1989) refer to the necessity of creating a matrix in the mindset of managers in order to deal with all the diversity and complexity involved in managing the transnational organization and argue that the socialization of managers in key positions at headquarters and subsidiaries is crucial.

All these studies emphasize the key role of CHR in GTM for the *top* talent across the company (Farndale, *et al.*, 2010; Kelly, 2001; Novicevic and Harvey, 2001). There is evidence that for European firms shortages of international management talent have been a significant constraint on the successful implementation of global strategies (Scullion and Brewster, 2001). In particular, a shortage of leadership talent is a major obstacle many companies face as they seek to operate on a global scale. The rhetoric of maximizing the talent of individual employees as a unique source of competitive advantage has been a central element of strategic HR policy in recent years (Scullion, 1994; Lewis and Heckman, 2006; Frank and Taylor, 2004). This reflects growing recognition both of the key role played by globally competent managerial talent in ensuring the success of MNCs given the intensification of global competition and the greater need for international learning and innovation in MNCs (Bartlett and Ghoshal, 1989). However, the extent to which organizations effectively manage their talent in this respect often fails to live up to the hype (Cappelli, 2008).

Research suggests that CHR must develop core management competencies focused on the talent management issues associated with senior management development, succession planning and developing a cadre of global managers (e.g. Evans, *et al.*, 2002; Scullion and Starkey, 2000; Sparrow, 2007). MNCs increasingly demand highly-skilled, highly-flexible, mobile employees who can deliver the desired results, operating sometimes in difficult circumstances (Roberts, *et al.*, 1998). This requires innovative responses from the CHR function. New tools, processes and coordination capabilities are required to focus in particular on the sourcing, retention and career planning of the key talent across the global network. This represents a major challenge and opportunity as CHR managers seek to redefine their role in a context of downsizing, restructuring and outsourcing. Failure to achieve this by the CHR function can have major consequences for the implementation of the internationalization strategy, and for achieving the levels of competitive advantage which a firm's talent can create (Evans, *et al.*, 2002).

Research also suggests CHR can make a vital contribution to support the strategic learning mission of the organization. Pucik (1992) argued that the transformation of the HR system to support the process of organizational learning is a key strategic task facing the HR function in the international firm and that the major challenge is to determine the best ways to transfer learning across different national units. Corporate HR therefore needs to demonstrate how it contributes to an environment in which learning can flourish and how HRM policies and practices contribute to the learning of new skills, behaviours and attitudes which support the strategic objectives of the organization (Cyr and Schneider, 1996; Scullion and Starkey, 2000).

Changing roles

CHR plays a significant role in coordination and monitoring the implementation of corporate GTM policies throughout overseas subsidiaries (Kelly, 2001). Based on the above review of the CHR function, we identify four important roles (see also Figure 3.1):

1 *Champion of processes.* Research at the major drinks multinational Diageo showed the importance of building the commitment of top management, providing coaching and training for managers, calibrating and equalizing talent across markets, enabling and aligning HR information systems, and monitoring talent management processes (Sparrow, *et al.*, 2004). The latter point highlights CHR's role as 'champion of processes' (Evans, *et al.*, 2002: 472). Given the global competition context, the demand for higher skill levels amongst staff has led to the need to specify more closely the sorts of capital (human, social, intellectual and political) that constitute 'talent'. Competitive forces are also requiring organizations to take control of the skills supply-chain through the use of more forward planning activity such as strategic workforce planning, market-mapping and employer-branding (Sparrow and Balain, 2008). These drivers have raised the need for

better horizontal coordination of tools, techniques and processes for talent management across internal functions. This in turn requires both effective management of global expertise networks and a designated champion of processes role to monitor the global implementation of a talent management strategy and related tools.

2 *Guardian of culture.* HR has a social responsibility to ensure the organization is sensitive and equipped to deal with global challenges. Social context theory explains how corporate culture represents an organizational social environment which influences the establishment of an HRM system (Ferris, *et al.*, 1999). It is also a form of social control which encourages behaviours and attitudes appropriate for an organization's members to display (O'Reilly and Chatman, 1996), for example, international mobility. This creates a role for CHR as guardian of culture (Brewster, *et al.*, 2005), overseeing the implementation of global values and systems when it comes to developing a talent management culture and employer brand across the organization (Ulrich and Smallwood, 2007). The role of CHR in MNCs has also been found to encourage a culture of trust and motivation to work together, through the design of appropriate practices, processes and structures (Gratton, 2005). This gives CHR the opportunity to focus on 'talentship' – better human capital decision-making (Boudreau and Ramstad, 2006). CHR can therefore play a key role in encouraging a 'joined-up' approach to GTM across the whole organization; the guardian of culture role could be key to ensure the right approach to GTM across the organization, creating a climate in which people feel encouraged to be mobile but valued for their difference. These are crucial steps in breaking down the silo mentality that exists within firms today within business and geographic regions (Gratton, 2005).

3 *Network leadership and intelligence.* Network leadership is a term used by Evans, *et al.* (2002: 471) indicating HR should have: an awareness of leading edge trends and developments in the internal and external labour market, the ability to mobilize the appropriate human resources, and a sense of timing and context (sensitivity to what is going on at both local and global levels). First, although 'leadership' may not be the most appropriate terminology here given the frequently cited limited powerbase of the HR function (Farndale, 2005), the importance of being well-networked is crucial. This includes being aware of events both inside and outside the organization, but also for CHR to take on the role of facilitating collaboration across the organization; HR's role in building social capital beyond organizational boundaries to encourage cooperation across the company and improve firm success has been recognized (Gratton, 2005; Lengnick-Hall and Lengnick-Hall, 2006; Mäkelä, 2007; Taylor, 2007). Mäkelä's (2007) study of expatriates has shown how social capital becomes important for global talent – their relationships are richer, more trustful and longer term than more arm's-length cross-border relationships, and these properties create more opportunities for knowledge-sharing, and have a multiplying effect by spreading ties more effectively across new units. Lengthened participation in the assignment unit typically leads to a higher level of shared cognitive ground, effectively facilitating knowledge. For Taylor (2007: 337) a pressing need now is then '. . . the identification, development and retention of managers, particularly those crossing geographic and cultural boundaries (high-value boundary spanners or HVBS), who can successfully develop social capital in multiple cultural settings'. She highlights the need for IHRM functions to manage both structural social capital (the configuration, density and strength of relationships between HVBSs) and cognitive social capital (shared goals and

shared culture, i.e. language, codes and narratives). She notes that the competencies needed to do this are little understood.

Second, we would add the dimension of intelligence about networks to this role. The majority of talent services (such as market intelligence, search capabilities, sourcing tools and techniques) are now distributed externally across a host of specialized or outsourced providers, or internally (within projects that have initiated new practices). We argue that taking a more proactive stance, and knowing both the talent markets and the capabilities created by different providers and practices, is a key role requirement for GTM. This creates a networking role for the HR function as a boundary spanner (Kostova and Roth, 2003) between external providers and the organization.

4 *Managers of internal receptivity.* Research on sectors (such as healthcare) that have learned how to source international labour into domestic markets, as well as research on inpatriation, shows that CHR can play an active role in the career management of international employees – encouraging mobility but also ensuring individuals are looked after in the process (in terms of the receptivity of the receiving units to manage diversity, career management, integration and work–life balance issues). The traditional male expatriate, mid-career, moving abroad possibly with family, is no longer the standard model. As more self-initiated movers and third country nationals/host country nationals become involved in international assignments, as well as these assignments taking different forms, a more complex but flexible approach to career management is required. CHR is ideally positioned to have the necessary overview across the organization to be able to manage this talent flow, by changing HR processes, challenging local mindsets and practices, and looking for new lower-cost forms of meeting international experience demands and skills shortages.

Looking in more detail at these four roles, we can also observe overlaps between them whereby complementarities create added value:

- the forward planning to attract and retain talent of the *champion of processes* role combined with the development of a brand culture of the *guardian of culture* role highlights the importance of *employer branding*;
- the combination of building a culture of mobility of the *guardian of culture* role and creating receptive business units for the flow of talent of the *managers of internal receptivity* role highlights the importance of *encouraging mobility*;
- having networks in place to move people around (*network leadership*) at the same time as managing the flow of people and their careers emphasizes (*managers of internal receptivity*) the importance of *managing staffing flows*;
- *global expertise networks* emerge based on the combination of the ability to build specialist networks (*network leadership*) and having experts in the processes which facilitate GTM (*champion of processes*);
- by combining the forward planning part of the *champion of processes* role with the career management of the *managers of internal receptivity* role, this results in strong *supply chain planning*;
- and finally, the combination of building an appropriate GTM culture (*guardian of culture*) with the creation of networks to support this (*network leadership*) highlights the ability to build strong *social capital* through both cognitive and structural means.

Despite the emergence of these CHR roles, there is still confusion regarding the specific role that HR professionals in particular should play in GTM processes, which places question marks over the ability of CHR professionals to manage their own destiny. Corporate HR professionals work alongside top management who has the option of outsourcing some of their activities. Although HR directors were found to be the primary decision-makers for outsourcing (GMAC, 2008), and can claim more insight into the risks involved in using external agencies given the complex compliance issues (such as immigration and taxes) involved in global resourcing, practitioner evidence suggests that HR's corporate impact is still declining (Guthridge, *et al.*, 2008). McKinsey found that the three key talent management activities carried out amongst high-performing firms are: ensuring global consistency in management processes, achieving cultural diversity, and developing global leaders (Guthridge and Komm, 2008). However, this evidence comes from reports from practice rather than empirical research.

There is empirical evidence that MNCs are putting in structural solutions to move what were previously only network linkages between International Mobility and Talent Management functions. For example, based on the 2008 Global Relocation Survey of 25 financial services firms and additional interview data from the senior international management (IM) functionaries of eight of these firms, Sparrow (2008) asked whether international mobility (or associated expatriation activity) should become a centre of excellence in its own right, or whether it should report via another such centre, such as talent management. The research showed that by far the most important influence on the relationship and division of responsibilities between central IM specialists, and in-country or in-business division HR partners, was the structural reporting relationship of the IM function. The solution chosen affords or denies the IM function entry into a range of HR issues also linked to international mobility. Many IM functions, by dint of history, still report into a compensation and benefits function that is responsible for the terms, conditions and financial package for expatriates. There is a trend, especially in those financial service organizations that have mature international markets, towards aligning IM under a talent management umbrella. A number of MNCs are already creating the structural solutions that will forge new talent management directorates that can manage these global mobility processes. A year later new flexibilities in policy offerings could be traced back to the structural solutions (Aldred and Sparrow, 2009a).

The importance of context

Given these new roles and practices, what might CHR do to enhance its role in GTM? To advance our understanding we explore relevant theory to explain how the approach of CHR to GTM varies in significant ways in different firms, based on their core competencies and strategies.

Our definition of GTM rests upon the resource-based view (RBV) (cf. Barney, 1991) of the firm, coupled with some premises from the organizational learning literature. The RBV of the firm argues that a series of organizational capabilities are necessary for successful globalization and that these capabilities require that a firm's internal processes, systems and management practices first meet customer needs and then direct both the skills and efforts of employees towards achieving the goals of the organization. Globalization is only possible when firms can transfer their distinctive knowledge-assets abroad into new international markets, and talent management is one way of transferring these assets. If there is any strategic advantage to be found in a firm's HRM capability (its philosophy, policies, and practices) then this HR capability itself must also be transferred into different geographies around the world. The capability to effect internal cross-border transfers of HRM practice (along with the knowledge needed to link this practice into local organizational effectiveness) becomes a core competence. This principle is considered to apply to a range of HR systems, talent management being one of the most important. The main differences that globalization makes to the nature of talent management are that firms must:

1 learn how best to co-ordinate and deploy their various capabilities and exploit them *in a large number of countries and markets*;
2 identify new resources *in untapped markets* that will strengthen their existing core competences; and
3 enhance existing competences by reconfiguring value-adding activities *across a wider geography or range of operations*.

In building these capabilities (akin to the Network Leadership and Intelligence and Managers of Internal Receptivity roles described above), we draw attention to three key issues: choice of capability strategy; political influence and control mechanisms; and regional co-ordination mechanisms.

Choice of capability strategy Meyskens, Von Glinow, Werther and Clarke (2009: 1448) argue that as MNCs have expanded their practices aimed at producing globally integrated but locally responsive staff, academic understanding has lagged behind: '. . . even though global talent management trends have evolved in practice, IHRM theorizing has not kept pace'. We believe this situation can be remedied by drawing upon an organization learning perspective. If the word 'talent' is substituted for the words 'knowledge' or 'resources' in the following outline, the dilemmas faced about the role of corporate HR functions in shaping GTM systems become clear. The RBV theory of the firm argues that although resources can provide a global advantage to the MNC as a whole, this is only true *if* the knowledge, skills, and capabilities possessed by these resources can be leveraged appropriately. Here two competing positions may be held (Sparrow, *et al.*, 2004). The *capability-recognizing* perspective argues that whilst MNCs possess unique knowledge-based resources, these are typically treated as being home-country based or belonging to central corporate functions and top teams, there only to be disseminated on a need-to-know basis. The *capability-driven* perspective (also called the *dynamic capability* perspective) is concerned with a much wider process of building, protecting and exploiting *mutual* capabilities across geographies (between a corporate HQ and local operations) whereby the world becomes an important source for new knowledge and new markets. As the need for more local sourcing increases, the more a *capability-driven* as opposed to just a *capability-recognizing* system is needed for talent management. It is important to note that we reinforce the need for a *capability-driven* perspective, which implies strong bottom–up, culture-driven processes of talent management in addition to a more strategic, centralized perspective.

Moreover, despite the impact of the recent economic recession, academic treatment still refers to there being a global race (if not war) for talent. Lewin, Massini and Peeters (2009) examined the offshoring of high-value knowledge-intensive work, noting that this has now become a routinized decision. Drawing upon research into the global location of R&D capabilities, they note that a capability-driven perspective (our language) can still mean that offshore assets may necessarily still be under central corporate control (as part of an *asset* or *home-base exploiting* approach, where it is necessary only to adapt to local markets and to enable firm-specific capabilities to be exploited in foreign markets). In contrast, an *asset augmenting* or *home-base augmenting* approach requires the development of local links in order to improve home-base capability, through the benefits of knowledge spillovers. Talent shortages, in turn reflecting the changing demographics and geography of educational provision, have produced a new management intentionality away from just cost-saving objectives towards knowledge-seeking objectives aimed at maximizing the value of human capital. Put simply, recessions and cost pressures will have increasingly limited impact on the pursuit of global talent management strategies. Empirical evidence seems to support this (Aldred and Sparrow, 2009b). Supply, not just demand, will ensure the continuation of a broadened and more strategic approach to the seeking of talent on a global basis. The analogy with the use of top–down and bottom–up global talent identification and deployment processes is clear.

Other IHRM researchers have also begun to adopt RBV-thinking to explain the advantages of adopting greater internal labour flexibility. Beltrán-Martín, Roca-Puig, Escrig-Tena and Bou-Llusar (2009) have recently applied RBV-thinking to the question of internal labour flexibility (ILF). They adopt Huang and Cullen's (2001) definition of ILF as being concerned with the adaptability of the organization's workforce to face non-routine circumstances and events that demand creativity and initiative. They draw attention to three dimensions of an ILF capability that become important in determining the efficacy of the HR function when promoting workforce adaptability – it requires intrinsic flexibility of a resource (defined as a resource's 'applicability in multiple situations' also called resource versatility); modification flexibility (defined as 'the extent to which a resource can be easily transformed (with low cost and time) in order to be used in new circumstances'); and relational flexibility (which 'facilitates the combinability of one resource with others') (Beltrán-Martín, *et al.*, 2009: 1581). We would note that such dimensions, without too much imagination, could be applied to the assessment of GTM processes and the way they build global talent, as one way of capturing the extent to which they truly draw upon multiple forms of international working and multiple talent populations.

Political influence and control mechanisms Different strategic approaches to GTM raise questions about the level of insight into business models and the formal versus informal methods of control for managing and aligning talent in MNCs, i.e. 'talent proofing' the organization (Sparrow and Balain, 2008: 121). The definition of who is deemed to have appropriate business insight is an important control mechanism inside globalizing organizations, and of course in the absence of well-designed talent identification systems, a political decision. Globalization, and in particular the spread of IT, has allowed the creation of unexpected and sometimes disruptive business models (Magretta, 2002; Schweizer, 2005). As the knowledge component of industries continues to grow, it is lowering the barriers to entry in many sectors (Christensen, *et al.*, 2004). The growth of emerging markets has accelerated the need to build capability in these markets. These capabilities reflect the need for component knowledge, which refers to an understanding of the nuts and bolts of the operations of the business often associated with specific products or functions (Henderson and Clark, 1990). They also reflect the need for architectural knowledge, which refers to the ability to understand how the various components of the business model fit together at a corporate level. It is becoming increasingly difficult to disentangle the process of globalization from associated changes being wrought in business models. The CHR function has to understand the implications of *both* these change processes. Concentrating on business process redesign and the changing location of work around the world can be misleading. A far more important driver of globalization, and one that will undoubtedly become more important in the future, is the process of business model innovation that is currently taking place. Clearly, this process has been made much easier once new options have been created through previous process streamlining, optimization or standardization of these processes, and decisions about sourcing and shoring.

Work on the role of CHR functions sheds some insight on how these capabilities are developed. In more polycentric MNCs where the degree of integration and co-ordination by the centre is weaker, and the central HR function smaller (Purcell and Ahlstrand, 1994; Scullion and Starkey, 2000), attempts are made to maintain control over the mobility and careers of international managers, however this is more fragmented and less systematic than in the globally integrated companies. Particularly in this environment there is thus a need for HR to become an 'effective political influencer' (Novicevic and Harvey, 2001: 1260) to be able to manage the internal labour market for global managers.

In addition, the co-ordination of international talent management strategies in highly decentralized MNCs is more problematic due to greater tensions between the short-term needs of the operating companies and the long-term strategic needs of the business (Scullion and Starkey, 2000). For example, in the French utilities firm, EDF, a new system was introduced group-wide for managing expatriation. However, being a highly decentralized MNC, this system relied mainly on the informal influencing capabilities of corporate HR rather than on the system itself. However, the corporate HR function can become increasingly influential in persuading the operating companies to support strategic talent management initiatives. Interestingly, in these situations, informal and subtle management processes (Doz and Prahalad, 1981) are used to introduce a degree of corporate integration to talent management approaches in decentralized multinationals.

The particular challenges of GTM in highly decentralized MNCs can be further illustrated through an examination of the problems of managing repatriation which are more complex than in the more centralized global companies (Scullion and Starkey, 2000): Corporate HR often has less influence on the operating companies and is frequently not responsible for finding re-entry positions for expatriates; and there are less well developed career and succession planning systems in the decentralized companies. However, as argued above, despite the formal organizational structures and decentralized philosophy of some firms, in practice the corporate HR function can exert significant informal influences to encourage operational managers and divisional managers to support corporate talent management activities (Storey, *et al.*, 1997).

For example, in a leading Irish building and materials MNC senior operating managers were required to report directly to top management on the extent of their co-operation with strategic talent management objectives which encouraged the development of a corporate rather than purely local perspective. This helped corporate HR managers to persuade divisional managers to release their high potential people for developmental international assignments or to employ expatriates who had worked for other divisions. In the same company networking meetings between HR directors of the different businesses were also encouraged to promote a more corporate outlook.

Regional co-ordination mechanisms Here the question is whether HRM integration processes involve the introduction of predominantly parent company HRM practices, or the introduction of a mix of locally and regional adjusted worldwide practices (Lu and Björkman, 1997). Much of the existing evidence suggests that MNCs actually, even in market terms, pursue regional not global strategies (Rugman and Verbeke, 2004, 2008), and this inevitably is reflected in a lack of truly global approaches to the management of talent. Semi-globalization implies a reality of 'neither extreme geographical fragmentation of the world in national markets nor complete integration' (Rugman and Verbeke, 2004: 6). However, the recent creation of new intra-regional and cross-regional flows of labour means that it now becomes important to ask whether regionalization helps organizations pursue a 'transnational' HRM strategy, especially with regard to GTM. Integrating HRM systems with the wider MNC network is often slowed by the challenges inherent in a country's institutional and cultural idiosyncrasies. Arregle, Beamish and Hébert (2009) examined the regional effect of location decisions by Japanese MNCs (from the semi-globalization perspective) finding significant and different considerations being exerted at this level. There were strong regional influences on agglomeration benefits (such as localized knowledge spillovers, social ties, transmission of knowledge and organizational practices) and on arbitrage decisions (reallocations of resources within an MNC's network of subsidiaries) between countries in the same region. There has been a lack of attention given to the regional dimension of internationalization processes (Enright, 2005). This observation clearly also applies to the globalization of talent management processes.

Yet research on the role of regional headquarters (RHQs) in 67 MNCs in one of the key regional markets, the People's Republic of China (PRC) has evidenced benefits of regional integration (Braun, *et al.*, 2003). Managerial talent was one of the scarcest resources within China, which meant that in order to attract and retain the best managers before the competition did, introducing world-class HRM practices within their affiliates became a core task. MNCs utilized either their RHQs or newly established PRC holding companies to drive forward this integration process. The competencies developed over time at their RHQs were valuable to further the integration process. Rather than being utilized simply to advance regional strategies, regional corporate centres for these firms functioned as implementation instruments and incubators for transnational HRM strategies. Those MNCs that managed broad HRM practice integration also differed from others in that top management at corporate headquarters showed a more favourable attitude towards the transfer of HRM practices across national borders: the pursuit of transnational or global HRM strategies is strongly dependent on top management viewing HRM competencies on a global level as a source of possible competitive advantage.

Collings, *et al.*, (2008) developed the Scullion and Starkey (2000) corporate level framework to pay more attention to regional international strategies. The study raised important challenges for corporate HR functions pursuing regional strategies:

- MNCs who follow regional strategies may still fall victim to the silo mentality in the sense that each region seeks to hold onto and protect their managerial talent within the 'regional silo'. This means that high potential and key talent may never reach their full potential due to the lack of a GTM perspective. This failure to develop high potential staff beyond the region limits the performance of the MNC.
- Regiocentric strategies fail to allow the MNC to source talent outside the home region. This potentially limits the performance of the MNC as there is a failure to exploit the best talent within the MNC and to gain greater knowledge of other regions.

Research on the actions of corporate HR functions (Scullion and Starkey, 2000) also questions whether intermediate regional capabilities may be learned. Corporate HR exerted a more centralized control of senior management talent management, including expatriates, in a number of decentralized MNCs, reflecting a shift away from the highly decentralized approaches popular in the early 1990s. Many MNCs attempted to achieve greater integration and co-ordination across their operating units in response to their strategy to reorganize on regional lines, but key talent management activities such as senior management development and the international transfer of high potential managers was increasingly controlled centrally.

MNC managers should reconsider the limitations of regional strategies in terms of the problems of exploiting regional talent through silo mentalities and a failure at corporate level to fully identify and utilize talent at the regional level (Collings, *et al.*, 2008).

Conclusion: the major challenges and constraints moving forward

Our review of the role of CHR in GTM in MNCs in different contextual settings highlights a number of important contingency variables: choice of capability strategy, political influence and control mechanisms necessary to develop appropriate business model insight, and alignment of talent management to the development of regional co-ordination. Each of these brings significant challenges. We now draw some conclusions about the major challenges and constraints facing the CHR role in the future and signal important areas for future research.

We have identified four specific roles for CHR in GTM: *Champion of process, Guardian of culture, Network leadership and intelligence*, and *Manager of internal receptivity* (see Figure 3.1). The ultimate aim of MNCs is to build a core competence of being able to transfer capability across multiple countries, which involves monitoring the implementation of relevant policies and practices, encouraging an appropriate corporate culture, establishing the necessary networks, and ensuring all parts of the organization are sensitive to the needs of international staff. This implies a formal role for both CHR and senior leadership. In general, we are seeing more centralization of talent management strategies, particularly at regional if not global level (Collings, *et al.*, 2008). However, the importance of informal control in decentralized structures has also been shown to be crucial (Scullion and Starkey, 2000). This informal approach may be more difficult to achieve but is highly effective. Future research should therefore focus in particular on the challenges and value of balancing both informal and formal forms of control over GTM in different types of MNC settings.

Trends towards increased local sourcing in GTM demonstrate the need to shift to a *capability-driven* perspective (Sparrow, *et al.*, 2004) which in turn entails a bottom–up focus across the firm to participate in mutual sharing of talent and joined-up thinking and action with regard to GTM. Therefore, in addition to the top–down role of CHR and senior leadership, there needs to be employee-led processes whereby employees take the initiative to be part of the talent flow. Two of CHR's roles – those of *Guardian of culture* and *Network leader* – become crucial in encouraging this,. As recent GTM research has shown, the focus may be better placed on the key *positions* in the organization rather than the star *people* (Collings and Mellahi, 2009). Future research should explore whether by combining this focus with the appropriate culture and networks, CHR can facilitate the bottom–up movement of talent around the organization.

Given the importance of the CHR role, it is perhaps surprising that there is little evidence or discussion about how the CHR function measures success for GTM in different contexts (we have identified three important contingent variables). Once more we must rely on evidence from practice. Where MNCs appear to fail to develop appropriate talent management strategies for recruiting and managing international talent, they have been shown to be less likely to succeed in international business (Guthridge and Komm, 2008). To support the case for closer measurement of GTM, McKinsey report that more activity in GTM activities across their ten dimensions was highly correlated with higher profit per employee (Guthridge and Komm, 2008). Further empirical research is needed in particular into how MNCs balance the short-term needs of operating businesses against the long-term strategic goals of GTM and alignment with corporate strategy and business models.

One particularly important aspect of GTM is retention: noted as being increasingly difficult, especially in the emerging markets (Yeung, *et al.*, 2008). Creating and maintaining high levels of employee engagement could therefore be one of the highest priorities for CHR. For example, in one UK-based large engineering multinational corporation operating in India and China, the CHR Director noted that it is corporate HR's role to encourage engagement with the corporate brand on a global level, as well as there being local HR responsibilities for ensuring employees are engaged with their local manager and work unit. It will be interesting to explore further the extent to which employer branding is indeed seen as part of a firm's GTM strategy.

There is also growing evidence that an MNC's corporate social responsibility (CSR) activities are becoming an increasingly important way to attract and retain high-potential and high-value employees (Macey and Schneider, 2008). It is suggested that employees identify with a company more when they think that it is acting in a socially responsible manner and that CSR contributes to employee identification and pride in the company (Bhattacharaya, *et al.*, 2008). We have noted the incorporation of marketing activity, such as employer branding, into the GTM function and CHR role, but future research should also examine the links between CSR and talent management. This could be particularly fruitful in the emerging markets such as India and China which have seen the infusion of managerial practices from around the world due to the increased openness to international trade and de-regulation.

We raise some research issues relating to the implications of the current global financial and economic crisis which began in 2008. First, researchers will need to address wider issues such as how the organization and management of the MNC is affected by the crisis. International mobility and talent management models currently in vogue in the west may be questioned increasingly. Given that the economic crisis at the time of writing may well be over by time of publication, we ask some retrospective questions that we hope research will have answered. As we look back on these times from future history, were we able to answer the following key questions: Did the crisis represent an opportunity for CHR to demonstrate the contribution of HR to the business strategy by helping to develop managers with the capabilities to develop new industries? What role did CHR play in helping MNCs to best use their talent to capitalize on the strategic new opportunities that would arise in the future? What impact did the crisis have on the demand and supply for talent? And, how were patterns of global staffing and forms of international mobility affected by the global crisis?

Related to the financial crisis is the role of the CHR function in governance and risk management around GTM processes. For example, the forward planning of talent streams can reduce risk for the organization. However, ensuring a broader governance remit whereby the CHR function is accountable for ensuring fair, ethical and appropriate processes are in place to move talent around the organization may also become crucial as the firms directly affected by the financial crisis are having to exhibit stronger regulation of their activities (Boselie, *et al.*, 2009). The coming years will show just how strong this dimension becomes within the CHR role.

We might also expect the crisis to impact future mobility strategies and the opportunities for high-potential knowledge workers and managers to move between leading MNCs. Future research should examine how strategies of employee retention and engagement operate in the very different context of the financial crisis.

There is also an urgent need for more empirical research on GTM strategies and practices in the emerging markets due to the rapid growth of these markets and the acute nature of the talent management challenges faced in these markets (Lane and Pollner, 2008). A new geographical ecology of mobility will alter the relevance and applicability of many constructs deemed important in western cultures, but operating to different dynamics in non-western cultures (Luthans, *et al.*, 2006; Sparrow and Budhwar, 1997).

Finally, in joining the debate around what the GTM literature adds above and beyond the broader IHRM literature, from the perspective of the role of the CHR function, it appears that managing talent and knowledge-flows across the organization may be crucial. A key aspect of GTM is about having systems which are integrated across the firm. This requires replication of systems through the alignment of information systems, application processes, and strategy (Morris, *et al.*, 2009). GTM goes beyond the notion of having policies and practices in place, to ensuring a seamless flow of talent, and hence a seamless system to support this. The extent to which organizations can actually achieve GTM rather than having a set of IHRM policies in place will thus be an interesting focus for future research.

We raise some research issues relating to the implications of the global financial and economic crisis which began in 2008.

References

Aldred, G. and Sparrow, P.R. (2009a) *International Mobility: Introducing Flexibility Into Policy Structures*. Global Relocation Trends Report. London: Brookfield Global Relocation Services.

Aldred, G. and Sparrow, P.R. (2009b) *International Mobility: Impact of the Current Economic Climate*. Global Relocation Trends Report. London: Brookfield Global Relocation Services.

Arregle, J.-L., Beamish, P. and Hébert, L. (2009) The regional dimension of MNEs' foreign subsidiary localization. *Journal of International Business Studies*, 40: 86–107.

Ashton, C. and Morton, L. (2005) Managing talent for competitive advantage. *Strategic HR Review*, 4(5): 28–31.

Barney, J. (1991) Firm resources and sustained competitive advantage. *Journal of Management*, 17: 99–120.

Bartlett, C. and Ghoshal, S. (1989) *Managing Across Borders: The Transnational Solution*, 2nd edition. London: Random House.

Beechler, S., and Woodward, I. C. (2009) The global 'war for talent'. *Journal of International Management*, doi: 10.1016/j.intman.2009.01.002.

Beltrán-Martín, I., Roca-Puig, V., Escrig-Tena, A. and Bou-Llusar, J.C. (2009) Internal labour flexibility from a resource-based view approach: definition and proposal of a measurement scale. *International Journal of Human Resource Management*, 20 (7): 1576–1598.

Bhattacharaya, C.B., Sen, S., and Korschun, D. (2008) Using corporate social responsibility to win the war for talent. *MIT Sloan Management Review*, 49: 37–44.

Boselie, P., Van den Brule, P., Farndale, E., Paauwe, J. (2009) *HR Governance and Risk Management*. Faculty of Social and Behavioural Science, Tilburg University, The Netherlands.

Boudreau, J.W., and Ramstad, P.M. (2006) Talentship and HR measurement and analysis: from ROI to strategic organizational change. *Human Resource Planning*, 29: 25–33.

Braun, W., Sparrow, P.R. and Schuler, R. (2003) Integrating the HR activities of Chinese affiliates through regional or transnational integration strategies? *Worldlink*. 13 (3): 2–3.

Brewster, H. (1994) The integration of human resource management and corporate strategy. In C. Brewster and A. Hegewisch (eds.) *Policy and Practice in European Human Resource Management: The Evidence and Analysis from the Price Waterhouse Cranfield Survey*. London: Routledge.

Brewster, C., Sparrow, P.R., and Harris, H. (2005) Towards a new model of globalizing human resource management. *International Journal of Human Resource Management*, 16: 953–974.

Cappelli, P. (2008) Talent management for the twenty-first century. *Harvard Business Review*, March: 74–81.

Christensen, C.M., Roth, E.A. and Anthony, S.D. (2004) *Seeing What Is Next: Using Theories of Innovation To Predict Industry Change*. Boston, MA: Harvard Business School Press.

Collings, D.G., and Mellahi, K. (2009) Strategic talent management: A review and research agenda. *Human Resource Management Review*, doi: 10.1016/j.intman.2009.04.001.

Collings, D.G., Morley, M., and Gunnigle, P. (2008) Composing the top management team in the international subsidiary: qualitative evidence on international staffing in US multinationals in the Republic of Ireland. *Journal of World Business*, 43: 197–212.

Cyr, D.J. and Schneider, S.C. (1996) Implications for learning: human resource management in East–West joint ventures. *Organization Studies*, 17 (2): 207 026

Doz, Y., and Prahalad, C.K. (1981) Headquarters influence and strategic control in MNCs. *Sloan Management Review*, 23: 15–30

Enright, M.J. (2005) The role of regional management centers. *Management International Review*, 45 (1): 83–102.

Evans, P., Pucik, V., and Barsoux, J. (2002) The global challenge. *Frameworks for International Human Resource Management*. New York: McGraw-Hill.

Farndale, E. (2005) HR department professionalism: a comparison between the UK and other European countries. *International Journal of Human Resource Management*, 16(5): 660–675.

Farndale, E., Paauwe, J., Morris, S. S., Stahl, G. K., Stiles, P., Trevor, J., and Wright, P. M. (2010) Context-bound configurations of corporate HR functions in multinational corporations around the globe. *Human Resource Management*, 49(1): 45–66.

Ferris, G.R., Hochwarter, W.A., Buckley, M.R., Harrell-Cook, G., and Frink, D.D. (1999) Human resources management: some new directions. *Journal of Management*, 25: 385–415.

Frank, F.D. and Taylor, C.R. (2004) Talent Management: trends that will shape the future. *Human Resource Planning*, 27(1): 33–41.

GMAC (2008) *Global Relocation Trends. 2008 Survey Report*. Woodridge, IL: GMAC Global Relocation Services.

Gratton, L. (2005) Managing integration through cooperation. *Human Resource Management*, 44(2): 151–158.

Guthridge, M., and Komm, A.B. (2008) Why multinationals struggle to manage talent. *The McKinsey Quarterly*, May: 1–5.

Guthridge, M., Komm, A.B., and Lawson, E. (2008) Making talent a strategic priority. *The McKinsey Quarterly*, 1: 49–59.

Harvey, M., Speier, C., and Novicevic, M.M. (2001) A theory based framework for strategic global human resource staffing policies and practices. *International Journal of Human Resource Management*, 12: 898–915.

Henderson, R.M. and Clark, K.B. (1990) Architectural innovation: the reconfiguration of existing product technologies and the failure of established firms. *Administrative Science Quarterly*, 35, 9–30.

Huang, H.J. and Cullen, J.B. (2001) Labour flexibility and related HRM practices: a study of large Taiwanese manufacturers. *Canadian Journal of Administrative Sciences*, 18: 33–39.

Hunt, J. and Boxall, P. (1998) Are top human resource specialists strategic partners? Self-perceptions of a corporate elite. *International Journal of Human Resource Management*, 9(5): 768–81.

Kelly, J. (2001) The role of the personnel/HR function in multinational companies. *Employee Relations*, 23: 536–557.

Kim, K., Park, J-H., and Prescott, J.E. (2003) The global integration of business functions: a study of multinational businesses in integrated global industries. *Journal of International Business Studies*, 34: 327–344.

Kochan, T., Batt, R. and Dyer, L. (1992) International human resource studies: a framework for future research. In D. Lewin *et al.* (eds.) *Research Frontiers in Industrial Relations and Human Resources*. Madison, WI: Industrial Relations Research Association.

Kostova, T., and Roth, K. (2003) Social capital in multinational corporations and a micro–macro model of its formation. *Academy of Management Review*, 28: 297–317.

Lane, K. and Pollner, F. (2008) How to address China's talent shortage. *McKinsey Quarterly*, 3: 2008

Lengnick-Hall, M.L., and Lengnick-Hall, C.A. (2006) International human resource management and social network/social capital theory. In G.K. Stahl and I. Björkman (eds.), *Handbook of Research in International Human Resource Management*. Cheltenham: Edward Elgar.

Lewin, A.Y., Massini, S. and Peeters, C. (2009) Why are companies offshoring innovation? The emerging global race for talent. *Journal of International Business Studies*, 40: 901–925.

Lewis, R.E. and Heckman, R.J. (2006) Talent management: a critical review. *Human Resource Management Review*, 16(2): 139–154.

Lu, Y. and Björkman, I. (1997) HRM practices in China–Western joint ventures: MNC standardization versus localization. *International Journal of Human Resource Management*, 8: 614–627.

Luthans, F., Zhu, W., and Avolio, B.J. (2006) The impact of efficacy on work attitudes across cultures. *Journal of World Business*, 41: 121–132.

Macey, W.H., and Schneider, B. (2008) The meaning of employee engagement. *Industrial and Organizational Psychology*, 1: 3–30.

Magretta, J. (2002) Why business models matter. *Harvard Business Review*. 80 (5): 86–93.

Mäkelä, K. (2007) Knowledge sharing through expatriate relationships: a social capital perspective. *International Studies of Management and Organisation*, 37: 108–25.

Meyskens, M., Von Glinow, M.A., Werther, W.B., and Clarke, L. (2009) The paradox of international talent: alternative forms of international assignments. *International Journal of Human Resource Management*, 20 (6): 1439–1450.

Morris, S. S., Wright, P. M., Trevor, J., Stiles, P., Stahl, G. K., Snell, S. A., Paauwe, J., and Farndale, E. (2009). Global challenges to replicating HR: the role of people, processes, and systems. *Human Resource Management.*

Novicevic, M.M., and Harvey, M. (2001) The changing role of the corporate HR function in global organizations of the twenty-first century. *International Journal of Human Resource Management*, 12: 1251–1268.

O'Reilly, C., and Chatman, J. (1996). Culture as social control: corporations, cults, and commitment. Pp. 157–200 in B. Shaw and L. Cummings (eds.), *Research in Organizational Behavior* (vol. 18). Greenwich, CT: JAI Press.

Pucik, V (1992) Globalization and Human Resource Management. In Pucik, V., Tichy, N. and Barnett, C.K. (eds.) *Globalizing Management*, New York: Wiley.

Purcell, J., and Ahlstrand, B. (1994) *Human Resource Management in the Multi-divisional Company.* New York: Oxford University Press.

Roberts, K., Kossek, E.E. and Ozekei, C. (1998) Managing the global workforce: challenges and strategies. *Academy of Management Executive*, 12(4): 93–106.

Rugman, A. and Verbeke, A. (2004) A perspective on the regional and global strategies of multinational enterprises. *Journal of International Business Studies*, 35 (1): 3–18.

Rugman, A. and Verbeke, A. (2008) A new perspective on the regional and global strategies of multinational service firms. *Management International Review*, 48 (4): 397–411.

Schuler, R.S., Budhwar, P. and Florkowski, G. (2002) International human resource management: review and critique. *International Journal of Management Reviews*, vol. 4(1): 41–70.

Schweizer, L. (2005) Concept and evolution of business models. *Journal of General Management*, 31(2): 37–56.

Scullion, H. (1994) Staffing Policies and Strategic Control in British Multinationals. *International Studies of Management and Organization*, 24 (3): 18–35.

Scullion, H., and Brewster, C. (2001) Managing expatriates: messages from Europe. *Journal of World Business*, 36: 346–365.

Scullion, H., and Starkey, K. (2000) In search of the changing role of the corporate human resource function in the international firm. *International Journal of Human Resource Management*, 11: 1061–1081.

Sparrow, P.R. (2008) *International Mobility in the Financial Services Sector: The Challenge of Emerging Markets*. GMAC Global Relocation Trends Report. London: GMAC.

Sparrow, P.R. (2007) Globalisation of HR at function level: Four UK-based case studies of the international recruitment and selection process. *International Journal of Human Resource Management*, 18: 144–166.

Sparrow, P.R., and Balain, S. (2008) Talent proofing the organization. Pp. 108–128 in C.L. Cooper and R. Burke (eds.), *The Peak Performing Organization*, London: Routledge.

Sparrow, P.R., and Budhwar, P.S. (1997) Competition and change: Mapping the Indian HRM recipe against world-wide patterns. *Journal of World Business*, 32: 224–242.

Sparrow, P.R., Brewster, C., and Harris, H. (2004) *Globalizing Human Resource Management*. London: Routledge.

Storey, J., Edwards, P., and Sisson, K. (1997) *Managers in the Making: Careers, Development and Control in Corporate Britain and Japan.* London: Sage.

Taylor, S. (2007) Creating social capital in MNCs: the international human resource management challenge. *Human Resource Management Journal*, 17: 336–54.

Taylor, S., Beechler, S., and Napier, N. (1996) Toward an integrative model of strategic international human resource management. *Academy of Management Review*, 21: 959–985.

Ulrich, D., and Brockbank, W. (2005) Role call. *People Management*, 11: 24–28.

Ulrich, D., and Smallwood, N. (2007) *Leadership Brand: Developing Customer-focused Leaders to Drive Performance and Build Lasting Value.* Boston MA, Harvard Business School Press.

Yeung, A. K., Warner, M., and Rowley, C. (2008) Growth and globalization: evolution of human resource management practices in Asia. *Human Resource Management*, 47: 1–13.

4 The identification and evaluation of talent in MNEs

ANTHONY McDONNELL AND DAVID G. COLLINGS

Introduction

In this chapter, we focus on how multinational enterprises (MNEs) identify and evaluate talent. In so doing, we highlight the key opportunities and challenges in effectively identifying and evaluating global talent across the MNE's network of operations. More particularly we analyse the talent identification and evaluation process and consider the issues around whether talent should be made or bought.

These are critical issues as organisations continue to be faced with mounting global workforce challenges. Key amongst these challenges is the requirement for organisations to effectively manage their global talent (Scullion *et al.*, 2010). Indeed, the 'great financial crisis' of the early twenty-first century has placed increased pressure on MNEs to more successfully leverage their global talent base whilst balancing labour costs. Of concern is that organisations continue to report shortages of sufficient talent to fill their pivotal positions which is having a negative effect on implementing global growth strategies (Ready and Conger, 2007). Consequently, it is unsurprising that global talent management (GTM) has become a hot topic amongst practitioners and academics alike. Unsurprisingly in light of the field's relative infancy there remains a lack of consensus on an exact definition of GTM (see Lewis and Heckman, 2006 on talent management and Scullion *et al.*, 2010 on global talent management). Nevertheless there are many recurring themes that arise across the existing literature. The identification, development, appraisal, deployment and retention of high performing and high potential employees globally are often considered key aspects of a MNE's GTM system (e.g. Collings and Scullion, 2007; Collings and Mellahi, 2009; McDonnell *et al.*, 2010a and b; Tarique and Schuler, 2010). For this chapter we define global talent management as:

> Global talent management includes all organizational activities for the purpose of attracting, selecting, developing, and retaining the best employees in the most strategic roles (those roles necessary to achieve organizational strategic priorities) on a global scale. Global talent management takes into account the differences in both organizations' global strategic priorities as well as the differences across national contexts for how talent should be managed in the countries where they operate.
>
> (Scullion *et al.*, 2010)

It may be argued that talent shortages are less of an issue in the current climate, owing to the mass organisational restructuring of recent times. However, owing to global demographic trends, supply issues will continue for some time (see Chapter 2, this volume; Schuler *et al.*, 2010). In addition, and in line with the resource base view we recognise that as traditional sources of competitive advantages such as technology and process are eroding, human capital is increasingly becoming one of most critical corporate resources (Barney, 1991). The unique context of the MNE is the ability to resource talent across its international operations. However a key challenge for MNEs is that the 'availability of talent per se is of little strategic value if it is not identified, nurtured and used effectively' (Mellahi and Collings, 2010: 5). In the context of maximising the strategic advantage of the global workforce through the inclusion of a range of talented individuals of different nationalities reflecting the organisation's global footprint, the challenge for the MNE is to effectively identify those high potential and high performing employees and ensure they fill the key positions.

As already noted, this chapter focuses on talent identification and evaluation and associated issues in this process. The next section discusses talent in terms of how organisations define what they mean by talent. We then consider the specific factors that MNEs are likely to evaluate in terms of identifying talent. More specifically, we focus on the idea of leadership talent. Following this, we discuss whether talent should be treated as an internal facet or whether the external labour market also needs to be incorporated. After that, we turn to the identification and evaluation process and the tools that may be utilised before discussing the global versus local issue. Finally, we conclude with some suggestions for future empirical investigation.

Talent

Defining talent: who are you looking for?

Before an organisation can determine how to evaluate and identify talent, they need to have a clear idea on what they actually mean by talent. McKinsey, the pioneers behind talent management, define talent as 'the sum of a person's abilities . . . his or her intrinsic gifts, skills, knowledge, experience, intelligence, judgement, attitude, character and drive. It also includes his or her ability to learn and grow' (Michaels *et al.*, 2001: xii). Boudreau and Ramstad (2007: 2) suggest talent is 'the resource that includes the potential and realised capacities of individuals and groups and how they are organised, including within the organisation and those who might join the organization'. These definitions recognise the importance of both capability and potential. However they fail to consider the importance of the relevance of their skills and competences vis-à-vis the organisation in which they work and the contribution they make to it. In this regard Ulrich (2006) progresses the debate by suggesting that talent should be identified as a mix of competence, commitment and contribution. Both competence and contribution relate to inputs. Competence refers to the knowledge, skills and values that individuals bring to their role. Commitment refers to the application of these competencies in the workplace and the engagement of employees with their work role. Contribution on the other hand relates to employees' outputs and their role in organisational success and ensuring they themselves find meaning and value in their work.

As a consequence, we suggest that talent and talent management are primarily concerned with employees who add value to the organisation. There will be those with the greatest potential to move into senior, strategic roles although they may not always do so. In other words, those employees that possess the potential to have a differential impact on organisational success. Hence, we argue that talent management should be focused, rather than including every employee in the organisation. Rather than focusing solely on inputs, talent management requires a change in mindset to focusing on potential outputs (Huselid *et al.*, 2005). In other words, do the employee's competences fit with the strategic requirements of the organisation and if deployed appropriately can they contribute to organisational performance? It is critical for each organisation to establish what talent means to them, which means that it needs to be intrinsically linked with their corporate strategy. Talent requirements are likely to vary considerably between organisations because of this. Further, while top management roles are always likely to be key positions, other key positions emerge at different levels of the organisational hierarchy.

Similarly, Collings and Mellahi (2009: 4) argue that organisations should identify the most critical, strategic roles 'in terms of potential outputs or the potential for roles to contribute to the organisational strategic intent'. This suggests that recruitment ahead of the curve is most appropriate (Sparrow, 2007; Collings and Mellahi, 2009). In other words, organisations should move away from vacancy-led recruitment to proactively recruiting high potential individuals that can fill roles when they become available. This approach resonates with professional sports where talent spotting is a key aspect of ensuring team longevity and success (Smilansky, 2006). For example, the financial services MNE, Zurich, identify their future business requirements in terms of the knowledge, skills and competencies that will be required to ensure long-term corporate success but which they do not currently possess in-house. Organisations that proactively analyse their needs and their current capacities will be better placed than those that do not. This resonates with Peter Cappelli's linking of talent management to supply chain management. Specifically Cappelli (2008b: 77) argues: 'how employees advance through development jobs and experiences [is] remarkably similar to how products move through a supply chain'. A key failure of many traditional talent management systems is a mismatch between supply and demand. This results in an oversupply of management talent resulting in employee turnover, or layoffs and restructuring, or an under-supply where key positions cannot be filled (Cappelli, 2008a). Recruiting ahead of the curve with future competence requirements in mind may facilitate managing this potential mismatch.

Identifying talent

We suggest that organisations should adopt a contingency approach in identifying talent according to their corporate strategy and objectives. While we acknowledge that talent can be defined differently, for the purposes of this chapter we focus on the identification of leadership talent, a critical talent segment across all organisations. This section explores the factors that organisations should take into account in identifying leadership talent.

There seems to be an increasing use of leadership competency profiles by MNEs (Beardwell, 2007a; Stahl *et al.*, 2007). For instance Stahl and colleagues (2007) found that organisations developed a profile of competencies their leaders required and employees were then graded against this. Positively, they also found that even within MNEs there was not a universal competency profile utilised. Instead different profiles were utilised for different categories of staff or talent which links to our argument about adopting a contingency approach to talent based on organisational requirements.

Clearly a key issue in establishing competency profiles is what should be included and what competencies and skills do you require your leaders to possess. In respect to this, we have seen a growing argument about leaders possessing a global mindset (Briscoe and Schuler, 2004; Osland *et al.*, 2006). While a relatively new research arena, the primary characteristics of a global mindset include being able to communicate and work with different cultures, manage uncertainty and global complexity (Briscoe and Schuler, 2004). This global mindset enables a shift away from an ethnocentric managerial approach to a more diverse management team and decision-making. The exploitation of talent from different countries and the diverse decision-making it enables has for some time been posited as a potential source of competitive advantage for MNEs (Macharzina *et al.*, 2001). Indeed, some organisations, including IBM and Ernst and Young, measure their managers' ability to retain and advance minorities and women (Jacobs, 2005), such is the increasing importance placed on diverse talent (Hewlett, 2009). Notwithstanding this, it has been suggested that many more organisations are failing to embrace the positive results that may arise from embracing a more diverse pool of talent instead continuing the preference for employees with a home passport (Nohria, 1999).

Cultural fit has also emerged as a criterion for identifying and selecting the right people for the organisation. In other words, an employee's personality and values were considered in determining their potential fit with the corporate culture (Stahl *et al.*, 2007). For example, Google is well known for the sophistication of its recruitment practices. Employees generally go through numerous rounds of successive interviews to maximise the fit of employees with the organisational culture.

Considering the focus on leaders, a further criterion that should be included in talent identification relates to an individual's ability to build and sustain relationships and networks (Beechler and Woodward, 2009). The importance of possessing networks with key stakeholders is becoming a critical aspect of many strategically important organisational positions. Farndale and colleagues (2010) note that increasing attention is being paid to the possession of social, political, cognitive and human capital. Social capital basically refers to having necessary connections to be able to perform boundary spanning roles (Kostova and Roth, 2002). Political capital is concerned with having the legitimacy necessary to be confirmed as talent (Harvey and Novicevic, 2004). Cognitive capital represents the possession of effective mental models of how knowledge needs to be shared across the globalizing organization (Murtha *et al.*, 1998) and human capital means possessing the competencies necessary to operate in cross-cultural contexts (Earley and Mosakowski, 2004).

It is clear that the skills and competencies required for MNE leadership positions are considerably more idiosyncratic and demanding than what is required working in a single national context (Collings *et al.*, 2009). There will be specific skills and competencies required depending on the organisation and position involved. However we contend that there are a number of generic competencies required by global leaders. The work of Osland and colleagues (2006) is useful in highlighting the range of competencies which the global leader may need to possess (see Table 4.1). These are categorised as: cross-cultural relationship skills, traits and values, cognitive orientation, vision, and global organizational expertise (Osland *et al.*, 2006). It is likely that particular competencies will be disproportionately important in specific organisations and thus organisations should differentiate between the competencies in terms of their relative importance in the specific organisational context. Indeed, it is important that organisations decide on the most critical competencies and focus their efforts on these over those of lesser importance. In addition, talent and competencies are not an end state. In other words, it is possible they might become out-dated – hence the importance in regularly reviewing the competencies and talent required by the organisation. Further, Karaevli and Hall (2003) suggest that what is particularly important is to develop the individual's ability to learn from the experience, which they argue will better serve the organisation than rigid competency frameworks.

The miss-identification of top performers and promotion of these employees can have grave consequences, as witnessed by the demise of Enron in the 1990s. Top performers in Enron received excessive rewards and were promoted without any great regard for an individual's experience or seniority (Michaels *et al.*, 2001). They used a system of identifying A, B, and C players, where A players received the extravagant rewards, B players encouraged to reach A level and C players were removed if they didn't substantially improve. However evaluation of performance was predominantly based on

Table 4.1 Global leadership competencies

Global leadership dimension	*Associated competencies*
Cross-cultural relationship skills	Cultural sensitivity, Appreciates diversity, Constructive dialogue, Motivates/rewards others, Develops others, Empowering others, Shares leadership responsibility, Social literacy, Cultural literacy
Traits and values	Inquisitiveness/curiosity, Resourcefulness, Optimism, Character/Integrity, Energetic, Emotional intelligence, Resilience to stress, Tenacious, Stable personal life, Life balance, Personal literacy
Vision	Articulates a tangible vision and strategy, Articulates values, Catalyst for cultural change, Catalyst for strategic change
Cognitive orientation	Global mindset, Open-minded, Thinking agility, Cognitive complexity, Managing uncertainty, Behavioural flexibility
Global business expertise	Global business savvy, Technologically savvy, Business literacy, Customer orientation, External orientation, Results orientation, Maintains competitive advantage
Global organizing expertise	Team building, Builds partnerships, Architecting/designing

Adapted from: Osland *et al.* (2006: 209).

subjective appraisals which resulted in employees being promoted for a false view of how an individual was performing with little regard for customers and shareholders (Gladwell, 2002). We contend it is important for organisations to derive formal identification criteria as per the requirements of their most critical future business roles. We maintain that Reitsma's (2001: 140) contention that 'a manager knows the criteria the business uses to come to a judgement about potential, which skills, it considers important in the various jobs, what the business-view is about his potential etc.' is misplaced as it places too much pressure on individual [subjective] judgements. While there will be an element of subjectivity in talent identification even with a formal set of identification criteria we argue that organisations with formal measures are likely to be better placed than those that adopt a more laissez-faire subjective approach.

Making or buying talent?

The vast majority of the talent management literature, implicitly at least, focuses on internal talent. However it is important to get the correct balance between internal and external talent. There is a long-standing body of research which highlights the importance of this and the dangers of being overly reliant on internal labour markets which can lead to a lack of new ideas and creativity in the organisation (Beardwell, 2007a). Buying talent from the external labour market may be particularly useful when an organisation needs a new way of thinking or the organisation is poorly networked with respect to service or product innovation (Rao and Drazin, 2002). Collings and Mellahi (2009), in their conceptual model of talent management, argue against solely relying on the internal labour market. In particular, they point to the emergence of the boundaryless career reflecting the decrease of the long-term career within a single organisation and greater movement between organisations during one's career (DeFillippi and Arthur, 1994) and reduced job and work identity (Weick and Berlinger, 1989). On the other hand, focusing on the internal labour market has benefits including improved morale, commitment and job security for employees and provides greater opportunity to assess an individual's ability and potential (Sparrow and Hiltrop, 1994).

We contend that organisations will be better placed by filling talent pools through a combination of internal development through the internal labour market and sourcing from the external labour market where appropriate (Cappelli, 2008a). This will help reduce some of the quantitative risks of not having sufficient talent or having an over-supply and the qualitative risks by ensuring there are people available to move into roles when required (ibid). Further, Hiltrop (1999) notes utilisation of the external labour market assists in preventing a silo type, single mindset from plaguing the organisation. A key step in this process relates to possessing a clear understanding of the firm's current talent base and the likely future requirements to facilitate decision-making with regard to an appropriate strategy for the operationalisation of talent management. We now turn to the identification and evaluation process.

The identification and evaluation process

HR planning

The strategic HRM literature suggests HR/manpower planning represent the critical tool linking an organisation's strategic business plans and strategic HRM (Iles, 2001). We also suggest it plays a key role in MNEs effectively managing their talent. Effective HR planning provides management with vital information which can facilitate decision-making with regard to increasing or decreasing investment in recruitment, training and development and so forth. Armstrong (2005) suggests a number of specific ways that the organisation can benefit from effective HR planning:

- better at attracting and retaining the required people with appropriate skills, experience and competences
- anticipate issues surrounding surpluses or deficits of talent reduce dependence on the external labour market.

Through understanding the talent the organisation needs and possesses, as well as availability from the external labour market, the organisation will be able to identify areas of particular vulnerability. We contend that these areas of key strategic impact should then be prioritised.

HR planning, however, should be a dynamic process which is regularly revised in conjunction with changes in the micro and macro environment and corporate strategy and should consider a number of contingences (Ivancevich, 2007). The usefulness of HR planning has been questioned owing to the rapidly changing environments in which organisations now operate. 'Business strategies do not always result in a rational plan but may – sometimes serendipitously – evolve over time' (McDonnell and Gunnigle, 2009: 193–194; see Mintzberg, 1978 for greater detail on patterns of strategy formulation). Liff (2000: 96) contends that 'the more rapidly changing environment . . . makes the planning process more complex and less certain, but does not make it less important or significant'. What is imperative is that HR plans are treated as 'tentative, flexible and reviewed and modified on a regular basis' (Beardwell, 2007b: 173).

The first step should be similar to the way a store undertakes a stock-taking exercise. This involves identifying the number and type of people required at each organisational level to achieve the corporate objectives. Further, the skills, abilities, knowledge and other characteristics (KSAOs) required in particular positions should be identified. Essentially this is akin to the traditional job skills analysis. Considering our focus on leadership positions, we suggest that the predominant focus should be on the key generic-type competencies required for these roles. When there is a higher degree of certainty of an individual's potential and their likelihood of moving into a specific role then developing her/him for the more specific requirements of this position can take place. Second, demand and supply forecasting must take place which allows a gap analysis to occur – in other words, forecasting future people needs and the future availability of people. Once completed, management needs to analyse how the organisation is currently positioned to allow more effective prediction of the key issues likely to emerge in the future. This will allow management to determine current capabilities and areas that they may be lacking people of a sufficient calibre in. This also needs to incorporate an appraisal of the external labour market taking into account changing demographics, skills availability and the like. Considering that talent management's emergence as a key management concern was premised on changing demographics which had resulted in major talent shortages, it is evident that organisations may not have been paying enough attention to these analytics and appropriately developing talent pools.

Scenario planning acknowledges the difficulty of predicting the future and thus involves speculation on the variety of 'futures' which may evolve and consideration of how the organisation may respond (Mintzberg, 1994). Further, contingency planning, which has links to scenario planning, involves drawing up different plans to deal with potentially different scenarios and helps to a more proactive rather than reactive planning process (Taylor, 2005). More recently, it has been suggested that micro-planning might represent a useful option to overcome the ever-changing business environment MNEs face. Micro-planning involves organisations concentrating on key problem areas rather than the organisation as a whole (Beardwell, 2007b). Arguably this holds much salience for MNEs due to the size of many of these organisations. Focus should be on those critical segments of the business rather than attempting to manage every single area in such a strategic, proactive manner.

Through undertaking effective workforce analytics and HR planning:

> . . . you know who to recruit, who to develop, who to redeploy and where to redeploy them, whether you should hire someone externally or promote someone from within, and whether you should look for a contingent workers, a contractor, or full-time workers. Workforce analytics can help you make the best talent-management decisions and align those with your corporate objectives
>
> Schweyer, 2004, cited by Lewis and Heckman, 2006: 147.

Succession planning

Succession planning is one of the principal methods organisations can use to identify senior management talent. It can be defined as 'a deliberate and systematic effort by an organization to ensure leadership continuity in key positions and encourage individual advancement' (Rothwell, 1994: 6). At its most basic, succession planning refers to ensuring an organisation has the right people, with the right skills, in the right place, at the right time. It should provide a global overview of the key managerial positions, the people holding them, as well as their potential successors (Stiles *et al.*, 2006). A key criticism of succession planning as traditionally defined is the narrow focus it takes. Succession planning is particularly concerned with the recruitment and retention of the key senior managerial roles (Beardwell, 2007a). Consequently, there is a rather limited focus as a result of the reliance on identifying a small number of people who could take on the key positions. This type of approach assumes a stable environment coupled with long-term career plans of employees. However, neither situation now exists. In other words, MNEs do not operate in stable business environments and employees often envisage their careers unfolding over a number of different organisations as opposed to within the boundaries of a single firm (see Arthur and Rousseau, 1996 for a discussion of the boundaryless career).

It has been suggested that succession planning has evolved from the traditional, early year short-term focus on replacing senior managers if they happened to leave without prior warning. There is now a more long-term aim of developing a cadre of key talent who are able to take on higher level roles, potentially even roles that may not currently exist, underpinning succession planning (cf. Beardwell and Claydon, 2007). Figure 4.1 demonstrates a key issue with traditional succession planning where an organisation failed to identify a pool of talent who possess the potential to take on a role. The utilisation of talent pools consisting of employees with key generic type competencies and skills allows the organisation far greater scope when positions become available. Management will be able to select the most suitable person from a pool of candidates and train the person into the specific requirements of that particular role. We argue this approach is less likely to lead to the situation highlighted in Figure 4.1.

One London-based real estate finance and development firm, for instance, was gearing up for a major reconstruction job in Berlin – an effort that would represent not only a €500 million boost in revenues over two years, but also an opportunity to get in on the ground floor of many other projects in that part of the world. When the executive committee reviewed the list of people who might be ready to take on such an assignment, the CEO noticed that the same names appeared as the only candidates for other critical efforts under consideration. And when he asked his business unit heads for additional prospects, he was told that there weren't any.

Figure 4.1 Making the case for moving away from traditional succession planning to talent pool identification

Source: Ready and Conger, 2007: 2.

Talent pool segmentation

There seems to be a move towards identifying pools of talent that possess the potential to move into a number of roles (Karaevli and Hall, 2003). Talent pools focus on 'projecting employee/staffing needs and managing the progression of employees through positions' (Lewis and Heckman, 2006: 140). These talent pools will encompass high potential and high performing employees who are capable of moving into higher level strategic roles when required. Additionally, there may be vertical deployment of such talented individuals in the organisation. Stahl and colleagues' (2007) research found MNEs recruit the best people and then place them into positions rather than recruiting for specific positions. Consequently there is somewhat of a change in focus to recruiting the 'right people in the right place' rather than the traditional focus on one specific role (Stahl *et al.*, 2007). The use of talent pools also involves a shift of focus to identifying high potential at an earlier stage and casting a broader net across different categories of staff (Farndale *et al.*, 2010). Reitsma (2001) argues that the identification of talent should not begin at senior management level but should commence when an organisation starts recruiting involving different categories of talent pools. Identifying people with only a very specific future role in mind can be counter-productive and wasteful because if a business changes strategies, a different type of leader may be required. Consequently, identifying high potentials according to particular competencies seems a useful approach as it will involve a pool of individuals that possess sets of important competencies that will place the organisation in a better position when they require this talent.

Performance management: identifying/evaluating performance or potential?

A key dilemma for organisations in effective talent management is how potential is measured as opposed to past performance. Although performance management, and measuring past performance is imperative in any talent management system, an employee's future potential also needs to be evaluated. Obtaining accurate and timely information is vital to successfully identifying high potentials – hence the importance of having some level of objective, formalised measures. If personal relationships and subjective observations are solely relied upon to identify these then what may occur will be a strengthening of the established network instead of developing a more diverse pool of talent (Jacobs, 2005). Building clones of existing performers in roles may not be what is required to achieve future objectives – '. . . "best-fit" today may be the "misfit" tomorrow' (Karaevli and Hall, 2003: 71).

Performance management essentially involves measuring performance against pre-set objectives. Consequently, potential may not be captured to a great extent and even the performance objectives can be problematic. Performance management was initially an operational type process which built on the 'management by objectives' (MBO) approach (MBO) by Peter Drucker (1954). While MBO was a solely quantitative result system, performance management seeks to integrate all organisational actors and often uses a number of qualitative measures in addition to quantitative objectives (McDonnell and Gunnigle, 2009). For performance management to be effective in talent management it needs to develop a more strategically oriented focus. The performance objectives set must be linked to the overall corporate objectives (Costello, 1994; Sparrow and Hiltrop, 1994) but there is also a need to identify and evaluate employees against the competencies required in their current role and those required for higher level positions.

The objective of the performance management system will be critical to its success in evaluating and identifying talent. In particular we suggest that a critical in-built aspect of the performance management process should be to identify behaviours, skills and competencies that need to be developed. The appraisal or review should identify skills and competencies that require improvement and three to four areas should then be typically selected to develop. For example, Unilever assesses the competencies of an individual against the competencies and requirements of the next level of seniority (Reitsma, 2001). This assists in identifying employees who have the potential to move to the next work level. Other organisations have adopted slightly different criteria – Citigroup evaluate staff against their capability of moving two levels above their current role and/or those capable of leading a global business or function in the future (Karaevli and Hall, 2003).

Performance management systems invariably consist of the line manager reviewing performance – this highlights a key issue – whether the line manager is always the best placed person to identify the potential of employees (see McDonnell and Gunnigle, 2009 for a more detailed critique of performance management systems). We suggest this: predominantly, performance type data should be used in conjunction with higher level talent review meetings consisting of top and HR managers at different organisational levels to aid the identification process (Makela *et al.*, 2010).

Talent is not fixed and treating it as such is dangerous (Beechler and Woodward, 2009). Consequently, regular reviews are a critical aspect. The common appraisal system of sitting down with an employee once a year to evaluate performance against pre-determined objectives is insufficient in the long-run. Arguably regular reviews and feedback are even more important for the new generation of employees who are believed to look for continuous feedback on how they are doing and how they can further improve. We suggest that this is a significant challenge for organisations and argue that, without top management support, any talent management system introduced will struggle to fulfil its objectives.

However regardless of an MNE's objectives with regard to talent management, the system may not always be effective in identifying the best talent within the MNE. This issue is considered in detail by Mellahi and Collings (2010). They identify a number of challenges in the advancement of subsidiary talent in the MNE. At the subsidiary level, drawing on agency theory, they argue that in some instances managers are not incentivised to identify their top talent to higher levels in the MNE hierarchy. Specifically, self-serving mechanisms displayed by subsidiary managers might hinder effective talent management systems throughout the MNE. For example, wishing to retain key subsidiary talent within the subsidiary to maximise the performance of the subsidiary operation. This hinders the promotion of key subsidiary talent beyond their home subsidiary.

Additionally at the headquarters level, they consider the bounded rationality to explain how the decision-making processes, and information that top management teams use to make decisions about talent management results in overlooking talents at subsidiary level. In this regard, the information available is simply too vast and complex for HQ managers to accurately evaluate decision-making processes about talent deployment. Hence, key decisions about talent may be made on the basis of incomplete information or an incomplete analysis of available information.

Talent identification/evaluation tools

Tests and tools that assess knowledge, competencies, skills, abilities, personality traits, experience and judgement should all be considered and used for identifying and evaluating high potential. Having an effective talent management system is much more than utilising a plethora 'of off-the-shelf components, such as competency-profiling tools, 360-degree feedback, and online training' (Cohn *et al.*, 2005: 8). It needs to be a well thought-out system that is specific to a particular organisation. MNEs need to identify means to identify and evaluate employees against the predefined competencies and skills for roles, some of which may not even currently exist. Typically, evaluation tends to be by means of an annual appraisal involving the manager sitting down with the employee, analysing performance against previously agreed objectives and identifying developmental areas. We suggest that organisations which are serious about talent management will utilise a range of tools to provide a more holistic and effective means of identifying high potentials. In highlighting some of the techniques that may be used we stress the importance of linking tools to corporate objectives. It is also critical to be aware of the issues and challenges one is likely to face in particular positions, as well as being able to measure the competencies required to handle future roles. For example, Ready and Conger (2007) highlight the talent management system used by HSBC which includes 360-degree feedback, one-on-one interviews and psychometric tests, as well as standardised rating scales encompassing three years of performance statistics. The results then lead into regional or business unit talent pools which track and manage high-potentials within HSBC. We now briefly discuss some of the main tools for the identification and evaluation of talent.

360-degree assessment 360-degree assessment involves multiple sources of feedback including supervisors, peers and colleagues. While it has been used as a performance appraisal technique linked to pay, it is arguably far more appropriate and effective in the context of development. The use of a multi-faceted view of one's performance can be an excellent exercise in providing honest feedback on areas that an individual could improve and serves as a means to identify potential. Its use will help negate some of the weaknesses, while acknowledging there are potential problems with 360-feedback itself, of relying solely on a line manager to identify an individual's potential.

Assessment centres Assessment centres which are structured on specific, pivotal organisational roles are likely to play a key role in ensuring better identification and evaluation of high potentials. For example, assessing people on specific competencies, using scenario-based questioning, cognitive tests and work-style inventories can be useful. Such role-based assessments provide an additional insight into how a person might cope in a given situation. Whilst the use of hypothetical scenario questioning in interviews allows a candidate give an answer showing how they would respond, the use of a role scenario will provide a more thorough analysis of how the person would respond in a given situation.

Psychometric tests Psychometric tests are 'systematic and standardised procedure for evoking a sample of responses from a candidate, which can be used to assess one or more of their psychological characteristics by comparing the results with those of a representative sample of an appropriate population' (Smith and Robertson, 1986: 152). There are a number of different types of psychometric tools (see Sharma and Bhatnagar, 2009 for a list and brief explanation of these). For selection and talent identification purposes, ability or aptitude tests and personality inventories or tests are the most commonly used. Ability or aptitude tests seek to test an individual's maximum ability with regard to a particular area such as cognitive ability. However, there are criticisms of their use at senior levels as the difference in intelligence of highly qualified individuals is likely to be minimal making it difficult to differentiate candidates (see Robertson *et al.*, 2002 for a more detailed critique on these tests). Personality tests are used to collate information on an individual's way of thinking and acting in specified situations and are believed to be particularly useful given the increasing consensus regarding the relationship of some personality tests with job performance (Murphy and Bartram, 2002).

Talent management information systems Assessment and evaluation of employees is one of the most difficult tasks for an organisation and is even more complex for the MNE due to the global nature of its operations and the resultant greater diversity and issues this involves. While technology is increasingly being used as a means of facilitating GTM, Chaisson and Schweyer (2004: 6) warn that technology can add 'almost as much additional complexity to the task as it offers solutions to make it easier'. The usefulness and effectiveness of an information technology (IT) based GTM system should not be taken for granted but MNEs are likely to benefit from having one in terms of quickly identifying high potentials with the particular skills and competencies that may be suitable for a particular role and also in tracking candidates across the organisation's global operations.

For example, Procter and Gamble (P&G) use an IT based global talent management system which accommodates each of their 135,000 employees – with a key focus on 13,000 middle and senior management (Ready and Conger, 2007). This system holds succession planning information at country, business unit and regional levels. Further, individual career paths, education, and capabilities are all accommodated. This system allows quick and easy identification of high potentials. To ensure the system remains relevant P&G use global talent reviews where each function in every country is audited for its ability to identify, develop, engage and retain its key talent. Similarly, Hartmann *et al.* (2010) found some use of IT systems to store the résumés of employees who were deemed to possess the potential to undertake international assignments.

Global versus locally managed?

The global nature of MNEs makes talent management a particularly complex issue. For MNEs to achieve the purported benefits from global integration and local responsiveness (Bartlett and Ghoshal, 1990) having a culturally diverse management team is critical. Consequently, MNEs that fail to acknowledge and use talent available at subsidiary level are likely to struggle with achieving this because subsidiary level management are better equipped to deal with local issues (Gong, 2003).

A key dilemma is should MNEs implement standardised systems for assessing employees/high potentials or do they need to have locally based systems? For instance, what impact will different cultures have on standardised performance appraisal or rating instruments? Do MNEs need to take local differences into account in these situations? These are major issues MNEs face in effectively identifying, managing and leveraging their best talent from their global network. For example, standardised rating scales may be appraised in different ways due to the inevitable level of subjectivity they involve. Practices standardised across operations may also vary in their implementation across units. Hartmann and colleagues (2010) in their study of western MNEs in China observed no adaptation of performance appraisals to the host context. This resonates with the questioning above as to whether a line manager alone is the most appropriate person to identify potential. A performance management system involving an annual appraisal should not be used in isolation as there is no fool-proof system that can be used. Instead we suggest that a suite of practices that evaluate people against key competencies should be utilised and a higher level talent review should be incorporated to assist in identifying those who possess the potential to develop further competencies to take on more strategic roles (Makela *et al.*, 2010).

For example, HSBC utilise a hybrid system for talent management (Ready and Conger, 2007). Talent pools are locally managed and initially involve new assignments within the region or business unit but in time these high potentials (those viewed as possessing the potential to reach a senior managerial role with the region or business) will be involved in cross-boundary assignments. In addition to these talent pools, the local high-level managers will identify those who are viewed as having potential to become senior executives and top management team members. This is a pool managed by central management at head office. Gong (2003) has highlighted the issue of geographical distance in headquarter level management identifying talent at subsidiary level (see also Makela *et al*, 2010; Mellahi and Collings, 2010). Consequently, we suggest that a hybrid model of both global and local involvement is critical for MNEs to provide them with the opportunity to maximise the potential of talent from foreign operations. This is likely to involve greater local involvement in some talent pools over others as in the case of HSBC. However, it is also important to note that the dynamics by which global talent management is likely to play out will vary between different types of MNEs (see Scullion and Starkey, 2000; Farndale *et al.*, 2010). A more in-depth discussion of the challenges surrounding global talent management is provided in chapters 2 and 3.

Conclusion

This chapter has highlighted some of the key challenges in one of the most critical elements of a talent management system namely, the identification and evaluation of talent. Moreover, concentrating on the leadership talent we provided some insights on where MNEs should be focusing and the tools they may utilise to be effective. Through effectively identifying and evaluating talent, in conjunction with other elements of the GTM system (e.g. development), talent shortages can be much more carefully predicted and managed (Ready and Conger, 2007).

More particularly, we note the importance of identifying the specific talent organisations need and the skills and competencies one requires to be effective in particular roles. Further, we note the importance of fit with the organisational culture (Stahl *et al.*, 2007) and the increasing importance of social capital or the extent of relationships which the person has across the organisation (Beechler and Woodward, 2009). Rather than identifying one or two people for a specific role as the more traditional form of succession planning adopted, we contend that organisations should identify pools of talent and develop the key generic competencies in them. When a role becomes available, then the organisation should look at providing the selected individual with the more specific requirements for that role. However, we urge caution about organisations primarily relying on the internal labour market. We suggest that it is vital that organisations do not neglect the potential that is likely to exist on the open, external labour market (Cappelli, 2008a). Finally, we discuss the various tools that an organisation may utilise to identify and evaluate employees. In so doing, we suggest, rather than using an off-the-shelf talent management system as is often advertised, organisations need to strategically consider their own requirements and develop a system accordingly.

From revising the GTM literature it is apparent that there remains an empirical paucity and the area of talent identification is arguably one of the most under-explored. From our review of this area we propose that there are a number of areas worthy of future investigation, not least, the competency frameworks being utilised by MNEs to identify talent and whether there is a level of convergence across these. Further, an exploration of how this process takes place in an MNEs operational network would be useful as it would aid our understanding of what is a complex process. For instance, are global, local or hybrid type approaches being adopted? How successful are MNEs in increasing the diversity of their organisational talent? It would also be useful to explore the role of information technology systems in the identification process and the extent to which it facilitates or further complicates GTM.

Finally, we wish to point out that although this chapter was specifically focused on the identification and evaluation of talent it is imperative that MNEs do not treat this process in isolation from other key elements of their GTM system. For instance, identifying talent is also (or at least should be) intrinsically linked to development. Specifically, when an individual is selected as talent it should mean that the said person will then receive the development that future roles and challenges will bestow (Karaevli and Hall, 2003). Indeed it is unlikely that any GTM system will be effective if each element is not consistent and integrated with one another. Little is known on how the different elements of GTM link and work together, thus research that explores integrated GTM systems would have considerable merit for practitioners as well as researchers in the field.

References

Armstrong, M. (2005) *A Handbook of Human Resource Management*, 10th edition, London: Kogan Page.

Arthur, M. B. and Rousseau, D. M. (1996) *The Boundaryless Career: A New Employment Principle for a New Organizational Era*, New York: Oxford University Press.

Barney, J. (1991) 'Firm resources and sustained competitive advantage', *Journal of Management*, 17 (1): 99–120.

Bartlett, S. and Ghoshal, C. A. (1990) 'The multinational corporation as an interorganizational network', *Academy of Management Executive*, 15: 603–625.

Beardwell, J. (2007a) 'Recruitment and selection'. In J. Beardwell and T. Claydon, *Human Resource Management: A Contemporary Approach*, 5th edition (pp. 189–224), Essex: Pearson.

Beardwell, J. (2007b) 'Human resource planning'. In J. Beardwell and T. Claydon, *Human Resource Management: A Contemporary Approach*, 5th edition (pp. 157–188), Essex: Pearson.

Beardwell, J. and Claydon, T. (2007) *Human Resource Management: A Contemporary Approach*, 5th edition, Essex: Pearson.

Beechler, S. and Woodward, I. C. (2009) 'The global "war for talent" ', *Journal of International Management*, 15 (3): 273–285.

Boudreau, J.W. and Ramstad, P.M. (2007) *Beyond HR: The New Science of Human Capital*, Boston, MA: Harvard Business School Press.

Briscoe, D. R. and Schuler, R. S. (2004) *International Human Resource Management*, 2nd edition, New York: Routledge.

Cappelli, P. (2008a) *Talent on Demand*, Boston, Harvard Business School.

Cappelli, P. (2008b) 'Talent management for the twenty-first century', *Harvard Business Review*, March: 74–81.

Chaisson, J. and Schweyer, A. (2004) *Global Talent Management: Fostering Global Workforce Practices That Are Scalable, Sustainable and Ethical. 8 Principles and 7 Field Lessons for Success in Global Talent Management*, A Human Capital Institute Position Paper.

Cohn, J. M., Khurana, R. and Reeves, L. (2005) 'Growing talent as if your business depended on it', *Harvard Business Review*, October, 1–11.

Collings, D. G., McDonnell, A. and Scullion, H. (2009) 'Global talent management: The law of the few', *Poznan University of Economics Review*, 9 (2):5–18.

Collings, D. G and Mellahi, K. (2009) 'Strategic talent management: A review and research agenda', *Human Resource Management Review*, 19: 304–313.

Collings, D. G. and Scullion, H. (2007) 'Resourcing international assignees'. In C. Brewster, P. Sparrow and M. Dickman (eds.) *International Human Resource Management: Contemporary Issues in Europe*, Basingstoke: Palgrave Macmillan.

Costello, S. J. (1994) *Effective Performance Management*, New York: Irwin.

DeFillippi, R. J. and Arthur, M. B. (1994) 'The boundaryless career: A competence-based perspective', *Journal of Organizational Behaviour*, 15: 307–324.

Drucker, P. (1954) *The Practice of Management*. New York: Harper.

Earley, C. and Mosakowski, E. (2004) 'Cultural intelligence', *Harvard Business Review*, October: 139–146.

Farndale, E., Scullion, H. and Sparrow, P. (2010) 'The role of the corporate HR function in global talent management', *Journal of World Business*, 45 (2): 161–168.

Gladwell, M. (2002) 'The talent myth: are smart people overrated?', *The New Yorker*, July 22.

Gong, Y. (2003) 'Subsidiary staffing in multinational enterprises: Agency, resources and performance', *Academy of Management Journal*, 45: 728–739.

Hartmann, E., Feisel, E. and Schober, H. (2010) 'Talent management of western MNCs in China: Balancing global integration and local responsiveness', *Journal of World Business*, 45 (2): 169–178.

Harvey, M. and Novicevic, M. M. (2004) 'The development of political skill and political capital by global leaders through global assignments', *International Journal of Human Resource Management*, 15 (7): 1173–1188.

Hewlett, S.A. (2009) *Top Talent: Keeping Performance Up When Business is Down*, Boston, Harvard Business School Press.

Hiltrop, J. M. (1999) 'The quest for the best: Human resource practices to attract and retain talent', *European Management Journal*, 17 (4): 422–430.

Huselid, M. A., Beatty, R. W. and Becker, B. E. (2005) 'A players or A positions? The strategic logic of workforce management', *Harvard Business Review*, 83 (12): 110–117.

Iles, P. (2001) 'Employee resourcing'. In J. Storey (ed.), *Human Resource Management*, London: Thomson.

Ivancevich, J. M. (2007) *Human Resource Management*, 10th edition, New York: McGraw-Hill Irwin.

Jacobs, D. (2005) 'In search of future leaders: managing the global talent pipeline', *Ivy Business Journal Online*, 69 (4): 1–5.

Karaevli, A. and Hall, D. T. (2003) 'Growing leaders for turbulent times: Is succession planning up to the challenge?', *Organizational Dynamics*, 31 (1): 62–79.

Kostova, T. and Roth, K. (2002) 'Adoption of an organizational practice by subsidiaries of multinational corporations: Institutional and relational effects', *Academy of Management Journal*, 45: 215–233.

Lewis, R. E. and Heckman, R. J. (2006) 'Talent management: a critical review', *Human Resource Management Review*, 16 (2): 139–154.

Liff, S. (2000) 'Manpower or human resource planning – what's in a name?' In S. Bach and K. Sisson (eds.), *Personnel Management: A Comprehensive Guide to Theory and Practice*, 3rd edition, Oxford: Blackwell.

Macharzina, K., Oesterle, M. J. and Brodel, D. (2001) Learning in multinationals. In M. Dierkes, A. Berthoin Antal, J. Child and I. Nonaka (Eds.), *Handbook of Organizational Learning and Knowledge*, New York: Oxford University Press.

Makela, K., Bjorkman, I. and Ehrmrooth, M. (2010) 'How do MNCs establish their talent pools? Influences on individuals' likelihood of being labelled as talent', *Journal of World Business*, 45 (2), 134–142.

McDonnell, A. and Gunnigle, P. (2009) 'Performance management'. In D. G. Collings and G. Wood (eds.). *Human Resource Management: A Critical Approach*, Abingdon and New York: Routledge.

McDonnell, A., Hickey, C. and Gunnigle, P. (2010a) 'Global talent management: exploring talent identification in the multinational enterprise', *European Journal of International Management*, in press, accepted 23 November 2009.

McDonnell, A., Lamare, R., Gunnigle, P. and Lavelle, J. (2010b) 'Developing tomorrow's leaders – evidence of global talent management in multinational companies', *Journal of World Business*, 45 (2): 150–160.

Mellahi, K. and Collings, D. G. (2010) 'The barriers to effective global talent management: The example of corporate elites in MNEs', *Journal of World Business*, 45 (2): 143–149.

Michaels, E., Handfield-Jones, H. and Axelrod, B. (2001) *The War for Talent*, Boston: Harvard Business School.

Mintzberg, H. (1994) *The Rise and Fall of Strategic Planning*, Hemel Hempstead: Prentice Hall.

Mintzberg, H. (1978) 'Patterns in strategy formulation', *Management Science*, 24: 934–948.

Murphy, K. R. and Bartram, D. (2002) 'Recruitment, personnel selection and organisational effectiveness'. In I. T. Robertson, M. Callinan and D. Bartram (Eds.), *Organisational Effectiveness: The Role of Psychology* (pp. 85–113), Chichester, Wiley.

Murtha, T. P., Lenway, S. A. and Bagozzi, R. P. (1998) 'Global mind-sets and cognitive shift in a complex multinational corporation', *Strategic Management Journal*, 19: 97–114.

Nohria, N. (1999) 'The war for global talent', *Chief Executive Magazine*, 16.

Osland, J. S., Bird, A., Mendenhall, M. and Osland, A. (2006) 'Developing global leadership capabilities and global mindset: a review'. In G. K. Stahl and I. Bjorkman (eds.), *Handbook of Research in International Human Resource Management*, Cheltenham: Edward Elgar.

Rao, H. and Drazin, R. (2002) 'Overcoming resource constraints on product innovation by recruiting talent from rivals: A study of the mutual funds industry', *Academy of Management Review*, 45: 491–507.

Ready, D. A. and Conger, J. A. (2007) 'Make your company a talent factory', *Harvard Business Review*, June, 1–10.

Reitsma, S. G. (2001) 'Management development in Unilever', *Journal of Management Development*, 20 (2): 131–144.

Robertson, I. T., Bartram, D. and Callinan, M. (2002) 'Personnel selection and assessment'. In P. Warr (Ed.), *Psychology at work*, 5th edition (pp. 100–152), London: Penguin.

Rothwell, W. J. (1994) *Effective Succession Planning: Ensuring Leadership Continuity and Building Talent from Within*, New York: Amacom.

Schuler, R., Jackson, S. and Tarique, I. (2010) 'The global talent management challenge: drivers and strategic HR issues'. In D. G. Collings and H. Scullion (eds.), *Global Talent Management*, Abingdon and New York: Routledge.

Scullion, H., Collings, D. G. and Caligiuri, P. (2010) 'Global talent management', *Journal of World Business*, 45 (2): 105–108.

Scullion, H. and Starkey, K. (2000) 'In search of the changing role of the corporate human resource function in the international firm', *International Journal of Human Resource Management*, 11: 1061–1081.

Sharma, R. and Bhatnagar, J. (2009) 'Talent management – competency development: key to global leadership', *Industrial and Commercial Training*, 41 (3): 118–132.

Smilansky, J. (2006) *Developing Executive Talent: Best Practices from Global Leaders*, Chichester: John Wiley.

Smith, M. and Robertson, I. T. (1986) *The Theory and Practice of Systematic Staff Selection*. London: Macmillan Press.

Sparrow, P. (2007) 'Globalization of HR at function level: four UK-based case studies of the international recruitment and selection process', *International Journal of Human Resource Management*, 18 (5): 845–867

Sparrow, P. and Hiltrop, J. M. (1994) *European Human Resource Management*, London: Prentice Hall.

Stahl, G. K., Bjorkman, I., Farndale, E., Morris, S. S., Stiles, P., Trevor, J. and Wright, P. M. (2007) *Global Talent Management: How Leading Multinationals Build and Sustain Their Talent Pipeline*, Faculty and Research Working Paper. Fontainebleau, France: INSEAD.

Stiles, P., Wright, P., Paauwe, J., Stahl, G., Trevor, J. Farndale, E., Morris, S. and Bjorkman, I. (2006) *Best Practice and Key Themes in Global Human Resource Management: Project Report*, Global Human Resource Research Alliance (GHRRA).

Tarique, I. and Schuler, R. (2010) 'Global talent management: literature review, integrative framework, and suggestions for further research', *Journal of World Business*, 45 (2): 122–133.

Taylor, S. (2005) *People Resourcing*, 3rd edition, London: CIPD.

Ulrich, D. (2006) 'The talent trifecta', *Workforce Management*, September, 32–33.

Weick, K. E. and Berlinger, L. R. (1989) 'Career improvisation in self-designing organizations'. In M.B. Arthur, D. T. Hall and B. S. Lawrence (eds.), *Handbook of Career Theory* (pp. 313–328), New York: Cambridge University Press.

Embracing turnover: moving beyond the "war for talent"

DEEPAK SOMAYA AND IAN O. WILLIAMSON

Introduction

If you ask top executives across the globe what are the greatest challenges to competitive success they face, they will invariably bring up the so-called "War for Talent." Across a wide range of industries it is not just the ability to get business or the state of the economy that keeps executives up at night, but finding employees who have the leadership capacity and talent to implement new and more complex global strategies. Indeed, in the 2007 Conference Board Survey 79 percent of CEOs of successful U.S. firms rated availability of talent as their chief business problem (Corporate Authorship TCB, 2007). Talent shortage has also become a critical issue in fast-growing emerging economies, such China and India, where large low-skill labor pools mask severe shortages of truly high-quality candidates (see Part 3 of the current volume). For example, India's NASSCOM (National Association of Software and Service Companies) has warned that the Indian IT sector faces a shortfall of 500,000 professionals by 2010 that will threaten the competitiveness of the country's offshore IT services (Johnson, 2007). This looming talent shortage is so critical that the Indian IT provider HCL Technologies, with over 50,000 employees and revenues over $2 billion, has adopted the radical philosophy of putting "the employee first and the customer second," based on the belief that great employees have become scarcer than customers (Birkinshaw, Crainer and Mol, 2007).

While the war for talent has many causes, first and foremost it has been driven by an economic shift from an industrial age to a knowledge-based one. In the past organizations generated large portions of their profits by acquiring and leveraging hard assets, such as machinery and land; but more and more intangible assets, such as the knowledge and relationships possessed by employees, have become key to organizational performance. However, unlike tangible assets, employees are not owned by firms, and are free to move between organizations and take their knowledge and relationships with them.

Despite the large amounts of money and time firms have invested in talent retention programs, at a macro-level there is little to suggest that the retention problem has improved. On the contrary, there is substantial evidence that in many labor markets employee mobility is actually increasing. A survey of United States companies conducted by the Society of Human Resource Management (SHRM) concluded that from the beginning of 2005 to the end of 2006 firms lost nearly 30 percent of their human capital (SHRM, 2007). In China, recent surveys have revealed that 43 percent of senior managers and leaders voluntarily leave their organizations each year. It is also estimated that the average tenure of Chinese employees between the ages 25 to 35—the age group most sought out by multinationals—has *decreased* in recent years from 3–5 years to 1–2 years (Amble, 2006). These findings reaffirm that inter-company mobility has become the career path norm for employees. Perhaps it is time to declare that the "War for Talent" is over . . . talent has won!

In the face of this new reality, what are companies to do? They can, as before, try to adjust their internal employee retention programs with the hope that these changes will curb employee mobility and help them win the talent war. However, there are limits to this more-of-the-same approach. Instead, based on our research (Somaya, Williamson, and Lorinkova, 2008) we suggest taking a more radical step—companies should embrace employee turnover as a fact of life, and deploy a portfolio of HR strategies that focus employee retention efforts more narrowly and effectively on the one hand, and leverage potential opportunities created by turnover on the other. At its core, our strategic framework is built on two key ideas: that all types of employee mobility are not the same, and that former employees can be a strategic asset if ties to them are developed and utilized appropriately. Therefore, it behooves companies to not approach all employee mobility with a war mentality, and to "pick their battles" more carefully.

The rest of this chapter is organized as follows. We begin with a description of our thinking about employee mobility and how it departs from the conventional view. We then outline some conventional strategic approaches for dealing with employee mobility, before advocating a relational strategy that is a superior alternative in certain situations. In the following section, we present a portfolio-based framework to help managers identify different types of employee mobility and target appropriate strategies in response to each type. Finally, we conclude with a brief discussion of the applicability of our framework in the emerging talent-driven business environment of the future.

Rethinking employee mobility

Conventional HR approaches to organizational turnover tend to view all employee mobility alike and treat all employees with the same broad brush. The goal then becomes one of meeting an overall turnover target, using one-size-fits-all policies of compensation and job satisfaction. However, in recent years, there has been a serious reevaluation of the conventional HR toolkit for managing mobile talent. One recommendation that has emerged is to use a market-based approach to manage who leaves and when; to wit, employees who are most likely to be poached away and who generate difficult-to-replace value for the firm should be targeted for the most intensive retention efforts (Cappelli, 2000). Other suggested strategies draw on the idea that a company's management of talent should be segmented or differentiated based on its strategic business impacts. For example, retention efforts can be focused on talented employees in so-called "A" positions that are critical for the firm's strategic capabilities and have a major impact on executing the firm's strategy (Huselid, Becker, Beatty, 2005). Similarly, talent needs can be segmented based on strategic business needs, and staffing or retention efforts focused on where the talent is "pivotal" to alleviating critical business bottlenecks (Boudreau and Ramstad, 2005). Yet another approach is to accept that employee mobility and the demand for talent are both highly uncertain, and employ "talent on demand" strategies that include better forecasting, outsourcing, uncertainty management, and internal labor markets to address these uncertainties (Cappelli, 2008).

These newer HR strategies help companies engage in the "war for talent" more strategically; however, they do not address the broader structural issues driving employee mobility. So, we think companies need to move beyond the mentality of constantly fighting over talent, and learn how they can exploit employee mobility to their advantage as well. For this to occur, organizational leaders need to fundamentally rethink some of the key principles underlying the "War for Talent" perspective. Traditionally, employee mobility has been framed as a win or lose scenario: a firm "wins" if it keeps its employees and it "loses" if its employees join another company. Turnover hurts firms because of the increased administrative expenses associated with recruiting, hiring and training replacements. These costs have been estimated to be 100 percent–150 percent of the salary of a high performing employee with unique skills. Firms also lose when they have turnover because employees are repositories of human capital—a firm's *talent* and *skill*, as well as its *knowledge* and *know-how*. Thus, if a valuable employee leaves her current employer to join a new firm along with her generic knowledge (talent) and company specific knowledge (e.g., trade secrets), she increases the human capital of her new employer while simultaneously decreasing the human capital of her former employer. In many industries, talented (and mobile) employees are significant drivers of firm performance, reinforcing the war-for-talent mentality towards employee turnover among top managers.

The recent case of a semiconductor company clearly illustrates this traditional "War for Talent" framing. The company lost both the project lead and chief architect working on a new integrated circuit (IC) product for the firm. From a human capital perspective these two former employees were perhaps the two most important assets for the fledgling business being developed within the company. They knew more about the IC product than anyone else in the firm, and walked out of the door with significant proprietary knowledge about markets and technologies as well. Naturally, in the midst of scrambling to replace these employees the company's managers framed these departures as a huge loss for the firm.

Win-win scenarios: social capital

While the managers in the semiconductor company example above were rightly concerned about the administrative and human capital costs created by the departure of these employees, they overlooked the potential opportunities created by the social capital embedded in their relationships with these employees. Social capital is defined as the sum of the actual and potential resources embedded within, available through, and derived from relationships (Nahapiet and Ghoshal, 1998). When employees move between firms they often maintain the relationships they shared with former colleagues. By virtue of the trust, mutual knowledge and reciprocity embedded in these ties, employee mobility can create a conduit for information and knowledge flows between two companies, and even serve as the basis for future business relationships between them. Because individuals possess knowledge about their former employer's capabilities, work practices and processes, cross-company endeavors between the two firms are also likely to be more efficient. Therefore, if harnessed, the inter-organizational social capital created by the movement of employees to other companies can represent a valuable source of competitive advantage for firms.

An implicit assumption of the War for Talent perspective is that employees are lost to or gained from competitors. Yet, employee movements also routinely occur between potential "cooperators" such as customers and suppliers, which may facilitate the creation or strengthening of business relationships with these cooperator firms. In practice, firms often utilize ties with former employees who have joined cooperators to develop new and profitable economic relationships. For example, in 2004 several high performing traders left the investment banking firm Goldman Sachs to start several multi-billion dollar hedge funds. The announcement of these departures produced concern that the exodus of talent would decrease Goldman Sachs' performance. However, the exact opposite happened as these new hedge funds became important *new* Goldman Sachs clients (Santoli, 2006).

Similarly, in 1998 Michael Jacobson, a securities lawyer with Cooley Godward LLP, announced his retirement from the firm to become general counsel for, at that time, a little known online auction site called eBay. Mr. Jacobson had over 12 years experience in the firm's securities division and the managing partners of the firm believed his loss would severely damage the practice. However, a few months later, due in part to the firm's ties with Mr. Jacobson, Cooley Godward was selected as lead counsel for eBay's record $1.3 billion initial public offering (Rich, 2005).

These examples challenge the notion that employee mobility is always a win or lose scenario. While employers may lose access to former employees' human capital they may still retain access to the social capital they share with former employees. Depending on the types of organization former employees join, this social capital can have significant value and increase firm performance. Therefore, in order to understand the performance implications of employee mobility, it is important to differentiate between different types of organizations that former employees may choose to join. In particular, it is vital to distinguish between employees that leave firms to join competitors and those joining cooperators, namely potential clients or partners.

Research findings

In our research we found systematic evidence about the benefits of social capital shared with former employees who leave to join cooperators. By examining the mobility of patent attorneys from 124 leading U.S. patent law firms, we found that these law firms actually did more business with clients (Fortune 500 companies) after their former employees moved to the client (Somaya *et al.*, 2008).[1] Losing attorneys to other law firms, on the other hand, was bad for business due to the loss of social capital shared with specific clients through the firm's former employees. Similarly, law firms also benefited from hiring individuals away from competitors and accessing their social capital, which directly translated into the hiring law firm getting more business from that competitor's clients. Similar to other professional service industries such as accounting, advertising, financial services, IT consulting, management consulting and public relations, a key component of law firms' competitiveness is their ability to develop relationships with potential clients and thus generate business from them. Our research findings clearly highlight that the social capital embedded in employees' ties to clients is a critical source of competitive advantage in these businesses. While employee movement to rivals results in a loss of social capital, employee movement to clients can increase the social capital shared with those clients and more than make up for the human capital losses incurred when a talented employee leaves. Therefore, there is a balance to be struck in human resource strategy between human (and social) capital losses that arise from turnover to rivals, and social capital gains that can accrue when employees leave to join cooperators.

Maintaining positive relationships

It should be noted, however, that the potential social capital gains from departing employees are premised on retaining positive and constructive ties with them. These ties can easily be destroyed and become invested with so-called negative social capital if firms take aggressive actions that alienate their former employees (Labianca and Brass, 2006). Consider the example of the semiconductor firm discussed earlier. What we did not mention above was that the two key employees who left the firm did so to create a start-up company that would develop systems built around integrated circuits (ICs) like the one they were developing at their former employer. As such, by virtue of the social capital shared with these former employees, the start-up they founded was a likely potential customer and/or partner for the semiconductor company's IC product. In the semiconductor industry, the fixed capital costs of product development and fabrication are extremely high, and competition often revolves around establishing one's product as an "industry standard" that is widely adopted by downstream firms. In this environment, building early ties with system integrators and inducing them to adopt one's technology is vital to product success. And here the company had been offered a golden opportunity on a platter; its own former employees had gone out to start a systems integrator. However, the turmoil created by the loss of two key employees and the pain and disruption of having to replace them on a time-critical project may cause top managers to lose sight of this bigger picture. If the employees' departures are followed by recrimination and retaliation the semiconductor firm could destroy its social capital with these former employees and lose the potential opportunity to lock down an early adopter of its technology.

Strategic responses to employee mobility

Thus far, we have established two key principles. First, not all types of turnover are harmful to companies; departing employees may sometimes provide firms with opportunities to develop valuable social capital ties with other firms (cooperators) that can more than make up for the human capital losses that they suffer. Second, retaliatory actions taken in response to turnover can have a downside; they may actually undermine a firm's ability to leverage opportunities with potential cooperators that their former employees choose to join.

Given that not all employee mobility is created equally, it is incumbent upon organizational leaders to develop different types of strategies for managing different types of turnover. Traditionally, firms have adopted two types of strategic response to employee turnover;

defensive actions and/or retaliatory actions. Defensive actions refer to the steps taken by organizations to reduce current employees' motivation to leave, thus, preventing future turnover. This would include changes to internal HRM practices, such as raising salaries, improving internal communication, developing succession plans, or offering employees training in an effort to increase worker satisfaction. The underlying logic of this approach is that by making the firm's work environment as appealing as possible, employees will be less likely to pursue or accept job offers from other organizations.

Retaliatory actions refer to the measures taken by companies to threaten or harm employees that leave the organization or the employers that hire them. For example, firms could aggressively enforce employee non-compete clauses and/or file lawsuits against companies that hire away their employees. These actions are designed to restrict the ability of former employees to use their knowledge and relationships, thus reducing the incentive for other firms to poach them. For example, in retaliation to Google poaching a key vice-president, in 2005 Microsoft filed a lawsuit demanding that the former vice-president be restrained from working on specific projects at Google that overlapped with his previous work at Microsoft (Delaney, 2005). This lawsuit was widely seen as an attempt by Microsoft to discourage Google from hiring Microsoft employees in the future.

The aim of both defensive and retaliatory responses is to reduce employer turnover, the latter by increasing the costs associated with leaving (i.e., lawsuits), while the former attempts to increase the benefits employees gain by staying with a company (i.e., better working environment). As such, these actions are primarily concerned with managing the administrative and human capital costs associated with employee mobility. However neither approach formally addresses the role of social capital in employee mobility. Instead, we suggest that firms may benefit from adopting a third type of strategic approach, which involves *relational actions*. This approach differs from traditional defensive or retaliatory actions in that, as opposed to stopping employee turnover, the focus is on leveraging the social capital that the firm shares with former employees.

A relational approach

Relational actions refer to the steps taken by firms to maintain positive relationships with former employees. One effective example of a relational action is the development of formal alumni programs. In recent years several multinational firms, across a wide range of industries have adopted such programs. This includes such firms as Procter & Gamble, Capital One, Microsoft, KPMG, Bearing Point, Accenture, McKinsey & Company, Children's Healthcare, and Shell. Alumni programs typically entail the creation of different company-sponsored opportunities (e.g., conferences, social gatherings, online electronic forums) for former employees to interact with each other and with current employees. Companies adopting alumni programs actively market this service to former employees and in some cases even provide former employees with incentives for joining their alumni groups (e.g., product discounts).

When implemented effectively relational approaches to employee mobility can provide firms with benefits in a number of areas, including: 1) access to clients, 2) access to human capital, 3) generating goodwill.

Client access

As illustrated by the Cooley Godward LLP example above, many former employees may accept prominent decision-making roles in their new organizations and become excellent points of contact for client development. Investments in relational activities may be particularly useful for organizations attempting to break into new markets where their reputation and visibility are low. Also, former employees may not only be influential in decision-making within their own organizations, but also valuable for their contacts and influence with other companies and clients. For example, one Germany-based technology consulting company attempting to expand into new foreign markets was able to obtain references for jobs in Indonesia, Egypt and Brazil from just one former employee. The CEO of the organization was quick to recognize that the firm would have never have had access to these projects had it not been for this former employee (Glückler, 2006).

Human capital access

Relational actions may also help firms access alternative sources of human capital and reduce the administrative costs associated with hiring. Often individuals leave organizations to pursue different types of career experiences not available with their current employer, or their decision to leave could be influenced by non-work occurrences (e.g., relocation of spouse, child care, or elder care). However, over time these issues may no longer be relevant, or new opportunities may appear in an organization that would be appealing to a former employee. Maintaining a relationship with alumni may make it easier to communicate new opportunities in the firm, thus, making it easier to recruit them back.

The recruitment of former employers, commonly referred to as "boomerang hires," offers several important benefits. Employers face much less uncertainty when making boomerang hires compared to hiring an individual without prior experience in the firm. Hiring managers will have great clarity about the skills, aptitude and cultural fit of former employees, which can inform decisions about where the person can best fit with the organization. There is also evidence that the use of boomerang hires can be 50 percent less expensive than normal recruitment channels (e.g., headhunters, formal job postings). These savings stem in large part from a reduction in the advertisement expenses associated with recruitment due to the use of network ties to attract former employees. For example, the accounting firm Deloitte estimated that in one year it saved $3.8 million in search firm fees by hiring former employees (Workforce Management, 2006). Boomerang hires may require less initial training than other hires, producing further cost savings. Boomerang employees can even play an instrumental role in developing new workers by serving as mentors. Former employees are also less of a turnover risk the second time around. Just as the company will have a clear understanding of what a boomerang hire can provide the firm, individuals who decide to rejoin their former employers have very little uncertainty about the culture of the firm, the job expectations and the organization's rewards. As a result, there is likely to be greater commitment in their employment choice.

In addition to filling full-time positions, former employees can also provide firms with short-term human capital flexibility by performing contract work. Given their tacit knowledge of the organization's norms, procedures and processes and their intra-firm network ties, former employees can more quickly come up to speed on projects and work in a more collaborative manner with current employees than contractors lacking previous experience with the organization. One company in particular that has experienced success in using former employees in this manner is Shell Oil Company. The company launched a website titled "AlliancexShell" to support corporate business development and recruitment and to provide alumni with an online networking platform (Weaver, 2006). The site allows ex-employees living around the world to post their résumés detailing their Shell and other work experiences. As the company identifies its short-term human resource needs, this database is searched for alumni candidates with the relevant skills for various projects. This has allowed the organization to fill contract positions quicker and the individuals filling these positions are able to complete projects faster and with greater quality. In addition, AlliancexShell is viewed positively by alumni, who see this as an excellent means to stay engaged in the industry and make additional income.

Goodwill assets

Finally, the implementation of relational actions can also be an excellent way to generate organizational goodwill. To the extent that individuals are in a good relationship with their former employer, they can be excellent references and serve as ambassadors for the firm. Companies can benefit from the goodwill embedded in these relationships in a number of ways, including attracting new talent and recruitment efforts. For example, one law firm provides lawyers it is interviewing access to their alumni directory and encourages them to contact these individuals during the selection process. The goodwill generated by effective alumni relations can also generate knowledge exchanges between current and former employees. Inviting alumni to attend company conferences allows for a cross-fertilization of ideas and gives current employees exposure to industry trends. Former employees may also eventually find themselves in positions of influence in government, academia, or other public roles. For example, Kai-Fu Lee, the Microsoft Vice President over whom the company had a protracted legal battle with Google, left Google in September 2009 to start a major angel investing venture in China. Someday soon, Microsoft will more than likely find itself interested in a company that Lee has funded, as a customer, alliance partner, acquisition target, or for some other strategic purpose. It will also likely find that the acrimony over Lee's departure from Microsoft has left a bitter aftertaste that is not easy to overcome.

A portfolio approach to managing employee mobility

While the adoption of relational tactics can provide firms with several benefits, in practice it is unlikely that firms will only adopt one type of response to employee mobility. Indeed, it is our recommendation that organizational leaders develop a portfolio of defensive, retaliatory and relational actions. In selecting which type of response to adopt, managers need to strategically balance the administrative and human capital costs generated by turnover with the potential social capital benefits that can be created by employee mobility.

There are two factors managers should consider when selecting strategic responses to employee mobility. First, managers need to consider the strategic importance of the knowledge departing employees carry with them. In some cases departing employees carry generic knowledge, which while valuable to the firm, is of low strategic value and can be replaced via new hires or the training of current employees. For example, an information technology (IT) firm might derive valuable performance from the generic programming knowledge possessed by a talented software engineer; however, if the engineer left the firm it might be possible to find another engineer who possesses a similar knowledge base. Conversely, the same may not be true for an engineer who possesses intimate, unique and critical knowledge about company-specific technologies. To the extent that this strategically important company-specific knowledge was developed through a combination of project experience, co-worker interactions and innate abilities, it may be very difficult and costly, if not impossible, for the IT firm to find a replacement engineer possessing a similar stock of knowledge.

Managers should also consider the destination of their former employees, that is, whether they are leaving to join a cooperator or competitor firm. As discussed above, losing employees to cooperator firms may represent a positive opportunity for firms to generate new capital with potential clients, suppliers, or strategic partners. However, if an individual leaves to join a competitor this may have a detrimental impact on a firm's competitive position because competitors are likely to use a firm's former employees in an adversarial manner.

Decision criteria

In Figure 5.1 we present a two-by-two decision matrix illustrating four scenarios for how these two factors might influence the types of strategies organizations adopt in response to employee exit. In the first situation, where employees with low strategic knowledge leave to join competitors, we recommend that firms emphasize the use of defensive actions. The loss of employees with generic knowledge to competitors may hinder a focal firm's productive capacity while increasing the productive capacity of their competitors. It may be possible to find replacements for these employees, however, the recruitment and/or training expenses may be substantial, especially in a tight labor market. In addition, it is unlikely that individuals who leave to work for competitors, who are inherently adversarial to the firm, will generate much social capital benefit for their former employer. Thus, a top priority for firms in this situation is reducing the administrative and adjustment costs associated with replacing employees. While it is not possible for a firm to prevent its competitors from gaining access to generic knowledge, it is in a firm's interest to limit competitors' access to their pool of employees. Defensive actions are designed to keep existing employees, thus these actions may be an effective means of reducing recruitment and/or training costs and restricting competitors' access to generic labor.

In situations where employees possessing knowledge that has low strategic importance leave to join cooperators, it may be most appropriate for firms to use relational actions. In this scenario the focal firm will incur administrative costs and human capital costs due to employee turnover. However, these costs are counterbalanced by the social capital benefits

	Quadrant 1	Quadrant 2
Low	Defensive actions	Relational actions
High	**Quadrant 3** Retaliatory and defensive actions	**Quadrant 4** Defensive and relational actions

Strategic importance of departing employees

Competitor	Cooperator

Figure 5.1 Destination of former employees

created by former employees joining potential clients, which may produce new business opportunities. Moreover, the skills of these employees, while valuable, are relatively easy to replace through recruitment from the labor market. Thus, the adoption of relational actions that both support individuals' decisions to join a cooperator and ensure that the firm maintains a positive relationship with these former employees can be very effective. In order to increase the probability of realizing these social capital benefits, companies may even take proactive steps to help individuals who wish to leave find new positions in cooperator firms. For example, it is not uncommon for partners in consulting and law firms to assist junior employees who for whatever reason will not reach partner status to find positions with current or potential clients.

The loss of employees with strategically important company-specific knowledge to competitors is potentially the most damaging form of turnover for an organization. Due to the unique and critical knowledge possessed by these employees, organizations will likely incur very high administrative and human capital costs if they depart. Not only are the talents of the focal employee lost, but their departure may create negative spillovers for the performance of the rest of the organization as well. If these employees share their proprietary knowledge with competitors, this will clearly hurt their former company's competitive advantage. Furthermore, as opposed to generating social capital, former employees may take to competitors key network ties with clients or supplies, further damaging the firm's competitive position. Thus, in these situations firms certainly need to engage in defensive actions. For example, a firm may wish to match external offers in order to prevent a key employee from joining a close competitor. In those situations where defensive actions are unsuccessful or not viable firms may need to additionally employ retaliatory actions. For example, similar to the Microsoft example discussed above, firms may seek to sue poaching firms or departing employees to restrict their ability to use company proprietary knowledge or access client relationships. Retaliatory actions may be particularly important in those situations where the departing employee possesses time-sensitive product information or key client contacts that could confer an immediate competitive advantage to a competitor in the marketplace. Therefore, the optimal mix of strategies in this situation would likely be a combination of defensive and retaliatory actions targeted towards retaining employees who are key contributors.

While not as potentially damaging as losing an employee to a competitor, the loss of employees with strategically important company-specific knowledge to cooperators produces an interesting challenge for firms. The loss of an employee who possesses critical company information will create significant administrative and human capital costs for the organization. Thus, firms will have a strong incentive to adopt defensive strategies to reduce the turnover of these types of employees. However, the movement of these employees to cooperators may also represent a substantial opportunity for firms to expand their social capital with important clients or suppliers. Because these individuals possess intimate knowledge of their former employer, they may be well suited to convey information about their former employer's operations, products, and services. Furthermore, individuals with highly specialized and valued skills may be more likely to take high-level positions in their new firms. Thus, they may have more decision-making ability concerning the choice of external partners, potentially increasing the likelihood of business exchanges between an employee's current and former employers. Moreover, employees themselves may have individual goals and constraints that may compel a shift in their career trajectories. Therefore, if defensive actions fail, firms will still have a strong incentive to engage in relational activities in order to maintain positive relationships with these key employees as they transition into their new organization. Indeed, adopting defensive actions geared towards improving employee's satisfaction with their job may actually generate goodwill that will help facilitate the formation of a positive relationship if individuals ultimately decide to join other companies.

Managerial judgment

Managers should use the four turnover categories as a guide, but use their discretion to determine what type of turnover situation they are facing. In practice, the distinction between knowledge with high versus low strategic importance will vary, and similarly placed individuals may fall into different categories in different situations. For example, even an employee with generic skill may be strategically important if he or she is involved in an important time-critical project. Moreover, depending on a firm's industry it may also be quite difficult to distinguish between who is a competitor and who is a cooperator. In many industries, competition and cooperation often proceed along parallel tracks—a competitor today may be an alliance partner tomorrow. All of these situations require that managers exercise careful judgment as to where they fall in our decision matrix and calibrate their actions accordingly.

Furthermore, over the course of their careers former employees may go on to join both competitors and cooperators. As the example of Microsoft's Kai-fu Lee illustrates, even employees who initially join competitors may eventually end up with potential cooperators. Thus, while employee mobility may not generate valuable social capital initially, the value of adopting a relational strategy may be realized later. Take for example, the case of one IT consulting firm we interviewed. The organization lost a highly skilled and capable software programmer to a competitor. Because the firm had invested a great deal of time and money in training and developing this employee, management viewed her departure very seriously, and sought to restrict her employability by suing her, alleging violations of employment non-competes and trade secrecy misappropriation. However, even before the litigation was settled, the former employee had left the competitor to work for a very large company that was a potential client of the IT firm. Unfortunately for the firm, the bitter experience of litigation made it impossible to approach the former employee for potential business opportunities.

As the example of the IT firm illustrates, managers might do well by adopting a longer-term view when balancing the potential gains and losses from social capital, human capital and administrative costs. The IT firm adopted the traditional win-or-lose approach to employee exit, looking at employee exit through the lens of administrative and human capital costs. Accordingly, management used retaliatory tactics as a means to fight the employee and the poaching competitor. That approach, however, ultimately resulted in the firm destroying a potentially valuable source of social capital—connections to a prospective client.

Conclusion

Despite concerted efforts by organizations to fight the "War for Talent" the evidence shows that employee mobility continues to increase. While talent shortages may have abated in the short term as recessionary economic conditions create a cyclical oversupply of skilled professionals, the trend towards increasing mobility is here to stay. Ultimately, employee mobility is likely to become more pronounced in the future due to increased globalization, demographic shifts, changing career norms, and the ongoing transition to a knowledge-based economy. Individuals in knowledge-based work face careers filled with potential job mobility, and employers in knowledge-driven industries face an existence of constantly seeking new talent. It is time for companies to move beyond the "War for Talent," and develop a new mindset towards employee mobility. Instead of the old "war" mentality, which frames all employee turnover as a win-or-lose scenario, companies should adopt a more holistic perspective by considering the entirety of administrative, human capital *and social capital* implications of employee mobility. A balanced consideration of these factors will help managers adopt strategies that not only minimize the damage caused by employee turnover, but also take advantage of situations where the loss of an employee can actually create economically beneficial business relationships for their firms.

Note

1   Law firms realized these performance benefits even when controlling for law firm reputation, law firm size, the human capital costs or gains law firms experienced from losing or hiring attorneys (regardless of source), and Fortune 500 firm attributes (e.g., size, R&D spending, and number of internal attorneys).

References

Amble, B. (2006) "Chinese employers face retention melt-down," *Management Issues*, September 1.
Birkinshaw, J., Crainer, S. and Mol, M. (2007) "Employees first," *Business Strategy Review*, Spring: 82–87.
Boudreau, J.W., Ramstad, P.M. (2005) "Talentship, talent segmentation, and sustainability: A new HR decision science paradigm for a new strategy definition," *Human Resource Management*, 44(2): 129–136.

Cappelli, P. (2008) *Talent on Demand: Managing Talent in an Age of Uncertainty*. Boston, MA: Harvard Business Press.

Cappelli, P. (2000) "A Market-Driven Approach to Retaining Talent," *Harvard Business Review*, 78(1): 103–111.

Corporate Authorship TCB (2007) "CEO Challenge 2007: Top 10 Challenges."

Delaney, K.J. (2005) "Microsoft wins small battle in Google suit," *Wall Street Journal*, July 29, p. B4.

Gardner, T. (2005) "Interfirm competition for human resources: Evidence from the software industry," *Academy of Management Journal*, 48(2): 237–256.

Glückler, J. (2006) "A relational assessment of international market entry in management consulting," *Journal of Economic Geography*, 6: 3: 369–393.

Huselid, M.A., Becker, B.E., Beatty, R.W. (2005) *The Workforce Scorecard: Managing Human Capital to Execute Strategy*, Boston, MA: Harvard Business School Publishing.

Johnson, J. (2007) "How India raises an army," *Financial Times*, May 22.

Labianca, G. and Brass, D.J. (2006) "Exploring the social ledger: Negative relationships and negative asymmetry in social networks in organizations," *Academy of Management Review*, 31: 596–614.

Nahapiet, J. and Ghoshal, S. (1998) "Social capital, intellectual capital and the organizational advantage," *Academy of Management Review*, 23: 242–266.

Rich, L. (2005) "Don't be a stranger," *Inc. Magazine*, January.

Santoli, M. (2006) "Minting money the Goldman Sachs way," *Barron's 86*, no. 15: 22.

SHRM (2007) *SHRM Human Capital Benchmarking Study*, Society of Human Resource Management, Alexandria, VA.

Somaya, D., Williamson, I.O. and Lorinkova, N. (2008) "Gone but not lost: The different performance impacts of employee mobility between cooperators versus competitors," *Academy of Management Journal*, 51(5): 936–953.

Workforce Management (2006) "The boom in boomerangs," *Workforce Management*, January.

Weaver, P. (2006) "Tap ex-employees' recruitment potential," *HR Magazine*, 51: 7: 89–91.

Employer branding and corporate reputation management in global companies: a signalling model and case illustration

GRAEME MARTIN AND SASKIA GROEN-IN'T-WOUD

Introduction

In this chapter our main aim is to shed further light on our earlier attempts to combine ideas from HRM, marketing, organisational behaviour and communications to show how employer branding might work in theory and practice in multinational enterprises (MNEs). In so doing, we hope to bridge a research-practice gap in this field. First, we have amended and developed our previous context, content and process framework of employer branding (Martin, 2009a) by linking it to signalling theory and incorporating new ideas on employee engagement (Balain and Sparrow, 2009). Second, we illustrate different features of our revised framework drawing on a case study of employer branding in a global construction materials company. The case shows how one firm is developing a sophisticated approach to employer branding and talent management. It also highlights key tensions in this on-going process, especially in resolving the dual logics of *global integration* and *local responsiveness* faced by most MNEs (Rosenzweig, 2006).

Towards a theory of employer branding

Employer branding has been an important part of HR strategy and practice in global organisations for more than a decade (Backhaus and Tikoo, 2004; Martin and Beaumont, 2003; Martin and Hetrick, 2009; Schultz, *et al.*, 2005). As such it has gone beyond the faddish status that some sceptical HR academics initially attributed to it, which reveals a potentially important research-practice divide. However, research is beginning to catch up with the practice of employer branding (Chun, 2005; Edwards, 2005; Lievens, 2007; Lievens, Van Hoye and Anseel, 2007) as academics with close links to industry realise the extent to which employer branding may even be synonymous with HRM itself rather than just another 'tool in the box'.

Perhaps more importantly, employer branding can be seen as an essential element in building and sustaining corporate reputations, a strategic agenda item that is increasingly important for global organisations (Fombrun and Van Riel, 2003; Hatch and Schultz, 2008; Highhouse, Brooks and Gregarus, 2009; Martin and Hetrick, 2006). In this context employer branding has been linked with a trend towards 'corporateness, a term coined by Balmer and Greyser (2003) to describe a developing interest in corporate level integration and identity management. However, the focus on corporateness also results in tensions among brand *differentiation* (being different from others) and organisational *legitimacy* (being seen as respectable and securing the approval of others) (Highhouse, Brooks and Gregarus, 2009; Martin 2009a; Martin, 2009b).

In 2008, we conducted an extensive review of the literature to develop a theory of employer branding (Martin, 2009a; Martin and Hetrick 2009). Since then we have refined our ideas and tested them in research and practical settings in four MNEs which provide particular challenges for employer branding. As a result, we believe employer branding is best explained by incorporating insights from signalling theory (Armbrüster, 2006; Cronk, 2005; Highhouse *et al.*, 2009). Second, we believe that recent research on two foci of employee engagement – *work engagement* and *organisational engagement* – are key to understanding and measuring the impact of employer branding signals and talent management practices in organisations (Beijer, Farndale and van Veldhoven, 2009; Martin, Pate and Bell, 2009).

Signalling theory and its application to employer branding

Signalling theory, which has its origins in the biological sciences, has been used for decades in a range of social sciences to explain communications between individuals and organisations (Goffman, 1956; Highhouse, Thornbury and Little, 2007; Spence, 2002). Central concerns of signalling theory are the *honesty* of signals, especially as interpreted by receivers, the *costs* associated with communicating honestly, and the possibility of *faking* honesty. At one level, honesty in signalling theory refers to little more than communicating information that might be of use to receivers, such as cues about the instrumental rewards employees can expect when they join an organisation. From an HRM perspective, however, honesty refers to the symbolic and cultural cues employees can expect to find from good employers, including deeply held cultural values, assumptions and beliefs, and the meaning that they can expect to derive from working in an organisation (Davies and Chun, 2007). For such messages to be perceived as honest and trustworthy by receivers, communications specialists have identified novelty, credibility and authenticity, and sustainability as important variables (Van Riel, 2003). The more these exist, the more employees are likely to buy into the cultural and symbolic cues which organisations attempt to signal. Novelty is important to make organisational signals distinctive from other, although this also creates a built-in incentive to fake honesty. Credibility, authenticity and sustainability are needed to create a sense of legitimacy, respectability, approval, prominence and prestige, the typical criteria used by external and internal stakeholders to assess the legitimacy dimension of corporate reputations (Highhouse *et al.*, 2009; Martin, Gollan and Grigg, forthcoming).

However, honesty in signalling theory terms refers not only to the content of the signal but also to its source, structures, processes and the channels used to convey and engage participants in messages. For example, leadership can be re-interpreted in this light: strategic leadership has been defined in terms of constructing and communicating novel, compelling and credible stories created by leaders for key stakeholders, including investors, the business press, employees and potential employees (Barry and Elmes, 1997). This signalling role of leaders has been brought to the fore because of recent events in the financial services industry and the furore over senior executive pay, thus requiring leaders to effectively re-brand themselves as a source of honest signals (Hamel, 2009; Martin, Hodges and McGoldrick 2010; Ulrich and Smallwood, 2007). There is further evidence that employees have less faith in official corporate communications channels for honest signals about organisations, instead turning to the internet for credible information about prospective employers and, indeed, their own employers, especially from social media such as employee blogs and employee social networking sites (Martin, Reddington and Kneafsey, 2009).

Whether signals are read by receivers as being honest usually, but not always, means that they are costly (Cronk, 2005). Honesty refers to the intention behind and perception of messages by, in this case, prospective and existing employees, as novel, credible and authentic, and sustainable. The costs of signalling honest messages are not only financial but are also connected with their *strategic* impact. In addition, they are also associated with major *handicaps*, such as the multiple organisational and national cultural milieux in which MNEs operate. Honest signals also depend on their *strength* and *consistency* over time. Weak signals and/or inconsistent signals are typically seen by employees as mixed messages and therefore dishonest. For example, we have found in recent research that the failure of senior leadership teams to communicate strong and consistent honest signals is one of the main reasons for employees in healthcare holding negative attitudes to their employers (Martin, Pate and Bell, 2009).

Consequently, organisations frequently engage in high cost signalling, sometimes bordering on 'conspicuous consumption' or ostentatious advertising to communicate messages they hope will be seen not only as honest in the short term but also in the long term by creating reputational capital, which may subsequently be drawn on to reduce future signalling costs. One of the reasons used by HR and corporate communications staff for engaging in competitions run by media such as *Business Week*, the *Financial Times* and the Best Place to Work Institute is the future leverage they gain from honest messages by doing well in such 'games'. However, as Cronk (2005) has also argued, honest signals are not always costly, especially if there is a natural convergence of interests between the signaller and receiver. This point can be illustrated by the extent to which bonus payments to key employees in the investment banking sector have become ingrained in the culture of the global financial services industry. Bonuses, while imposing short-term financial costs on many profitable banks, have not traditionally invoked strategic costs and handicaps precisely because they are an industry-wide norm. However, governments in a number of countries are now attempting to impose strategic, reputational costs on the banking sector by fuelling public outcry over excessive bonuses for 'fat cats' in addition to financial costs through windfall taxes.

Engagement

We have also woven into our model two key foci of engagement, which we argue have a major impact on how employees perceive honest employer brand signals, on employer brand capital and reputational capital. The first is the well-researched and empirically verified concept of *work engagement* (Schaufeli and Bakker, 2008; Salanova and Schaufeli, 2008) The second is *organisational engagement*, initially developed by consultants but which is now being treated in academic literature as an important driver of organisational performance (Beijer *et al.*, 2009; Edwards and Peccei, 2007; Macey and Schneider, 2008; Martin, Pate and Bell, 2009). Distinguishing between these two foci of engagement is an important step forward in making engagement a more useful concept to academics and practitioners.

Work engagement

Work engagement studies are increasingly based on a *demand-resources model of work engagement*, (Schaufeli and Bakker, 2008). This model has identified three forms of engagement that people have with their work. These are the levels of *vigour* employees invest in doing the job, their levels of *absorption* or immersion and attachment to their work, and their *dedication* to their work. Work engagement has been shown to predict valuable outcomes such as positive evaluations of organisations, lower job turnover and higher levels of individual and unit performance. These forms of engagement are thought to be positively driven by the existence of key job resources and challenge demands, but negatively driven by hindrance demands, in turn resulting in employee burnout.

Organisational engagement

Recent academic work has sought to define organisational engagement in terms of emotions and attitudes (state engagement) and behaviour engagement (the traditional interest of management consultants). Key components of these different types of engagement with the organisation, include organisational satisfaction and commitment, vigour and absorption displayed towards an organisation and positive organisational citizenship behaviours (Beijer *et al.*, 2009; Macey and Schneider, 2008). To these we would add employee identification with an organisation, drawing on the well-established concept of organisational identification (Douglas Pugh and Deitz, 2008). This idea has been developed further by Edwards and Peccei (2007) and Edwards (2009), who proposed three distinct but related factors comprising employee identification with their organisations. The first refers to how employees self-categorise their personal identities. For many staff, their employment in an organisation plays a major role in their answer to the question: who am I? The second refers to their sense of attachment and belonging to their organisations, often related to how long they have worked in it. The third refers to the extent to which employees share the goals and values of the organisation and incorporate them into their own goals, values and beliefs. High levels of organisational identification were shown to predict all categories of workers' helping behaviours, turnover intentions and feelings of being involved in the organisation.

Modelling employer branding

Our revised model is set out in Figure 6.1, and in the first part of this chapter we explain these *signal design, signal evaluation* and *outcomes* stages of the model in some detail.

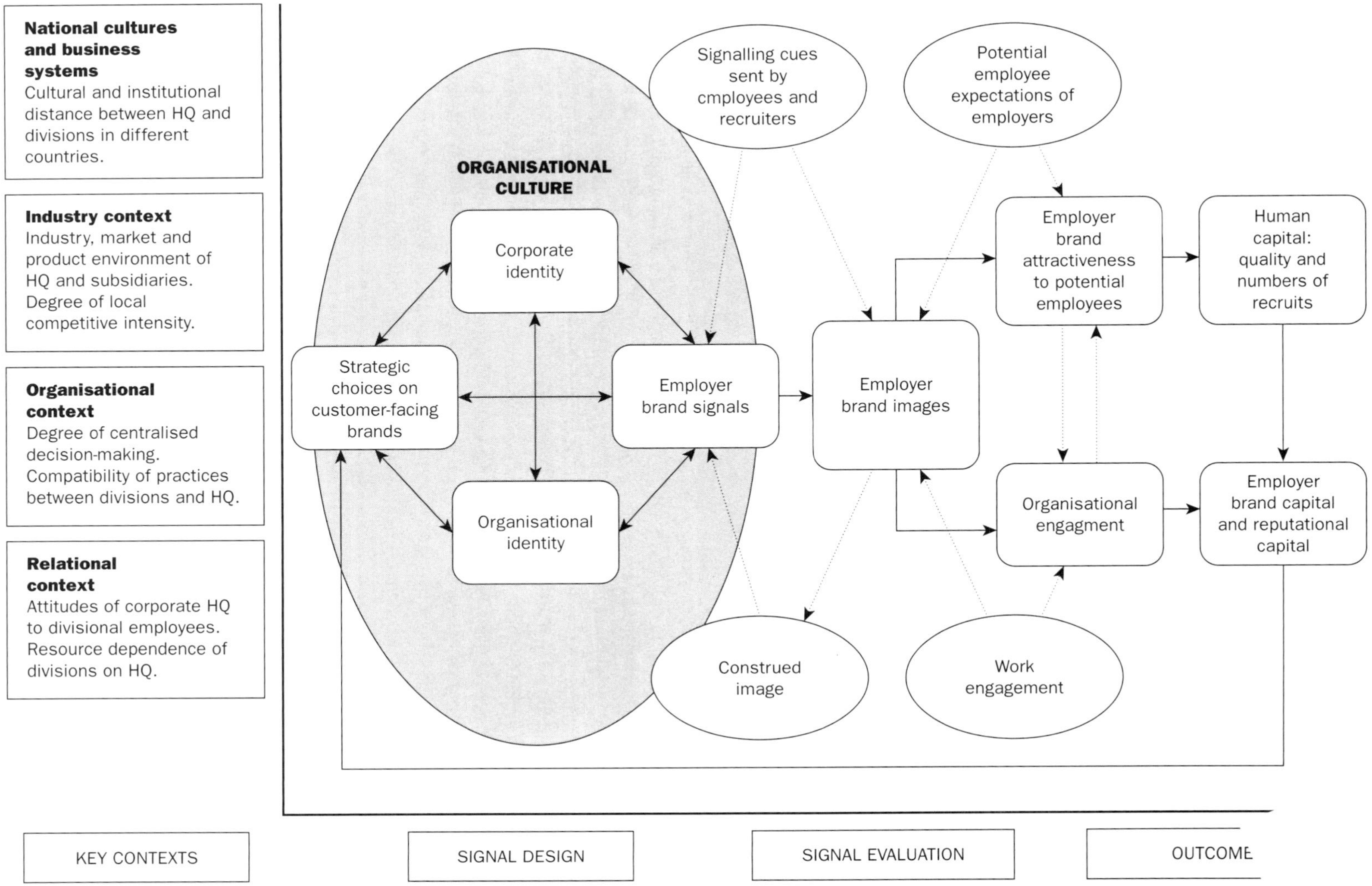

Figure 6.1 A Context–Process–Content model of employer branding

KEY CONTEXTS

National cultures and business systems
Cultural and institutional distance between HQ and divisions in different countries.

Industry context
Industry, market and product environment of HQ and subsidiaries. Degree of local competitive intensity.

Organisational context
Degree of centralised decision-making. Compatibility of practices between divisions and HQ.

Relational context
Attitudes of corporate HQ to divisional employees. Resource dependence of divisions on HQ.

SIGNAL DESIGN

ORGANISATIONAL CULTURE

Corporate identity

Organisational identity

Strategic choices on customer-facing brands

Employer brand signals

SIGNAL EVALUATION

Signalling cues sent by employees and recruiters

Construed image

Potential employee expectations of employers

Work engagement

Employer brand images

Employer brand attractiveness to potential employees

Organisational engagment

OUTCOME

Human capital: quality and numbers of recruits

Employer brand capital and reputational capital

6

Following a well-established logic of model building in business and management described by Whetten (2002), in which he argues that what needs to be explained should come before the explanation, we begin our discussion with the intended outcomes of employer branding.

The outcomes of employer branding

The intended outcomes of employer branding can be defined as the creation of two forms of capital assets in organisations. These are *employer brand capital*, which refers to the extent of employee advocacy of the organisation, its products, services and reputation as an employer of choice (CIPD, 2007; Joo and McLean, 2006), and *reputational capital*, which refers to the degree of (a) corporate differentiation and prominence in product and labour markets and (b) legitimacy with key stakeholders for good corporate governance, leadership and corporate social responsibility (Deephouse and Carter, 2005; Highhouse *et al.*, 2009; Lievens, Van Hoye and Anseel, 2007; Martin and Hetrick, 2006; Martin, Gollan and Grigg, 2009; Ulrich and Smallwood, 2007). These capital assets are increasingly thought to be critical to the short-term and long-term performance and sustainability of organisations. This is particularly so in certain sectors of the economy, including the knowledge sector (Kaye, 2004), high-technology firms (Birnik and Bowman, 2007), the service sector, international consulting firms (Armbrüster, 2006), the public services (Martin, Hodges and McGoldrick, 2008), and in the financial services industry (Burke, Martin and Cooper, forthcoming).

To achieve these positive outcomes, organisations need to secure and manage *human capital* – the appropriate quality of stocks and flows of individual skills and competences. This is sometimes characterised as having the right people, at the right time with the right skills in the right place (Dyer and Ericksen, 2007). Human capital, in turn depends on (a) attracting the right numbers and kinds of people in the right locations and right time frame interpreting positive and honest signals about working in the organisation, and (b) having existing employees accept the honesty, consistency and value of the signals sent by employers. It also depends on securing high levels of work and organisational engagement as detailed in the previous section. These two foci of engagement are related but distinct. While work engagement is likely to be associated with organisational engagement, employees can be engaged in their work without being engaged in the organisation (Martin, Pate and Bell, 2009). Of course, the reverse situation is also evident: employees can feel pride in their organisation without being particularly engaged in their work.

Designing employer brand signals: the interactions among organisational culture, corporate identity, organisational identity and strategic choices on branding

The first stage of the model comprises five interacting factors: the existing *organisational culture* shaping and being shaped by a collective sense of *organisational identity, strategic choices* on the customer-facing brand and a *corporate identity* to produce an *employer brand image*. It is these conscious and unconscious signals that create employer brand images among prospective employees and existing employees.

Organisational identity, culture and strategic choice

Identity has become a core but contested concept in management research over the last decade (Hatch and Schultz, 2004; Oliver and Roos, 2007). For our purposes in developing this model we use a definition of organisational identity as the collective answer by employees and managers to the 'who are we?' question, revealed in the organisation's shared knowledge, beliefs, language and behaviours (Whetten and MacKey, 2002). This organisational self-concept is not just a collection of individual identities but has been described as having a metaphorical life of its own, independent of those who are currently employed in a corporation. In other words, it is a 'social fact', capable of having an impact on an organisation's abilities to attract and retain resources, cause individuals to identify with its values, handle critical incidents, including brand advocacy, and prevent organisations from fragmenting (Oliver and Roos, 2007). In contrast, the marketing-related concept of corporate identity has been depicted as an organisation's projected image of 'who we want to be', expressed not only in the form of tangible logos, architecture and public pronouncements, but also in its communication of mission, strategies and values (Balmer and Greyser, 2003). In relation to employment, this notion is often described as the employee value proposition (EVP) or employment proposition (Martin and Hetrick, 2006).

Both of these drivers of employer brands are essentially products of the more deep-seated root metaphor of organisational culture, for our purposes best described by Schein's (2004) classic definition as the often hidden values, assumptions and beliefs of organisations that shape external adaptation and internal integration. This adaptation-integration definition highlights the two faces of organisational culture – the customer and employee-facing functions – so linking the disciplines of marketing and HR in particularly useful ways. Hatch and Schultz (2004) make a strong case for organisational identity being the link between organisational culture and its image with outsiders. Culture shapes how organisational members define themselves collectively, and through time, employees and managers self-consciously reflect on cultural values and assumptions develop a collective sense of 'we'. In turn, organisational identity reflects back on culture to form a two-way relationship.

Both organisational and corporate identity, however, are also a consequence of strategic choices by key decision-makers. These choices are shaped by and reflect back on the culture of an organisation. They include the clarity of strategic objectives, especially in firms characterised by unrelated diversification, across international boundaries, and the feasibility of developing standardised customer or employee-facing branding (Martin and Hetrick, 2009; CIPD, 2007); and, in an international context, choices over how to segment markets.

Employer and employee authorship of the employer brand signals

These cultural, identity and strategic drivers shape the intended design of *employer brand signals*, which comprises the signals senior managers intend to communicate to existing and potential employees about the package of extrinsic functional and economic benefits and intrinsic psychological benefits on offer (Martin and Hetrick, 2009). As we noted early, however, it is not just the communications content of message that comprises the signal but the cues associated with the bundles of HR practices put into place to reinforce the signals. These include the use of bonuses to reinforce the importance of key outcomes, workplace architecture to signal, for example, the importance of team working, career development to signify relational psychological contracts. This 'autobiographical account' signals to employees the company's intentions, so forming expectations among employees and potential employees of the psychological contract 'deal' on offer (Conway and Briner; 2005; Rousseau, 1995). However, just as strategy and autobiographies can be intended/official and unintended/unofficial (Mintzberg, 1994), so too are employer brand signals. As a number of authors have noted (Dowling, 2001; Knox and Freeman, 2006; Mangold and Miles, 2007), often the most powerful source of signals about the employer brand are the messages employees communicate to outsiders and new recruits about the 'reality' of working in the organisation, and their views of the honesty of the signals, including the material, symbolic and cultural signals (Dowling, 2001; Highhouse *et al.*, 2009). Mangold and Miles (2007) suggest that the failure of employees to understand and/or treat as honest the intended signals of employers' internal branding is one of the main points of fracture in this design phase of the employer brand promise or employment proposition (Martin and Hetrick, 2006; Whetten and MacKey, 2002). As signalling theory predicts, dishonest signals are relatively easy to send but can incur enormous future costs in the evaluation of any organisation. Moreover, honest signals are typically costly in terms of the amount of senior management commitment needed to make them credible and authentic, and in removing barriers to change such as unnecessary organisational politics and bureaucracy, 'turf wars', perceptions of procedural injustice, bullying or incompetent line managers, all factors which inhibit employee engagement with their work and their organisations (Crawford *et al.*, in press).

Researchers have also identified *construed identity* as an important influence on employer brand signals. This notion refers to how employees view external stakeholders' perceptions of their organisation, including family, friends, employees of other organisations, the press and other media. Press influence in shaping the reception of employer signals is one of the main rationales underlying the establishment of corporate communications departments in institutions as diverse as financial services, universities and healthcare, and for developing 'employer of choice' award schemes such as the those produced by national media such as *Business Week* and the *Financial Times* (Joo and MacLean, 2006; Van Riel, 2003). These communications and award schemes raise the costs of signalling initially but, as noted earlier, are deemed by participating organisations to reduce them in the longer run because of the reputational capital they create.

The evaluation of the employer brand signals by employees and potential applicants

Employer brand reputations as biographies

If the employer brand signal is self-authored, employer brand images refer to multiple receivers' perceptions of the honesty, credibility, consistency and strength of these signals. In earlier work we have likened these to the multiple *biographical accounts* of what an employer brand holds in terms of meaning for potential and new employees who, along with others, begin to write different stories about the signals. In doing so, they form themselves into distinct segments of interest and lifestyles. This notion mirrors debates in the literature on psychological contracting (Conway and Briner, 2005; Martin and Beaumont, 2003), whereby employee psychological contracts are sometimes defined in terms of their expectations arising from perceived promises or obligations on behalf of employers (the employer brand image), what value employees place on these promises, obligations or employment propositions, and the extent to which they perceive employers to have delivered on the psychological contract deal (Martin and Hetrick, 2006). The critical point here is that just as psychological contracts are essentially individual phenomena, so too are the signals received and the biographies written about an organisation. In the literature on reputation management, images are seen as plural (Dowling, 2001); different groups of people are likely to expect and attribute different values to particular employer brand signal cues and view them differently in signal strength, honesty, credibility and benefit.

The instrumental and symbolic aims of employer branding

In discussing meaning, a further important feature of shaping the reception of employer brand signals is that they are intended to fulfil two levels of expectations, needs and meaning – the *instrumental* and *symbolic* levels – both of which have been identified as forming employees' views of their psychological contract (Conway and Briner, 2005) and the honesty with which signals are treated. These distinctions also parallel developments in the branding literature (Holt, 2004; Lievens and Highhouse, 2003; Lievens, Van Hoye and Anseel, 2007). Instrumental needs and expectations of employees refer to objective, physical and tangible attributes that an organisation may or may not possess (Lievens, 2007; Lievens, *et al.*, 2007). These might include the ability to provide rewarding jobs, high salaries, opportunities for career advancement, job security, job satisfaction, all elements of high performance work systems. Symbolic needs broadly translate into perceptions and emotions about the abstract and intangible image of the organisation, for example, employees' feelings of pride in the organisation, the extent to which it gives them a sense of purpose, beliefs about its technical competence and honesty in dealing with clients and employees, the extent to which it is an exciting or innovative place to work, and the extent to which it is seen as chic, stylish and/or as aggressively masculine or competitive (Davies and Chun, 2007; Lievens, Van Hoye and Schreurs, 2005). Distinguishing between instrumental needs and symbolic meaning mirrors recent trends in branding models. These models have moved away from a focus on so-called *mind-share approaches*, which refers to a brand's capabilities to occupy a central, focused appeal to individuals (through specific employee value propositions on rewards, career development, etc.) to an *emotional* level, in which the brand interacts and builds relationships with people (Holt, 2004).

Contextualising the employer branding process

Four levels of context

Like all HR policies, the design of employer brands, assessment by potential recruits and existing employees, and the outcomes of employer brands are often context-dependent. This dependency is also evident in the marketing and branding literature (Birnik and Bowman, 2007). In our previous work we have identified four, overlapping levels of contexts (Martin and Beaumont, 2001; Martin and Hetrick, 2006, 2009), which can be defined as more or less receptive to strategic HR change and employer branding in domestic and international organisations. These are the *industry context* of the organisation and its subsidiaries, the *corporate context* or relationships between HQ and its divisions, the *relational context*, which refers to the nature and quality of personal relations among managers and levels of resource-dependence of subsidiaries on organisational headquarters (HQ), and, in the case of MNEs, *the national cultural and business system context* of HQ and its subsidiaries.

To illustrate the influence of context, the marketing and strategy literature have been particularly strong in showing that industry context is influential in shaping key strategic decisions and industry recipes (Spender, 2007) and key elements of the marketing mix (Birnik and Bowman, 2007). However, this literature also shows that different types of brands tend to be more standardised than others across international boundaries though certain consumer products that are perceived to be culture bound or related to use in the home tend to be less standardised. In addition, the degree of local competitive intensity among subsidiaries in a country or region has been found to be related to local adaptation of branding and marketing strategies and one might reasonably expect that such a finding would be especially important in labour market competition.

We have also shown how the nature of relationships among managers in a US-based MNE was influential in shaping strategic choices on branding and organisational culture and in the outcomes of a major rebranding exercise (Martin and Beaumont, 2003). In this case, attempts by the US headquarters to impose a corporate branding strategy on local subsidiaries failed because of the greater international experience of managers in the subsidiaries and because they enjoyed less dependence on financial resources from head office (Martin and Beaumont, 2001).

The tensions between corporateness and the search for authenticity

There is good evidence pointing to standardisation of brand signals and a growing corporateness as the preferred strategy of most MNEs (Stiles *et al.*, 2006). Yet, many organisations seek to promote and benefit from authenticity and to give customers and employees a greater voice, which is an important limitation on one-size-fits-all branding strategies. So marketers have turned to the interactivity of Web 2.0 (Martin, Reddington and Kneafsey, 2009) and the street to 'discover' their own 'authentic' brands (Gladwell, 2000). Authentic brand images are typically local in origin, thus what is authentic in one community is not necessarily so in others. For example, the same MNE can attract quite different reputation rankings in countries as close in national culture and institutional make-up as, for example, Sweden, Norway and Denmark, as different criteria are used in these same countries (Apéria, Simcic Brønn and Schultz, 2004). Thus in signalling theory terms, one of the most difficult decisions facing organisations is securing an appropriate balance between honesty and the costs of signalling in relation to one-size-fits-all versus segmented employer brands. Since honesty is most likely to be achieved when there is a close co-incidence between the signaller and individuals receiving the signals, the likelihood, especially in complex organisations such as MNEs, is that initially higher cost, tailored signals – based on extensive research into the values, expectations and desires of different groups of employees – will be less costly in the long run. Investment in honest signalling in employer branding helps reconcile the contradictory logics of integration and local responsiveness (Rosenzweig, 2006). Such investments are also contingent on the degree of value creation potential and unique market position of different groups of employees (Highhouse *et al.*, 2009; Lepak and Snell, 2002).

How does employer branding work in practice?

Thus far we have attempted to set out a model of how employer branding might work in theory and practice. In this next section our model helps to explain one major MNE's 'real time' attempts to integrate employer branding into their strategic HR and global talent management processes. The company operates in the industrial products sector of the global economy, and has grown rapidly through acquisitions over the last few decades. Like many companies following such a strategy, it is wrestling with the problems of reconciling the dual logics of global integration and local responsiveness (Rosenzweig, 2006), which we have argued are inconsistent and dynamic logics that all MNEs need to resolve if they wish to benefit from global integration of their acquisitions and obtain leverage from their corporate brand while retaining and building on mid-level strategic advantages among business units (Lengnick-Hall, *et al.*, 2009; Martin, Gollan and Grigg, forthcoming).

To present the case, we follow the logic of our model by setting out the context of employer branding for the company and the different stages and processes which have been involved to date. The case illustrates a range of issues found in many MNEs, including the problems of the limited formal influence of headquarters HR in decentralised MNEs and compatibility of practices and data, the problems of designing effective employer brands that meet the demands of global integration and local responsiveness, the relational problems of HQ and local managers, resource dependence, and the problems of measuring engagement and the outcomes of employer branding.

The company history, strategy and organisation

The case study company is CONCO, a pseudonym for one of the world's largest construction materials companies formed in the early 1900s. Since its inception, CONCO has focused on growth as a strategic aim, and its interests have expanded to include a network of holdings in North and Latin America, the Asia Pacific Region and Eastern

Europe. Today CONCO operates in over seventy countries with a workforce in excess of 85,000 people. Its head office is situated in a major central European city, employing a multicultural workforce which is reflected in a multicultural corporate HR team made up of 50 people from 15 countries with English as the official language of the company.

One of the key strategic challenges facing the organisation is that it is a group of acquired and partly owned operating companies, more resembling a 'house of brands' than a globally integrated, 'branded house' (Martin and Beaumont, 2003). In marketing terms, CONCO has adopted a mixed branding strategy, with elements of a master brand, co-branding, endorsed branding and independently named brand strategies under a corporate 'house of brands'. Some recently acquired companies retain significant power and influence as independent brands in their own right due to their prior brand strength; others have been left as independent companies because head office has taken a view that allowing them to adopt the corporate brand at this stage in their development creates reputational risk for the CONCO corporate brand.

This mixed branding strategy has led to tensions between CONCO's European corporate HQ management team and operating company managers, which are also exacerbated by divergent geographic, national and organisational cultural pressures. As a consequence, head office operates both as a controlling and consulting function in relation to the operational businesses, which is reflected in the 'transitional' status of its corporate HR department (Starkey and Scullion, 2000). The company is run by an executive board and each geographical region has an executive committee member responsible for it. Regional and local autonomy is heavily influenced by the beliefs and decisions of responsible committee members, though these are shaped by the power of local operating companies and their dependence on corporate HQ for financial and managerial resources (Martin and Beaumont, 2001).

Industry context

The industry under discussion supplies basic construction materials across the world using a mix of local, regional and global markets that logistically align product supply with demand. It is subject to changing macro-economic influences resulting from international variations in housing and public infrastructure spending, and the specific economic dynamics of developing countries and regions. Typically, manufacturing processes are located near raw material quarries and in turn supply a hub of plants that are close to dispatch locations. As a result, the industry was traditionally highly fragmented with many small players, though it is gradually becoming more concentrated through mergers and acquisitions, with four companies, including CONCO, accounting for 23 per cent market share in 2009.

A further important element influencing employer branding is CONCO's strong sustainability agenda, which is incorporated into the vision and mission statement, proclaiming that the company 'has a major interest in provid(ing) a foundations for society's future'. In addition, high importance is placed on achieving 'zero harm' in the workplace, developing innovative environmental products that contain recycled or co-processed materials, utilising other industries' waste products as alternative fuels and ensuring maximum value is returned to the communities in which CONCO operates through employment, employee training and development, community involvement and a commitment to human rights. CONCO also aspires to be one of the world's most respected and attractive companies in its industry (company website) through an employer of choice policy. These aspirations play a large part in CONCO's decisions on whether and when to integrate acquired companies under the corporate brand.

Organisational context

As a result of its rapid growth by acquisition and the dominance of local brands CONCO has traditionally operated a decentralized business model and organisational architecture. As noted earlier, key decisions on autonomy are taken by specific executive committee members with regional responsibilities, and operational decision-making responsibility is largely devolved to operating companies grouped in the countries or regions. In certain regions, where local brands are strong, CONCO's strategy has been to leave local operating company managers to make key decisions to reflect relevant market conditions. In others, where local brands were deemed to be weak, CONCO has attempted major rebranding to incorporate newly acquired companies into the global CONCO brand. This mixture of local, endorsed and global branding, mix of ownership models and the stages of development reached by particular operating companies in meeting the corporate sustainability agenda presents significant challenges for the integration of the HR function and people management policies. The decentralised nature of much of the business is also evident in the budget and target-setting process. Once performance targets are agreed with head office, operating company managers are given a high degree of autonomy to deliver them.

Thus at this stage in the company's development, most of CONCO's head office functional management, including its corporate HR function, is in a transitional stage (Starkey and Scullion, 2000), combining elements of both centralisation and decentralisation. This reflected the corporate HR function's early development in a basic transactional role restricted to managing staff in corporate HQ. Therefore, until a few years ago, the relatively small corporate HR function was largely cast in the role of a consulting function to the operating companies, providing advice on most strategic HR issues, including talent management, career development, leadership development, training and e-HR rather than exercising centralised direction over these roles. An internal market system operated, which provided a significant test for corporate HRs' worth to the operating group companies through a 'recharge model' for central HR services. In effect, operating companies had and still have the power to purchase corporate HR services, develop their own internally, or choose not to have the service. The long-term aim of the corporate HR function, however, was to demonstrate their worth so that operating companies would gradually recognise the benefits of releasing power and control over HR services to the centre, including employer branding.

Recently, however, the corporate HR function was given a boost through recognition from key members of the executive committee team that the function would have to be redesigned to meet the strategic global integration aims of a growing but fragmented business (Starkey and Scullion, 2000. These changes in strategy and organizational architecture are gradually resulting in a more centralised, stronger corporate HR function, though it still operates its basic consulting, re-charge model. Personal dynamics and leadership have played an an important role here. Corporate HR's sponsorship by an influential executive committee member who assumed responsibility for the HR, corporate branding and knowledge management as well as certain geographical areas, has been critical. His dual responsibility has assisted corporate HR implementation of employer branding and talent management initiatives because of the influence he has exercised with the executive committee and the operating company HR directors who are responsible to other executive committee members. These regional HR directors are directly responsible for people management policies and practices in their region, and it is this historic importance accorded to regions and regional HR directors that has restricted corporate HR to playing a largely consulting role to date.

Another key appointment in the executive committee's integration strategy and the emerging influence of corporate HR is its current head, who is a former accountant and plant manager with experience as a CEO in one of CONCO's South American business units. He was deliberately chosen to head up the function to give it more credibility with operating companies and regions. At the time of writing, the corporate HR function has five departments providing a mixture of centralised direction and consulting advice on 'Talent Acquisition', 'Talent Leadership and Development', 'International Assignments and Remuneration', 'HR Processes', and 'Training and Learning'.

Relational context

Although CONCO has a geographically distributed business and has grown rapidly, it also has a history of being a 'family' business based on personal relationships, particularly among the management hierarchy. Training events such as corporate inductions, leadership and management programs have historically brought people together from around the world. High retention rates amongst employees over the past 20 years, together with the approach of rotating senior managers across its group company portfolio has created a strong web of inter-personal relationships. The limitations of these strong networks, however, are evident in the difficulties that newcomers have in breaking into the relationship systems and the ways in which these personal relationships influence appointments for management succession

The design stage

Background research

As part of the corporate integration strategy and a perceived need to improve the position of CONCO in relevant labour markets, a decision was taken in 2008 to appoint a new global talent acquisition team who had previous experience of employer branding in a similar Australia-based company. Following their appointment, the team developed a set of proposals for submission to the executive committee intended to assist in the corporate employer branding process as well as retaining the benefits of local autonomy. In determining CONCO's employer brand, they quickly found little consistency in the HR approach across the business and in how 'touchpoints' were being managed, which are those organisational, HR and leadership behaviours and actions that impact prospective and existing employees. Touchpoints comprise the HR processes relating most directly to employer branding signals as well as the attraction, selection, on-boarding, deploying, developing, engaging and exiting of staff (see Figure 6.2). As a consequence of this inconsistency across the group and problems in generating a cohesive employer brand, a programme of extensive research was undertaken into all stages and processes connected with the talent pipeline, a metaphor based on the concept of career in organisations.

Focusing on the 'funnel and tunnel' of the talent pipeline, the employer branding team decided to re-design the package of economic and psychological rewards to all employees before beginning on the design of a new employer brand itself. This involved working with the leadership and development team to understand how key functions such as succession management, performance management and leadership development needed to be structured, and to construct transparent criteria to create fairness and equality for these processes. Traditionally, the strength of personal relationships had a strong influence on who was selected for key positions, which had on occasion resulted in appointing staff who lacked the necessary capabilities and capacities for leadership positions. Addressing this issue formed an important element of CONCO's leadership strategy for meeting the demands of a continually growing business. By investing in this process at an early stage, the employer branding team is currently striving to ensure that the eventual employer brand signals or 'promises' on attraction, engagement and retention purposes will be seen as honest.

Running in parallel, an extensive research project was undertaken to gain a better understanding of local labour markets. Not only has this research been much needed for the corporate HR function but it has helped establish its credibility with the strategic planning function in corporate headquarters, the executive committee team and other business units. In addition, the employer branding team has adopted a benchmarking approach, collecting key HR data on five industry and five cognate, non-industry competitors for talent. These data were collected to gain insight into competitor companies' employer value propositions (EVPs). Extensive labour market intelligence data was gathered from a range of sources, including recruitment consultants, media and rating websites to assess the strength of each competitor. Ten benchmarking criteria were used, which were identified by the Corporate Leadership Council (an established consulting firm in the industry) as being strongly associated with company performance. These criteria were company mission, values and distinctive competences, reward and compensation, role management, development opportunities, leadership, management support, communications, respect for people and the environment, and work–life balance. Subsequently, these criteria were turned into an HR and people management scorecard, and used to compare the competitor companies and CONCO. Interestingly, the research team was also tasked with providing a 'credibility' index for each company, assessing the differences between the organisational impressions that internal communications departments wished to create and the insights into company actions and behaviours provided by recruitment consultants, relevant business media and ex-employees. Undertaking such an extensive exercise has provided CONCO with the

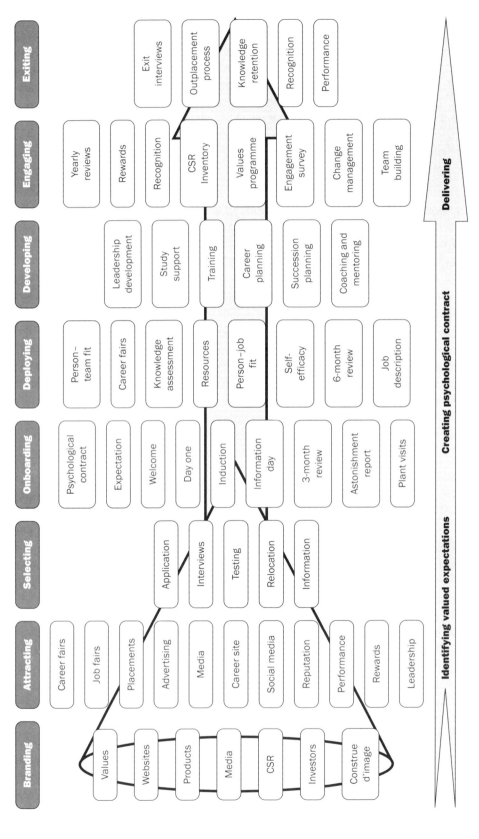

Figure 6.2 Stages in the talent pipeline and the 'touchpoints' at CONCO

necessary data to develop key points of differentiation from competitors, which represents an important step forward in creating a novel, credible and authentic employer brand.

A second programme of research was undertaken to assess operating companies' demographic workforce profiles and compare these with the country of operation's demographic profiles to identify any major gaps. Generational mapping was felt to be necessary because the data generated provided an insight into the future talent needs of CONCO, which were subsequently mapped against other research on key value propositions and the best recruitment media channels for different age groups conducted for the CIPD (Penna Consulting, 2008), with the aim of aligning EVPs with local employee demographics. For example, the demographics of the CONCO business in Vietnam showed over half the workforce was under thirty years of age, which contrasted markedly with developing markets in eastern Europe, where the average age of the operating companies' employees was forty-eight.

Linking the global and local

By undertaking research of this nature, CONCO hopes to be able to remain sensitive to the needs of local labour market demographics and recruitment media channels while retaining its global EVP on issues such co-worker quality, technology, values, organisational stability and depth of opportunity and experience. To achieve this aim, regional hubs have been seen as the key conduit for information flows between corporate headquarters and business units in specific countries. HR staff from different regions were selected for their interest in developing a local employer brand that would benefit from an association with CONCO's global brand. Regional hubs have now been made responsible for translating the corporate brand and corporate employer brand into locally relevant differentiation factors in the talent pipeline using tools like the local generational mapping and touchpoint analyses described above. At the same time, data from local touchpoint analyses is also fed back through the regional hubs to help provide a credibility check on the corporate employer brand.

What is gradually emerging from these activities is a dynamic capability for CONCO to gain substantial leverage from particular local business units by working with volunteer HR innovators who have the 'skill, will and opportunity' to adopt, adapt and implement local EVP projects. At the same time, creating in these subsidiary businesses of CONCO the capability to deliver candidates and employees with a locally relevant message and experience through the touchpoint analysis tool is allowing CONCO to build a consistent, honest and strong message globally. There has been a growing realisation that for CONCO to achieve a novel, credible, authentic and sustainable employer brand in all seventy countries in which it operates, it is also necessary for the company to invest substantial strategic effort and remove as many handicaps as possible. By so doing, it can ensure that it has the local insight and capability to deliver honest signals before 'going global'. It is also essential that these signals, in the form of an employer brand promise, are aligned to the market's expectations internally and externally.

The evaluation stage

The employer branding team have put into place plans for a four-stage evaluation process, which they see as a 'journey and not as a destination'. The first is an integrated 'Touchpoint Gap Analysis', which will assess each of CONCO's companies in relation to their touchpoint strengths and weaknesses in the internal and external labour market. These audits will then be used by the CHR team in conjunction with local HR teams to improve their service delivery across set criteria, resulting in increased consistency of HR performance across the business. These analyses will also act as tools for collating data from subsidiaries to promote sharing of 'promising' practices across the business.

The second stage is to development engagement measures as a key element of the Touchpoint Gap Analysis. This is currently done using a well-established values survey developed in conjunction with a major HR consulting firm. A pilot study conducted with eleven group companies has provided data for the Touchpoint Gap Analysis and will be used in the benchmarking process. These data are also being correlated with business performance measures and financial measures including earnings before tax to try to establish a link between HR variables and key metrics. The corporate HR team recognises, however, that the current values survey is limited and will need to be revised to reflect the measures of work and organisational engagement referred to earlier in this chapter. Adopting valid and reliable measures such as these will allow them to build better logic models and engage in more sophisticated predictive measurement (Cascio and Boudreau, 2008).

The third stage is a careers website benchmarking exercise. Each year CONCO participates in an international study carried out by a media company to identify how well the careers section of the website is performing. The careers website element is a major channel for engaging with prospective employees, currently accounting for 74 per cent of all enquiries to the company from applicants. CONCO's initial website ranking among comparator global companies for generating prospective employees was 81 out of the 100 selected MNEs. The corporate HR team have set goals for 2009 and 2010 to be in the top 50 and top 25 respectively. Finally, CONCO will participate in an international benchmarking exercise on 'Best Workplaces'. This well-respected study benchmarks companies internationally on a range of criteria, which will be used to measure progress and improve performance on key HR metrics arising from the Touchpoint Gap Analysis.

At this stage of the CONCO employer branding process, it is too early to provide an evaluation of progress. At the time of writing, however, there are signs that the investment in research and the sophisticated approach of the employer branding team is beginning to have an influence with the executive committee, which has commissioned further work in the field and continued to exercise sponsorship, and among the operating companies in 'trial' regions. The touchpoint approach has been well received and fully implemented by CONCO operating companies in Vietnam and Eastern Europe, whose HR staff have also begun to form links to share promising practices. Feedback from the HR teams in those regions has revealed how using the model has 'opened up HR's eyes to both the touchpoints and the time at which they occur in the employee lifecycle'. Securing 'early wins', a shibboleth of Anglo-Saxon change management literature (Martin and Beaumont, 2001), are deemed to be essential for developing a strong corporate brand and in establishing the credibility of corporate HR and the individuals whose careers are directly linked to it.

Conclusions for theory and practice

We have argued that employer branding has become an essential element in global HR talent management. Indeed HR high performance work systems and much leadership activity may be seen as an impression management exercise to create positive employer brand images among existing and prospective employees. Our revised model has incorporated signalling theory concepts, especially the need for honest signals which are seen as authentic by different groups of employees who view these messages through different lenses. It has also highlighted the complex interactions and relationships that shape employer branding in MNEs as they seek to engage new and existing employees to help the organisation build reputational capital. Thus our principal message for research in the field of talent management in global companies and, indeed, HR in general is to assess the relevance of signalling theory as a means of developing more sophisticated models of HR and HPWS.

Evidence from existing employer branding research points to the honesty of symbolic and culturally authentic features of employer brands being the most important to employees but also the most costly and 'hard-to-fake' signals. Currently much employer branding practice relies on rather simplistic, one-size fits all corporate messages and employer of choice propositions, which highlight instrumental benefits and corporate spin (Becker, Huselid and Beatty, 2009). The strength and consistency of signals, which are contingent on the sources, structures, systems and processes of employer branding, as well as the extent to which leaders and followers 'live the brand', will have a major impact on receivers' perception of the honesty of such signals and, through these, their willingness to engage with the organisation.

We also see employer branding and engagement being interrelated and interdependent, with more academic research needed to develop the potentially useful notion of engagement. Our model has made a distinction between work engagement and organisational engagement (Beijer *et al.*, 2009) as key influences on the creation of reputational capital by, amongst other outcomes, building brand advocacy and sending positive signals to potential employees. However, as we have also alluded to in the chapter, there are other potentially relevant engagement foci, including, as demonstrated in our case, the nature of the industry and its reputation for social responsibility and sustainability. Employer brand images and engagement are also an important test of the honesty with which employer branding signals are received by employees. Somewhat contrary to the trends towards global corporate branding, which is intended to reduce the costs of signalling vital messages to customers and employees, potentially more costly signalling of employer brands is more likely to reconcile the dual logics and negative capabilities inherent in the integration-responsiveness problems faced by global companies. Costly signals, in the form of extensive research, testing and evaluation, are likely to pay proportionately larger returns in the long run, which is the basic belief underlying the corporate HR team's efforts in the case study. Such costly signals are inherent in the need to strike a dynamic balance between standardisation and integration on the one hand and local responsiveness and authenticity on the other. Short-term costs are also inherent in giving employees greater voice in the design and implementation of employer branding, but doing so may reduce the long-term costs by improving local responsiveness and authenticity.

The case study has illustrated many of these points. However, it has raised other issues relevant to employer branding and talent management research and practice in global companies. The first is path dependency in shaping the relationships between corporate headquarters' HR teams and subsidiary companies' HR practices in MNEs. The CONCO case shows how the timing and nature of acquisitions has led to a mixed branding strategy and relatively decentralised organisational architecture, at least at this stage in the company's development. As a consequence the historically limited role of headquarters' HR has made it much more difficult for the newly-fashioned corporate HR team to perform anything other than a consulting role. In effect the traditional resource-dependency relationship between the centre and subsidiaries has been reversed (Martin and Beaumont, 2001), with the corporate HR team placed in a resource-dependent relationship on powerful regional and operating company managers and HR staff. As a consequence, corporate HR and the newly-established employer branding and talent management teams have had to be especially cognisant of this relationship, the complicated organisational politics it engenders, and change their management theory and practice to deal with it. Their approach, which has some important lessons for HR credibility in other companies, has been to develop a sophisticated, evidence-based talent management and employer branding strategy, based on extensive advice and research by from consultants *and* from HR academics – an important illustration of how to breach the perennial problem of the research-practice divide in HRM. This evidence-based practice has then been used to prove its credentials among sceptical senior executives in headquarters, the regional hubs and certain operating companies, using selective role modelling projects. It has also demonstrated a need for corporate HR teams to develop extensive internal and external networks with key executives and subsidiary managers to establish credibility, to implement initiatives and to increase their absorptive capacity for new knowledge.

References

Apéria, T., Simcic Brønn, P. and Schultz, M. (2004) A reputation analysis of the most visible companies in the Scandinavian countries, *Corporate Reputation Review*, 7: 218–230.

Armbrüster, T. (2006) *The Economics and Sociology of Management Consulting*, Cambridge: Cambridge University Press.

Backhaus, K. and Tikoo, S. (2004) Conceptualizing and researching employer branding, *Career Development International*, 9: 501–517.

Balain, S. and Sparrow, P. (2009) *Engaged to Perform: A New Perspective on Employee Engagement.* White Paper 2009–04, Centre for Performance-Led HR, University of Lancaster. Available online at http://www.lums.lancs.ac.uk/research/centres/hr/WhitePapers/

Balmer, J.T. and Greyser, S.A. (2003) *Revealing the Corporation: Perspectives on Identity, Image, Reputation, Corporate Branding and Corporate-level Marketing*, London: Routledge.

Barry, D. and Elmes, M. (1997) Strategy retold: toward a narrative view of strategic discourse, *Academy of Management Review*, 22: 429–452.

Becker, B.E., Huselid, M.A. and Beatty, R.W. (2009) *The Differentiated Workforce: Transforming Talent into Strategic Impact*, Boston: Harvard Business Review Press.

Beijer, S., Farndale, E., and van Veldhoven, M. (2009) *The Meaning of Employee Engagement: Towards an Integrative Typology for HR Research*. Paper presented to the Dutch Association of Work and Organizational Psychologists (WAOP), Amsterdam, the Netherlands, 5 November.

Birnik, A. and Bowman, C. (2007) Marketing mix standardization in multinational corporations: A review of the evidence, *International Journal of Management Reviews*, 9: 303–324.

Burke, R., Martin, G. and Cooper, C. (eds.) (forthcoming). *Corporate Reputations: Managing Opportunities and Challenges*, London: Routledge.

Cascio, W. and Boudreau, J. (2008) *Investing in People: Financial Impact of Human Resource Initiatives*, Upper Saddle, NJ: FT Press/Pearson Education.

Chun, R. (2005) Corporate reputation: meaning and measurement, *International Journal of Management Reviews*, 7: 91–109.

CIPD (2007) *Employer Branding: The Latest Fad or the Future of HR?*, London: Chartered Institute of Personnel and Development.

Collings, D.G. and Scullion, H. (2006) Approaches to international staffing. In H. Scullion and D.J. Collings (eds.) *Global Staffing*, London: Routledge.

Conway, N. and Briner, R.B. (2005) *Understanding Psychological Contracts at Work: A critical Evaluation of Theory and Research*, Oxford: Oxford University Press.

Crawford, E.R., LePine, J.A. and Rich, B.L. (in press) Linking job demands and resources to employee engagement and burnout: A theoretical extension and meta-analytic test, *Journal of Applied Psychology*.

Cronk, L. (2005) The application of animal signaling theory to human phenomena: some thoughts and clarifications, *Social Science Information/Information sur les Sciences Sociales* 44: 603–620.

Davies, G. and Chun, R. (2007) Employer branding and its influence on managers, *European Journal of Marketing*.

Deephouse, D.L. and Carter, S.M. (2005) An examination of differences between organisational legitimacy and reputation, *Journal of Management Studies*, 42: 329–360.

Douglas Pugh, S. and Dietz, (2008) Employee engagement at the organization level of analysis, *Industrial and Organizational Psychology*, 1: 44–47.

Dowling, G.R. (2001) *Creating Corporate Reputations: Identity, Image and Performance*, New York: Oxford University Press.

Dyer, L. and Ericksen, J. (2007) Dynamic organisations: achieving marketplace agility through workforce scalability. In J. Storey (ed.) *Human Resource Management: A Critical Text*, London: Thomson, pp. 263–281.

Edwards, M.R. (2005). Employee and employer branding: HR or PR?. In Bach, S. (ed.) *Managing Human Resources, Personnel in Transition*, Oxford: Blackwell, pp. 266–286.

Edwards, M.R. and Peccei, R. (2007) Organizational identification: development and testing of a conceptually grounded measure, *European Journal of Work and Organizational Psychology*, 16: 25–57.

Edwards, M.R. (2009) HR, perceived organisational support and organisational identification: an analysis after organisational formation, *Human Resource Management Journal*, 19: 91–115.

Fombrun, C.J. and Van Riel, C.B.M. (2003) *Fame and Fortune: How Successful Companies Build Winning Reputations*, Upper Saddle River, NJ: Financial Times/Prentice Hall.

Gladwell, M. (2000) *The Tipping Point: How Little Things Can Make A Big Difference*, Little Brown.

Goffman, E. (1956) *The Presentation of Self in Everyday Life*, University of Edinburgh Social Sciences Research Centre.

Hamel, G. (2009) Moonshots for management: What great challenges must we tackle to reinvent management and make it more relevant to a volatile world? *Harvard Business Review*, February: 91–98.

Hatch, M.J. and Schulz, M. (2004) *Organisational Identity: A Reader*, Oxford: Oxford University Press.

Hatch, M.J. and Schultz, M. (2008) *Taking Brand Initiative: How Companies Can Align Strategy, Culture and Identity Through Corporate Branding*, San Francisco: Jossey Bass.

Highhouse, S., Brooks, M.E. and Gregarus, G. (2009) An organizational impression management perspective on the formation of corporate reputations, *Journal of Management*, 35: 1481–1493.

Highhouse, S., Thornbury, E.E., and Little, I.S. (2007) Social-identity functions of attractions to organizations, *Organizational Behavior and Human Decision Processes*, 1003: 134–146.

Holt, D.B. (2004) *How Brands Become Icons: The Principles of Cultural Branding*, Boston, MA: Harward Business School Press.

Holt, D.B. (2007) *How Brands Become Icons: The Principles of Cultural Branding*, Boston, MA: Harvard Business School Press.

Huselid, M.A., Becker, B.E. and Beatty, R.W. (2005) *The Workforce Scorecard: Managing Human Capital to Execute Strategy*, Boston, Harvard Business School Press.

Joo, B.K. and McLean, G.N. (2006) Best employer studies: a conceptual model from a literature review and a case study, *Human Resource Development Review*, 5: 228–257.

Kaye, J. (2004) *The Truth about Markets: Why Some Countries are Rich and Others Remain Poor*, London: Penguin.

Knox, S. and Freeman, C. (2006) Measuring and managing employer brand image in the service industry, *Journal of Marketing Management*, 22: 695–716.

Lengnick-Hall, M.L, Lengnick-Hall, C.A., Andrade, L.S. and Drake, B. (2009) Strategic human resource management: the evolution of a field, *Human Resource Management Review*, 19: 64–85.

Lepak, D.P., and Snell, S.A. (2002) Examining the human resource architecture: the relationships among human capital, employment, and human resource configurations, *Journal of Management*, 28: 517–543.

Liden, R. (2007) Doing well by doing good in the employee–organisation relationship: current knowledge, future promise, *Academy of Management All Academy Symposium*, Philadelphia, August 5–9.

Lievens, F. and Highhouse, S. (2003) The relation of instrumental and symbolic attributes to a company's attractiveness as an employer, *Personnel Psychology*, 56: 75–102.

Lievens, F., Van Hoye, G., and Schreurs, B. (2005) Examining the relationship between employer knowledge dimensions and organisational attractiveness: an application in a military context, *Journal of Occupational and Organisational Psychology*, 78: 553–572.

Lievens, F. (2007) Employer branding in the Belgian army: the importance of instrumental and symbolic beliefs for potential applicants, actual applicants and military employees, *Human Resource Management*, 46: 51–69.

Lievens, F., Van Hoye, G. and Anseel, F. (2007) Organisational identity and employer image: towards a unifying framework, *British Journal of Management*, 18: S45–S59.

Macey, W.H., and Schneider, B. (2008) The meaning of employee engagement. *Industrial and Organizational Psychology: Perspectives on Science and Practice*. 1, 3–30.

Mangold, W.G. and Miles, S.J. (2007) The employee brand: Is yours an all-star? *Business Horizons*, 50: 423–433.

Martin, G. (2007) Employer branding: time for a long and hard look? In CIPD, (2007a) *Employer Branding: The Latest Fad or the Future of HR?* London: Chartered Institute of Personnel and Development, pp. 18–23.

Martin, G. (2009a) Employer branding and corporate reputation management: a model and some evidence. In C. L. Cooper and R. Burke (eds.), *The Peak Performing Organization*, London and New York: Routledge.

Martin, G. (2009b) Driving corporate reputations from the inside: a strategic role and strategic dilemmas for HR, *Asia Pacific Journal of Human Resource Management*, 47: 219–235.

Martin, G. and Beaumont, P.B. (2001) Transforming multinational enterprises. Towards a process model of strategic human resource management change, *International Journal of Human Resource Management*, 12: 1234–1250.

Martin, G. and Beaumont, P.B. (2003) *Branding and HR: What's in a Name?* London: Chartered Institute of Personnel and Development.

Martin, G., Beaumont, P.B., Doig, R.M. and Pate, J.M. (2005) Branding: a new discourse for HR?, *European Management Journal*, 23: 76–88.

Martin, G. and Hetrick, S, (2006) *Corporate Reputations, Branding and Managing People: A Strategic Approach to HR*, Oxford: Butterworth Heinemann.

Martin, G., Hodges, J. and McGoldrick, J. (2008) *Understanding Strategic Leadership in HR: A Model and Evidence from the UK Health Sector*. Paper presented to the annual conference of the University Forum for Human Resource Development, Catholic University of Lille, Lille, France, 21–24 May.

Martin, G. and Hetrick, S. (2009) Employer branding: the case of Finco. In P. Sparrow (ed.) *Handbook of International Human Resource Management: Integrating People, Process and Context*, Chichester, UK: John Wiley, pp. 293–320.

Martin, G. and McGoldrick, J. (2009) Corporate governance and HR: some reflections and a case study from the UK National Health Service. In Young, S. *Contemporary Issues in International Governance*, Melbourne: Tilde University Press.

Martin, G., Reddington, M. and Kneafsey, M.B. (2009) *Web 2.0 and Human Resources: 'Groundswell' or Hype?* Research Report. London: Chartered Institute of Personnel and Development.

Martin, G., Gollan, P. and Grigg, K. (forthcoming) Is there a bigger and better future for employer branding? Facing up to innovation, corporate reputations and wicked problems in SHRM, *International Journal of Human Resource Management*.

Martin, G. Pate, J.M., and Bell., S. (2009) *Images of Organization: Reputation Management, Employer Branding and HR in NHS (Scotland)*. Paper presented to a joint HRM and Healthcare Division symposium, British Academy of Management Annual Conference, Brighton, 16th September.

Martin, G., Hodges, J. and McGoldrick, J. (2010) The branding of leadership: can it resurrect leaders' full from grace? Paper presented to the 11th International Conference on Human Resource Development Research and Practice Across Europe, 2–4 June, Pecs, Hungary.

Miles, S.J. and Mangold, W.G. (2004) A conceptualization of the employee branding process, *Journal of Relationship Marketing*, 3: 65–87.

Mintzberg, H. (1994). *The Rise and Fall of Strategic Planning*, Hemel Hempstead, UK: Prentice Hall.

Oliver, D. and Roos, J. (2007) Constructing organisational identity multi-modally, *British Journal of Management*, 18: 342–358.

Penna Consulting (2008) *Gen-up: How the Four Generations Work*, Penna Consulting/Chartered Institute of Personnel and Development, London: CIPD.

Rosenzweig, P. (2006) The dual logics behind international human resource management: pressures for global integration and local responsiveness. In Stahl, G.K. and Björkman, I. (eds) / *Handbook of Research in International Human Resource Management*, Cheltenham, UK: Edward Elgar: 36–48.

Rousseau, D. (1995) *Psychological Contracts in Organisations: Understanding Written and Unwritten Agreements*, Thousand Oaks, CA: Sage Publications.

Schein, E. (2004) *Organisational Culture and Leadership* (3rd edition), New York: Wiley.

Salanova, M., and Schaufeli, W.B. (2008). A cross-national study of work engagement as a mediator between job resources and proactive behavior, *International Journal of Human Resources Management*, 19: 226–231.

Schaufeli, W.B. and Bakker, A.B. (2008) Positive organizational behaviour: engaged employees in flourishing organizations, *Journal of Organizational Behavior*, 29: 147–154.

Schultz, M., Antorini, Y.M. and Csaba, F.F. (eds.) (2005) *Corporate Branding: Purposes, People and Processes*, Copenhagen: Copenhagen Business School Press.

Spence, M. (2002) Signaling in retrospect and the informational structure of markets, *American Economic Review* 92: 434–459.

Spender, J.C. (2007) Structural adjustments and conflicting recipes in the US auto industry. In T. Hamalainen and R. Heiskala, *Social Innovations, Institutional Change and Economic Performance*, Cheltenham: Edward Elgar, pp. 123–158.

Starkey, K. and Scullion, H. (2000) In search of the changing role of the corporate human resource function in the international firm, *International Journal of Human Resource Management*, 11, 1061–1081.

Stiles, P., Wright, P., Paauwe, J., Stahl, G., Trevor, J. Farndale, E., Morris, S. and Bjorkman, I. (2006) *Best Practice and Key Themes in Global Human Resource Management: Project Report*, GHRRA.

Ulrich, D. and Smallwood, N. (2007) *Leadership Brand: Developing Customer-focused Leaders and Drive Performance and Build Lasting value*, Boston: Harvard Business Review Press.

Van Riel, C.B. (2003) The management of corporate communications. In J.M.T. Balmer and S.A. Geyser (eds), *Revealing the Corporation: Perspectives on Identity, Image, Reputation, Corporate Branding and Corporate-level Marketing*. London: Routledge, pp. 161–170.

Whetten, D.A. (2002) Modelling-as-theorizing: A systematic methodology for theory development. In D. Partington (ed.) *Essential Skills for Management Research*. London: Sage, pp. 45–71.

Whetten, D.A. and Mackey, A. (2002) A social actor conception of organisational identity and its implications for the study of organisational reputations, *Business and Society*, 41: 393–414.

Part 3

Global talent management: comparative perspectives

7 Talent management in India*

JONATHAN P. DOH, WALTER G. TYMON, JR.
AND STEPHEN A. STUMPF

Introduction

As emerging markets grow and become integrated into the global marketplace, management practices of developed countries are adapted to other country contexts. In the realm of talent management, as Western companies enter and expand in emerging economies, there is competition for talent as companies seek competitive advantage by leveraging their understandings of linkages between talent management and overall firm performance (Bowen and Ostroff, 2004; Burton, *et al.*, 2004; Corporate Executive Board, 2006; Fulmer, Gerhart, and Scott, 2003; Gelade and Ivery, 2003). Some companies use similar HR practices in different geographic markets with the belief that such practices, and the work climate that these practices partially create, help to attract and retain employees, cause employees to have positive attitudes, and increase employee performance (Neal, West, and Patterson, 2005; Patterson, Warr, and West, 2004; Rogg, Schmidt, Shull, and Schmitt, 2001). Others believe that adapting and adjusting to the country conditions and pursuing a "localization" strategy—including talent management—is more effective (Budhwar and Sparrow, 1997).

India is considered by some as an exemplar among emerging markets in its economic liberalization, dynamic growth, and integration of foreign and domestic business activity; yet, it is the poorest of the BRIC (Brazil, Russia, India, China) countries with per-capita GDP of less than $1,000 (Budhwar, 2001a; Economist Intelligence Unit, 2008). Fueled by the boom in the service sector, India has been the recipient of rapidly increasing levels of foreign direct investment (FDI) (Economist Intelligence Unit, 2008). The resulting landscape of national, international, and global organizations creates a rich setting to explore the "strength of the HRM system" defined by Bowen and Ostroff (2004: 203) as the extent to which "individuals share a common interpretation of what behaviors are expected and rewarded."

There are four key factors driving talent management concerns in the Indian context. First is the continued rapid growth of the Indian economy. In spite of the global recession, above average long-term economic growth is expected to continue in India. Second, there is a scarcity of talented knowledge workers possessing the necessary skills of a globally competitive workforce. Third is the retention of talent within firms when the demand for talent across Indian organizations is so great. These three factors combine to provide the challenge at the heart of talent management which is to meet their needs for human capital in positions that are difficult to fill (Cappelli, 2008; 2009) that are also critical to strategic success. Boudreau and Ramstad (2005) refer to human capital needs in these areas as "pivotal talent pools" (p. 129). Finally, there is a paucity of empirically based knowledge of best talent management practices within India. We elaborate on these key factors below. For organizations across the globe, talent management of knowledge workers and managers is of strategic importance. Organizations are facing severe difficulties recruiting and retaining the necessary talent to support global operations (Scullion, Caligiuri, and Collings, 2008). Although companies are facing talent management difficulties in several regions of the world, the challenges are most acute for young professionals and new managers in emerging markets—India is a prime example. There have not been enough qualified candidates to meet the demand for talent during periods of economic expansion, corporate growth, and low unemployment. For example, a McKinsey study reported human resource professionals would consider hiring only 10–25 percent of India's 14 million university graduates to work in multinational companies because they lack the necessary training, language skills, and cultural awareness required in global corporations (Holland, 2008). Equally challenging has been their retention of knowledge workers beyond 2–3 years. In India, the information technology (IT) and business process outsourcing (BPO) sectors experience annual attrition rates of 30 to 45 percent (Bhatnagar, 2007). The economic downturn of 2008–2009 has had little effect on the retention challenges for IT professionals in India. Their value has increased when firms reduce their labor costs by laying off unskilled and semi-skilled workers. Firms need their IT professionals to provide software and systems to replace these workers (Chopra, 2009).

The need for effective talent management is gaining attention in the area of cross-cultural influences on work motivation and job performance (Bhagat and McQuaid, 1982; Earley, 1997; Steers and Sanchez-Runde, 2001). Yet, there has been little research taking a comprehensive view of talent management in emerging markets, i.e., the best practices for the attraction, on-boarding, development, appraisal, motivation, retention and/or redeployment of professional talent.

Academic research and practitioner reporting suggest that HR practices tend to be less institutionalized, less structured, and less impactful in developing countries (Yeung, Warner, and Rowley, 2008). Despite the institutional pressures to adopt global HRM systems, there is reason to expect variation among the nationality (e.g., Sparrow and Budhwar, 1997) and scope of firms in the extent to which they are able to create a strong organizational climate through their HR practices that affects employee career success, job performance, and potential for advancement.

In this chapter, we survey recent research on talent management in India. We begin by reviewing the broad political, social, and economic context and business environment in India and explore the implications of this context for talent management. We review some of the most important contributions to understanding talent management in India, including the link between talent management and firm performance. We then report results from a comprehensive survey of talent management practices in India and offer some practical implications for that research. We conclude by suggesting areas for further research.

The Indian context

With a population of more than 1.1 billion and growth rates of 8 percent per year, India has been one of the most dynamic economies in the world. According to the Indian Central Statistical Organization (CSO), the real Gross Domestic Product (GDP) growth has accelerated from 9.0 percent in 2005–2006 to 9.2 percent in 2006–2007. According to the India Brand Equity Foundation (IBEF), the growth rate has been spurred by the industrial and services sectors, which have logged a 10.9 and 11 percent rise in 2006–2007 respectively, against 9.6 and 9.8 percent in 2005–2006. And India growth has been robust, even through the global economic downturn, with GDP increases of 8 percent in 2008, and forecasts of 6–7 percent in 2009 and 8–9 percent in 2010. This record has attracted MNCs to invest in many industry sectors, from infrastructure to pharmaceuticals, and from automotive to financial services. The fact that many Indian people speak English and are well educated makes India especially attractive to U.S. and British firms. Given the high levels of British and American FDI and colonial influence, it is reasonable to expect that, despite its low per capita income, India would be relatively advanced with regard to HRM systems and HR practices.

We use the term talent management to refer to those practices which potentially influence the acquisition, management, development, and retention of knowledge workers and that are key to the strategic success of the organization. As the editors of this volume have observed, organizations are facing severe problems in recruiting and retaining talent for their global operations. India continues to be a prime example of the talent management challenge facing organizations, even with the global recession. The acronyms HR and HRM are traditional in the academic literature, and can refer to almost any practice whose purpose is directed toward an employee, whether that employee is a knowledge worker or not. To be true to the literature, we use the terms HR and HRM when used in the literature referenced.

India was one of the first large, impoverished countries to choose a democratic government and to give priority to the development of technical skills via state-of-art education (Sen, 2007). The Indian government provides funds and incentives for economic development, adding to the attractiveness of this market to MNCs. Many firms have responded to this positive business climate by increasing their activity in India. IBM's Indian workforce increased from 9,000 in 2004 to nearly 50,000 in 2007. GE spun off its business process outsourcing (BPO) to Genpact, India's largest BPO organization with nearly 30,000 employees.

Organizations across industries in India have introduced talent management tools, often based on their understanding of the "best practices" used in successful multinational companies. The local units of multinational companies have been early adopters of talent management systems such as development centers, relative ranking of performance, and talent portfolio analysis. Large Indian organizations are following suit. Organizations are using employee surveys to measure employee engagement. Earning the designation of being one of the "best places to work" is a top agenda item for many CEOs. Yet, little research has been done in India to assess the effect of these talent management efforts on the retention of new professionals.

Most CEOs and talent management professionals agree that retaining quality professionals and developing the supervisory skills to effectively manage new professionals are both critical to their success in India. Below we look at new professional perceptions of the effectiveness of their organization's talent management efforts: performance management practices, professional development practices, the quality of supervision, and the organization's social responsibility posture. These four areas are under the control of the organization's leadership and affect new professionals' attitudes about the organization, including their intentions to leave and subsequent turnover.

This dynamism has created challenges for talent management. India's salaries rose rapidly from 2002–2007, with increases of more than 15 percent a year. Even so, companies have faced attrition rates of 15–30 percent per year in their labor force of young professionals. As the demand for professional talent increases faster than supply, the costs of attracting and difficulties in acculturating employees is increasing. While long-term growth should continue, the attrition and acculturation problems may limit the continued success of the India model (Rai, 2005).

A growing, but still limited, literature stream provides insights into the recent evolution of talent management in the Indian context. Sparrow and Budhwar (1997) highlight the challenges involved in the transfer of HR practices from one country to another. They compare practices in 137 Indian organizations with a global database of like practices; India emerges as a "cultural island" in terms of its application of these practices. By contrast, Budhwar and Sparrow (1997) analyze the levels of "integration" of HRM into corporate strategy and devolvement of responsibility for HRM to line managers in India, revealing that the integration-development levels of India were somewhat similar to several European countries, notably the UK, Italy, and Germany. Budhwar and Khatri (2001) investigate the dominant HRM practices in the Indian manufacturing sector using the five main models of HRM (the "Matching model;" the "Harvard model;" the "Contextual model;" the "5-P model;" and the "European model"). This research supports the existence of a formal HRM structure in the Indian context. Budhwar (2003) examined employment relations in Indian organizations, focusing on the role of management, unions, and the state. This study suggests that the competitive pressures created by the liberalization of the Indian economy were causing organizational transformation generally and the modernization of human resource practices in particular. Baruch and Budhwar (2006) found both similarities and differences in the career management systems of firms operating in both India and Britain.

Budhwar and Boyne (2004) compared HRM practices in Indian public and private sector organizations, somewhat unexpectedly finding that there were many similarities in practices between these two sectors in: (i) the structure of the HR department, (ii) the role of the HR function in corporate change, (iii) recruitment and selection, (iv) pay and benefits, (v) training and development, (vi) employee relations, and (vii) emphasis on key HRM strategies. However, they also found that in a few HR functional areas (for example, compensation and training and development), Indian private-sector firms have adopted a more "rational" approach than their public-sector counterparts.

Budhwar, Luthar, and Bhatnagar (2006) explored the dynamics of business process outsourcing (BPO) and the HRM practices associated with this phenomenon. Using a sample of 51 BPO companies in the New Delhi area, they found that formal HRM practices were integral to the success of the BPO industry. Saini and Budhwar (2008) explored how people management issues are addressed in Indian small and medium enterprises (SMEs). They highlighted the indigenous approaches to human resource management (HRM) that have surfaced in the Indian SME context, showing that indigenous realities in HRM in Indian SMEs relate mainly to the provision of financial, emotional and social support to the workforce; employee involvement practices; recruitment; skill development; managing employee relations; and managing vis-à-vis labor law. Importantly for our analysis of the differences in global, international, and indigenous companies, this study indicates that indigenous firms face unique challenges and must approach HRM practices accordingly.

Som (2006, 2007) suggests that, as a result of the challenge of increasing competition that has resulted from liberalization, Indian organizations have adopted HRM practices both critically and constructively to foster creativity and innovation among employees. By way of summary, Budhwar and Bhatnagar's (2009) book provides a comprehensive overview of HRM practices in India, including key developments in Indian HRM, determinants of Indian HRM, sector specific HRM, emerging themes, and future challenges and the way forward.

The challenges of talent management have led firms in India to implement HRM systems, often based on their understanding of the best practices used in successful MNCs (Yeung, Warner, and Rowley, 2008; Bjorkman and Lu, 2001). The local units of MNCs have been early adopters of annual performance appraisals, employee development programs, and relative (normalized) ranking of performance (Corporate Executive Board, 2006). Large indigenous Indian organizations are following suit in their implementation of talent management systems. However, the literature suggests that these indigenous firms often adapt and tailor these practices to the particular realities of the Indian context and the unique and challenging circumstances faced in this context. Our research was designed to better understand these practices and their impact on employee career success, performance, and potential.

Talent management practices and firm performance in India

Empirical research suggests that talent management practices have positive effects on employees and company performance, at least in Western countries (Arthur, 1994; Collins and Clark, 2003; Delaney and Huselid, 1996; Delery and Doty, 1996; Ferris et al., 1998; Guthrie, 2001; Huselid, 1995; Ichniowski and Shaw, 1999). When firms apply talent management practices that respond to their external environment and leverage their internal capabilities, they can achieve superior performance (Huselid, 1995; Lado and Wilson, 1994; Wright and McMahan, 1992). Devanna, Fombrum, Tichy, and Warren (1982) argue that HRM is a key element in strategy implementation. Schuler and Jackson (1995; 1999) highlight HR activities, such as performance appraisals and development programs, as essential to managing people so as to achieve organizational goals. What is not as clear is whether these practices yield similar employee and organizational outcomes in developing and emerging economies (Parker et al., 2003).

Recent research on one or more BRIC countries suggests differences in talent management practices are significant in their effects on employees. Gong and Chang (2008) investigated

HRM in the Chinese context, comparing the presence of HR practices and their impact on performance by different ownership and governance structures. They found that the provision of career opportunities in domestic private firms and Sino-foreign joint ventures was similar to that in wholly foreign-owned firms, but greater than that in state-owned firms, and such provision was positively related to employee organizational commitment, citizenship behaviors, and firm performance. Additionally, they found that the provision of employment security was greater in state-owned than in non-state-owned firms. Employment security was positively related to employee organizational commitment, but not to citizenship behaviors or firm performance. Similarly, Ngo, Lau, and Foley (2008) examined HR practices in China to assess their impact on firm performance and the employee relations climate. The levels of adoption of HR practices were lower in state-owned enterprises than in foreign-invested enterprises and privately owned enterprises. HR practices were found to have positive effects on financial performance, operational performance, and the employee relations climate. The moderating effect of ownership type was significant for financial performance only.

Singh (2004) surveyed 82 Indian firms and found a significant relationship between two HR practices (professional development and reward systems) with perceived organizational and market performance. A Corporate Executive Board (2006) study on HR practices included 58,000 employees from 90 member organizations and 10 countries. The study reported the percentages of respondents rating various practices in their top 5 for enhancing their psychological commitment to their organization. Top practices for India were: people management (14 percent), recognition (20 percent), development opportunities (29 percent), and meritocracy (10 percent). For the U.K. they were: people management (17 percent), recognition (18 percent), development opportunities (31 percent), and meritocracy (16 percent). For the U.S. they were: people management (8 percent), recognition (7 percent), development opportunities (18 percent), and meritocracy (12 percent). People management, recognition, and development opportunities were more important to employees in India and the U.K. than in the U.S., with meritocracy least important in India.

A recent survey of executives in India indicates a strong belief that robust HR practices in employee development are critical to building and sustaining a workforce needed to capitalize on business opportunities (Malkani, Pandey, and Bhagwati, 2007). HR practices that build workforce talent will determine whether or not companies are successful in harnessing India's demographic dividend (Knowledge@Wharton, 2008). For HR practices to yield tangible benefits to the firm in terms of employee career success, performance, and potential, they must be designed, executed, and perceived to be effective (Delery and Doty, 1996; Sparrow and Budhwar, 1997).

Consistent with this previous literature, Budhwar and Debrah (2009) suggest that future research should focus on factors that contribute to the efficient management of knowledge workers. Globalization and competitive pressures are pushing organizations in India to move towards Western systems. There has been a trend from collectivism to individualism in India. With this shift, we hypothesize that more individualized talent management practices will influence employee and employer assessments of individual employees, particularly for knowledge workers.

Findings from a recent survey

It is in this context of a dynamic labor market that we conducted a large-scale talent management study of the attitudes of 2,732 new professionals from 28 companies in India. Here we identify how the perceptions of talent management practices contribute to more prideful and satisfied professionals, and the factors that prompt these professionals to intend to leave, and their retention one year later (Steel, 2002).

Factors affecting intentions to leave and turnover include: (i) growth in the economy and low unemployment, (ii) demographic trends affecting the supply of labor, (iii) poor performance or a low organizational growth rate, (iv) the organization's reputation and socially responsible behaviors, (v) employer talent management practices (e.g., performance management, professional development, quality of supervision), (vi) attitudes and beliefs of the new professional (e.g., pride in the organization, satisfaction with the organization), and (vii) characteristics of the employee (e.g., length of service, age, gender, education). Many of these factors are beyond the control of the organization (e.g., state of the economy, labor market conditions, demographic trends), and others are likely to change slowly (e.g., organizational performance and growth) (Griffeth, Hom, and Gaertner, 2000; Maertz and Campion, 1998; Ng and Butts, 2009; Vandenberghe and Bentein, 2009). The findings relating retention to these factors are clear: organizations experience higher turnover rates in fast-growing economies, in tight labor markets, when demographic factors restrict the flow of talent, with weak organizational performance, and with slow growth.

We focus on talent management practices that organizations implement as part of their human resource strategy independent of uncontrollable exogenous factors. Our focus is twofold. First, we explore how specific talent management practices affect new professionals' pride in the organization and satisfaction with it. The practices, derived from both a review of the literature and discussions with company executives, were the organization's performance management practices, professional development practices, manager relationships with employees, and the organization's socially responsible behaviors (Turban and Greening, 1996). We also explore the likely effects of these practices on new professionals' intentions to leave and turnover as mediated by their pride in and satisfaction with the organization (Griffeth, Hom, and Gaertner, 2000; Maertz and Campion, 1998). Second, we examine contextual factors that might affect the talent management practices, affective responses, and retention: the degree of globalization of the firm (national, international, and global), and five demographic characteristics of new professionals that are frequently considered in the turnover literature (e.g., length of service, age, gender, position, education) (Steel, Griffeth, and Hom, 2002).

Each of the four talent management practices studied—performance management practices, professional development practices, manager support, and socially responsible actions— had a positive relationship with pride in and satisfaction with the organization; yet the size of these relationships varied substantially. Pride in the organization was most strongly associated with socially responsible actions (56 percent of the variance in pride was shared with socially responsible actions), and then by performance management practices (42 percent shared variance), professional development practices (36 percent), and manager support (21 percent). Satisfaction with the organization was most strongly associated with professional development (49 percent shared variance), socially responsible actions (48 percent), performance management (42 percent), and manager support (33 percent). The effects of the talent management practices on retention were significant, but substantially less strong than they were on pride and satisfaction (from 8 percent to 13 percent shared variance with intention to leave; from 7 percent to 11 percent with turnover). The new professionals' pride in and satisfaction with the organization were more strongly related to intention to leave (pride, 12 percent shared variance; satisfaction, 26 percent) and turnover (pride, 10 percent, satisfaction, 23 percent).

Of the new professionals that strongly agree with the quality of the performance management practices—42.6 percent express strong pride in the organization, 48.0 percent express satisfaction, 21.8 percent feel they will leave within one year, and 11.1 percent ultimately left within one year. Of those new professionals that do not agree or only slightly agreed with the effectiveness of the organization's performance management practices—only 11.4 percent feel strong pride in the organization; 6.8 percent feel strong satisfaction with the organization, 42.7 percent express a strong intention to leave within one year, and 32.2 percent actually left within a year. A 21.1 percent difference in attrition rate translates into about a million dollars greater human resource expense to replace these professionals for every 50 positions in the firm. A similar pattern exists with respect to the professional development practices, manager support, and social responsibility.

The new professionals' perception of these practices and their pride in and satisfaction with the organization have a strong relationship with their intention to leave and subsequent turnover. Of those expressing strong pride in the organization, 19.5 percent still expressed a strong intention to leave; only 10.3 percent left as of a year later. Of those expressing strong satisfaction with the organization, 14.4 percent express a strong intention to leave; only 6.5 percent left as of a year later. Professionals expressing satisfaction with the organization and pride in it are the least likely to leave, resulting in some of the lowest attrition rates reported in developing countries. It is the perceived effectiveness of the firm's HR practices that leads to such satisfaction and pride.

The firms studied varied significantly in the extent to which these practices were enacted— with those new professionals in firms perceived to be effective in executing one or more of these practices being less likely to intend to leave, or actually leave (see Table 7.1). Having high levels of professional development practices and manager support yielded the greatest retention (5 percent–10 percent). The importance of manager support provides evidence for Becker and Huselid's (2006) contention of the critical role of line managers in managing talent and implementing a workforce strategy—with high levels of performance management practices and social responsibility yielding the next best levels of retention (9 percent–15 percent). However, this was contingent on these new professionals also feeling high levels of pride in and satisfaction with the organization. The incremental benefit to a firm that was perceived to do all four practices "exceptionally" well by its new professionals was modest compared to firms doing at least two of these practices well.

The results support the idea that the influence of social responsibility is through its positive affect on new professionals' pride in and satisfaction with the organization (Burke and Logsdon, 1996). Within the literature, a consensus has emerged that "virtuous" firms are often rewarded in the marketplace for being socially responsible (Margolis and Walsh,

Table 7.1 India talent management survey: company differences on workplace study variables[1]

Company information	Organizational practice ratings	Employee affect	Intention to leave[1]
Cluster 1 (5 firms)	Av. performance management High professional development High manager support Av. social responsibility	High pride High satisfaction	Lowest (5%–10% turnover)
Cluster 2 (7 firms)	High performance management Av. professional development Av. manager support High social responsibility	High pride High satisfaction	Low (9%–15% turnover)
Cluster 3 (3 firms)	Av. performance management High professional development Av. manager support Av. social responsibility	Av. pride Av. satisfaction	Average (16%–22% turnover)
Cluster 4 (13 firms)	Low performance management Low professional development Av. manager support Low social responsibility	Low pride Low satisfaction	High (21%–36% turnover)

Note [1] These figures report an employee's active search for alternate employment and intention to leave within one year. We conducted a follow-up communication to determine actual employee departure and intention to leave was highly correlated with actual departure (r = 0.69).

2003; Orlitzky, Schmidt, and Rynes, 2003). One common thread is the role of social responsibility in building and enhancing firm reputation—the opinions about an entity which results in a collective image of it (Bromley, 2001). In addition, research suggests that a good corporate reputation can increase current employees' motivation, morale, and satisfaction (Branco and Rodrigues, 2006; Riordan, Gatewood, and Bill, 1997). Our research provides further support for the important role of a firm's reputation for social responsibility in the talent management domain. This research specifically provides evidence of its importance among employees in emerging markets, and specifically its importance for professionals working in India. In emerging markets, with India as an example, many employees have experienced poverty first hand. The social responsibility of their employer matters greatly to these professionals (Ready, Hill, and Conger, 2008). They are committed to a stakeholder perspective of the corporation, whereby the success of the firm must provide benefits to the larger community. Only when they see this virtuous cycle occurring, do they feel pride and satisfaction as employees of the firm, and become committed to it.

In addition, social responsibility and managerial support may work together in improving retention in Indian firms. Consider, for example, Tata Steel, a global firm that is part of the Tata Group. Tata Steel created a leadership competency framework to help identify high-potential managers. Knowing the importance employees placed on the organization's commitment to social responsibility, Tata included such competencies as "shows sensitivity and genuine concern for the eco system." They assessed the potential of managers around these dimensions to be groomed for more responsible assignments. One outcome is that Tata ranked highest among companies considered to have a larger purpose.

Because the relationship of satisfaction with the organization with intention to leave is strong, taking actions to increase employees' satisfaction tends to improve retention. One's pride in the organization is highly related with one's satisfaction with it. Elements of pride include being proud of the work you do and of the organization's reputation, being willing to speak highly of the organization's products and services, and being confident in this organization's ability to "do the right thing."

Organizations that may not have strong performance management practices or strong professional development practices, can still affect their employees' pride, satisfaction, intentions to leave, and retention through the support their managers provide to the employees and the social responsibility their organization exhibits. Socially responsible actions, in particular, are associated with a strong sense of pride in the organization (62.5 percent) and satisfaction with the organization (62.4 percent).

Five demographic "control" variables were considered to potentially relate to employee attitudes and behaviors: length of service, age, gender, position, and education. Employees with varying months or years of service may have different needs that they expect the firm's talent management practices to address; they may also experience varying levels of pride in and satisfaction with the organization based on their experiences. Older new professionals may have different needs due to their life and family situation than younger new professionals. The same can be said for men versus women. New employees in different positions (individual contributor, team leader, supervisor, or manager) may have different needs and experiences. One's education may affect one's expectations as to what one perceives as fair treatment and meaningful opportunities. We explored each of these factors for new professionals with respect to their evaluation of talent management practices, affective responses, and retention.

1 *The recruitment honeymoon is over within 6 months.* Newcomers report the highest ratings in the quality of support they receive from their managers, their belief in the social responsibility of the organization, their pride in the organization, and their satisfaction with the organization. They also report the lowest intention to leave. The recruiting process has its desired effect.

2 *Unmet expectations contribute to lower levels of satisfaction with the organization.* Between the second and fifth years of service, the attitudes and beliefs of new professionals regarding talent management practices are lower than those with less length of service. It may be that the high expectations of earlier years are not being effectively met, and this then contributes to lower levels of satisfaction with the organization, leading to intentions to leave.

3 *Older new professionals respond to different cues than do younger ones.* Younger new professionals (those under 30) report placing higher value on performance management and professional development than those from 31–40 years of age. The 21–25 age group report greater benefits of performance management than either the 25–30 or 31–40 age groups, and valued professional development more than all other age groups.

4 *Gender does not seem to matter.* There are no differences in any study variables based on gender.

5 *Professionals in positions that involve close supervision of others are more positive about the organization's talent management practices than are non-manager professionals/individual contributors.* Individuals in supervisory or management positions indicate significantly greater agreement with the positive effects of performance management, greater belief in the social responsibility of the organization, greater pride, greater organizational satisfaction, and less intention to leave than the professional/individual contributor and supervisor/team leader positions.

6 *Individuals with a technical /college degree or MBA are the most difficult to retain.* New professionals with a technical university/college degree or MBA have stronger intentions to leave earlier in their career compared to those with a non-technical college degree, or a graduate degree other than MBA.

A range of organizational actions that stimulate employee engagement and retention has been shown to also support firm financial performance. In a study of 50 multinational companies, Towers Perrin–ISR documented the impact of employee engagement on financial performance (Towers Perrin, 2008). Senior management's ability to demonstrate genuine interest in employees was the top engagement driver globally. Among the youngest employees (18–24), the ability of the organization to develop leaders at all levels was the top engagement driver while the availability of excellent career advancement opportunities was the top driver among those 24–34. Over 12 months, companies with higher levels of engagement outperformed those with less engaged employees in three key financial measures: operating income, net income growth and earning per share. These companies also experienced higher levels of retention. These findings provide added support to the relationship among employer practices, employee engagement, and retention.

Some companies in India are investing in these actions, often integrating several of the levers we have discussed here into a broader performance management initiative. For example, the Ingersoll Rand Engineering Center worked with technical employees who were in the early stages of their career to identify individuals with the potential to become business and technical leaders. As part of the process, the company worked with an HR consulting firm to create a 360° online tool, manage the assessment and feedback process, and provide consultative advice on mentoring and coaching. By doing so, they were able to find the best candidates as early as possible to jumpstart the development process. In addition, employees were assigned mentors, drawn from the ranks of global leadership, to provide support in implementing individual development plans. This combination of leadership assessment and mentoring was recognized as one of the top five global best practices by the company, according to the firm.

Infosys Technologies Limited developed a "Performance Engagement Skills" coaching program for 108 selected leaders from across the Infosys Development Centres. The 12 workshops included role-playing exercises, a development matrix based on the Infosys competency model, and an interactive electronic refresher course with key concepts for use after the program was over. These 108 managers were tasked with cascading the skills to over 1,000 managers throughout the organization for integration into their respective Development Centres. As Nandita Gurjar, Group HR Head for Infosys, explained, "Performance coaching is a key capability required in our senior managers to strengthen the high performance work ethic. Tools such as 'appreciate inquiry' and 'coaching' help sustain employee engagement throughout the year rather than a one-time intervention.

This helps us to focus more on the 'how' of getting results rather than just the results themselves" (Gurjar, 2009).

Although it is too early to tell if these actions are paying off, our study suggests that investments such as these can help to create an environment characterized by managerial support, employee development and reduce the incidents of unplanned turnover. More broadly, our study of new professionals in India supports the contributions of performance management practices, professional development, manager support, and/or having a strong reputation as a socially responsible employer to successful talent management in India. These traditionally Western talent management approaches are working in a non-Western culture. Our findings suggest that organizations in India can be successful by building a distinctive talent management profile closely aligned to the organization's business strategy.

At the same time, the most successful companies in India implement talent management practices with the cultural context in mind. For example, managerial support can involve what has been described as a nurturant-task leadership style (Sparrow and Budhwar, 1997). The strong element of nurturing is consistent with a culture high in "power distance," with Indians more comfortable with, and accepting of, power differences within a hierarchy than in the West (Hofstede, 2001). Likewise, a company's visible commitment to social responsibility in the local community in which new professionals work can be particularly salient. These professionals are reminded on a daily basis of the reality of economic inequality. For them, the pride that results (or does not result) from the social responsibility of their firms is rarely far from their minds.

In conclusion, our research and the examples provided above lead us to believe there will be an increased emphasis on, and diffusion of, the talent management practices discussed in this chapter across firms in India. Successful firms are leveraging their social responsibility reputations, implementing equitable performance management practices, attending to the professional development of employees, and training managers to provide the support necessary to lead professionals successfully. Successful companies operating in India have adopted fairly sophisticated systems that reflect these global best practices to meet the human capital challenges they face in India. With continued intense global competition, we foresee these talent management initiatives becoming more widespread.

While the Indian business environment is distinctive in many ways, the similarities in Asian and South Asian cultures, cultures sometimes characterized as "high context" (i.e., communications and interactions depend heavily on context), may suggest that our findings have broader applicability (Hall, 1976). As MNEs from the U.S. and Europe continue their penetration of emerging markets, and as emerging markets' MNEs broaden their scope to other emerging and developing countries, understanding the critical role of talent management practices in employee satisfaction and retention will continue to be an important element of firm strategy and success.

A future research agenda

We are in the early days of global diffusion of talent management practices. In the case of India, Indian academics anticipated liberalization policies would have wide-ranging consequences for business policies, practices, and procedures (Kalra and Gupta, 1999). In the first part of this decade, research showed that a majority of Indian managers believed the personnel function would be under severe pressure to improve productivity. With India's prominent role in the global competitive landscape, organizations have understood the need to develop the workforce into well-trained, motivated, and productive employees (Budhwar, 2001b). Indeed researchers (Debrah and Budhwar, 2001) observed that HRM was playing a noticeable role in bringing about changes in Indian organizations, and more recently noted that human resource management continues to be a key to success for organizations located in India (Saini and Budhwar, 2007). However, despite the contribution of human resource practices, the relevant literature on Indian talent management continues to be scarce.

Our research helps to address this need. We found that companies operating in India have adopted fairly sophisticated systems that reflect global best practices. This is consistent with Budhwar's (2009) recent conclusion that most foreign firms and an increasing number of local firms are adopting formal, structured, and rational approaches to talent management in India. He notes that the present economic context has forced changes in traditional Indian employment practices. Much like their Western counterparts, employees expect to be treated fairly, rewarded equitably, provided with growth opportunities, to know what is expected of them and be given fair and constructive feedback on their performance. This is a move away from previous traditional Indian work systems known to be based on the social connections of those belonging to a particular caste, religion or group, changing to those based on formalization, professionalism and a systematic approach (Budhwar, Varma, Singh, and Dhar, 2006).

Our research indicates that knowledge workers are for the most part reacting positively in their attitudes to more rationalized talent management systems in India. Budhwar (2009) noted the need for more rationalized systems across sectors in India, and our research suggests this is happening. Progress however continues to be somewhat unevenly distributed among different types of firms and different sectors, and not necessarily in a predictable way. Additional research is needed to better understand these patterns and whether or not they will (or should) converge over time (Budhwar, 2009). Moreover, the performance benefits that the literature suggests appear to be only partially realized in the current Indian context. Our research suggests the substantial challenges in adapting talent management practices to various institutional contexts, and underscores the need for more academic research on the efficacy of talent management practices in India in general, and in different firm types and sectors specifically. In addition to more quantitative research approaches, there also is a need for more qualitative research to more fully explore the mental models and behavioral dynamics at work in the implementation of talent management systems in India.

Future research should also explore other differences among firms operating in India in addition to those investigated here. For example, firms that are state-owned (versus privately owned) are more likely to maintain more rigid, colonial-influenced talent management practices. In addition, more technology-intensive firms may be early adopters of more progressive, performance-oriented practices. In addition, there may be geographic differences within India such that firms located in the North maintain different traditions and practices from those in the South, or whether, among the global contingent, Indian firms are more likely to adopt practices, such as normalization (ranking of employees), that are associated with a strong Anglo-American tradition than those of Continental Europe. These are a few of the questions that could be explored to better inform management on talent management in India and other emerging markets.

The process of India's integration into the global economy, including its adoption of "Western" management practices, is in process and will continue. There has been an explosion of management institutes and graduate business programs in India, most of which have adopted the Western education system (Budhwar, 2001b). Executive education programs are also increasing in number, suggesting leaders of companies operating in India are seeking the benefits of management education at multiple levels. We expect that the penetration of talent management practices common in the U.S. and Europe will continue. The degree to which their introduction and implementation generate the desired results needs to be the subject of ongoing study.

We do believe talent management practices are critical aspects of effective business management in emerging markets, and that practices from Western developed countries such as the U.K. and U.S. will continue to be adapted to the Indian national context. At the same time, while English is widely spoken in India, at least among certain educational and socio-economic classes, this apparent similarity to the business environment of the U.S. and U.K. may be deceptive. Managers in India attempting to adopt Western management theories and techniques can unwittingly produce resentment and other negative feelings in the workforce, contributing to inefficiency and lack of organizational effectiveness (Jaeger, 1990; Kanungo and Jaeger, 1990). This is most likely to occur when employees feel they are being forced to adopt and accept practices which run counter to deeply held values and assumptions of the Indian culture (Jaeger, 1990). Trouble can occur when managers attempt to implement talent management systems with a mindset of "managing people" instead of "assisting them" (Khare, 1999). For example, in implementing talent management practices in India, an effective manager would be wise to develop skill as a nurturant task leader, a style whereby the leader cares for an employee, takes a personal interest in his or her well-being, while at the same time makes nurturance contingent on the employee's task accomplishment (Jaeger, 1990; Mendonca and Kanungo, 1990). In doing so, successful managers will be blending the indigenous cultural ethos of India with the requirements of techno-economic systems (Khare, 1999). How best to manage employees in the various sectors of the developing Indian economy will remain a critical area of investigation for academic researchers, with important practical implications for managers and organizations.

A recent survey from McKinsey suggests that "companies that can satisfy their global talent needs and overcome cultural and other silo-based barriers tend to outperform those that don't" (Guthridge and Komm, 2008). While we fundamentally agree with this assessment, we would also emphasize the challenges involved. As Mendonca and Kanungo (1990) noted some years ago, performance management is not a set of simple, easy, and uncomplicated routines. Instead, performance management is a set of challenging tasks which demand considerable intellectual, emotional, and physical energy as both managers and employees bring to bear their time, talent, and skills on the fulfillment of these tasks. The same can be said about talent management practices in general, in addition to performance management specifically. When managed well, the outcomes derived from skilled implementation of talent management systems should make a significant positive difference for employees and their organizations.

Even with the recent global economic recession and its accompanying high unemployment, effective talent management of professionals in India remains a critical challenge. As we noted earlier in this chapter the downturn of 2008–2009 has had little effect on the retention challenges for IT professionals for example. Their value has increased when firms reduce their labor costs by laying off unskilled and semi-skilled workers. Firms need their IT professionals to provide software and systems to replace these workers (Chopra, 2009). Given these continuing challenges, more work needs to be done to better understand the effects of evolving talent management systems in India as well as in other developing and emerging regions of the world.

Acknowledgment

* This chapter draws heavily on the following: Stumpf, S.A., Doh, J.P., and Tymon, Jr., W.G. (2010). The strength of HR practices in India and their effects on employee career success, performance and potential. *Human Resource Management:* 49(3), 353–375; Tymon, Jr., W.G., Stumpf, S.A., Doh, J.P. (2010). Exploring talent management in India: The neglected role of intrinsic rewards. *Journal of World Business*, 45(2) 109–121; Doh, J.P., Haid, M. and Stumpf, S.A., and Tymon, Jr., W.G. Managing talent in high velocity environments: Insights from India. Working paper; Doh *et al.* (2009). *Stemming the Tide of Attrition in India: Keys to Increasing Retention*. Right Management White Paper.

References

Arthur, J.B. (1994). Effects of human resource systems on manufacturing performance and turnover. *Academy of Management Journal*, 37, 670–687.

Baruch, Y., and Budhwar, P. (2006). A comparative study of career practices for management staff in Britain and India. *International Business Review*, 15, 84–101.

Becker, B.E., and Huselid, M.A. (2006). Strategic human resources management: Where do we go from here? *Journal of Management*, 32, 898–925.

Bhagat, R.S., and McQuaid, S.J. (1982). Role of subjective culture in organizations: A review and directions for future research. *Journal of Applied Psychology*, 67: 653–685.

Bhatnagar, J. (2007). Talent management strategy of employee engagement in Indian ITES employees: Key to retention. *Employee Relations*, 29: 640–663.

Bjorkman, I., and Lu, Y. (2001). Institutionalization and bargaining power explanations of HR practices in international joint ventures: The case of Chinese–Western joint ventures. *Organization Studies*, 22, 491–512.

Boudreau, J.W., and Ramstad, P.M. (2005). Talentship, talent segmentation, and sustainability: A new HR decision science paradigm for a new strategy definition. *Human Resource Management*, 44, 129–136.

Bowen, D.E., and Ostroff, C. (2004). Understanding HRM-firm performance linkages: the role of the "strength" of the HRM system. *Academy of Management Review*, 29, 203–221.

Branco, M.C., and Rodrigues, L.L. (2006). Corporate social responsibility and resource-based perspectives. *Journal of Business Ethics*, 69: 111–132.

Bromley D.B. 2001. Relationships between personal and corporate reputations. *European Journal of Marketing*, 35: 316–334.

Budhwar, P.S. (2001a). Doing business in . . . India. *Thunderbird International Business Review*, 43, 549–568.

Budhwar, P.S. (2001b). Human resource management in India. In P.S. Budhwar, and Y.A. Debrah (Eds.), *Human resource management in developing countries* (pp. 75–90). London: Routledge.

Budhwar, P.S. (2003). Employment relations in India. *Employee Relations*, 25, 132–148.

Budhwar, P.S. (2009). Challenges facing Indian HRM and the way forward. In P.S. Budhwar, and J. Bhatnagar (Eds.), *The Changing Face of People Management in India* (pp. 288–301). London: Routledge.

Budhwar, P.S., and Bhatnagar, J. (Eds.), (2009). *The Changing Face of People Management in India*. London: Routledge.

Budhwar, P., and Boyne, G. (2004). Human resource management in the Indian public and private sectors: An empirical comparison. *International Journal of Human Resource Management*, 15, 346–370.

Budhwar, P., and Debrah, Y.A. (2009). Future research on human resource management. *Asia Pacific Journal of Management*, 26, 197–218.

Budhwar, P., and Khatri, P. (2001). HRM in context: Applicability of HRM models in India. *International Journal of Cross Cultural Management*, 1, 333–356.

Budhwar, P., Luthar, H., and Bhatnagar, J. (2006). The dynamics of HRM systems in Indian BPO Firms. *Journal of Labor Research*, 27, 339–360.

Budhwar, P., and Sparrow, P. (1997). Evaluating levels of strategic integration and development of human resource management in India. *International Journal of Human Resource Management*, 8, 476–494.

Budhwar, P.S., Varma, A., Singh, V., and Dhar, R. (2006). HRM systems of Indian call centres: An exploratory study. *The International Journal of Human Resource Management*, 17, 881–897.

Burke, L., and Logsdon, J. M. (1996). How corporate social responsibility pays off. *Long Range Planning*, 29 (4), 495–502.

Burton, R. M., Lauridsen, J., and Obel, B. (2004). The impact of organizational climate and strategic fit on firm performance. *Human Resource Management*, 43, 67–82.

Cappelli, P. (2008). Talent management for the twenty-first century. *Harvard Business Review*, 86, 74–81.

Cappelli, P. (2009). A supply chain model for talent management. *People and Strategy*, 32, 4–7.

Chopra, T. (2009). Personal communication with Tushar Chopra, CEO, ATS Services Ltd., May 19, 2009.

Collins, C.J., and Clark, K.D. (2003). Strategic human resource practices, top management team social networks, and firm performance: The role of human resource practices in creating organizational competitive advantage. *Academy of Management Journal*, 46, 740–751.

Corporate Executive Board (2006). *Attracting and Retaining Critical Talent Segments: Identifying Drivers of Attraction and Commitment in the Global Labor Market*. Washington, DC.

Debrah Y.A., and Budhwar, P.S. (2001). Conclusion: International competitive pressures and the challenges for HRM in developing countries. In P.S. Budhwar, and Y.A. Debrah (Eds.), *Human Resource Management in Developing Countries* (pp. 238–254). London: Routledge.

Delaney, J.T., and Huselid, M.A. (1996). The impact of human resource management practices on perceptions of organizational performance. *Academy of Management Journal*, 39, 949–969.

Delery, J.E., and Doty, D.H. (1996). Modes of theorizing in strategic human resource management: Tests of universalistic, contingency, and configurational performance predictions. *Academy of Management Journal*, 39, 802–835.

Devanna, M. A., Fombrum, C., Tichy, N., and Warren, L. (1982). Strategic planning and human resource management. *Human Resource Management*, 21, 11–17.

Earley, P.C. (1997). *Face, Harmony, and Social Structure: An Analysis of Organizational Behavior across Cultures*. New York: Oxford University Press.

Economist Intelligence Unit, (2008). *India: Country Profile 2008*. London: The Economist Intelligence Unit.

Ferris, G.R., Arthur, M.M., Berkson, H.M., Kaplan, D.M., Harrell-Cook, G. and Frink, D.D. (1998). Toward a social context theory of human resource management–organizational effectiveness relationship. *Human Resource Management Review*, 8, 235–264.

Fulmer, I.S., Gerhart, B. and Scott, K. S. (2003). Are the 100 best better? An empirical investigation of the relationship between being a "great place to work" and firm performance. *Personnel Psychology*, 56, 965–993.

Gelade, G.A., and Ivery, M. (2003). The impact of human resource management and work climate on organizational performance. *Personnel Psychology*, 56, 383–404.

Gong, Y., and Chang, S. (2008). Institutional antecedents and performance consequences of employment security and career advancement practices: Evidence from the People's Republic of China. *Human Resources Management*, 47, 33–48.

Griffeth, R.W., Hom, P.W., and Gaertner, S. (2000). A meta-analysis of antecedents and correlates of employee turnover: Update, moderator tests, and research implications for the next millennium. *Journal of Management*, 26, 463–488.

Gurjar, N. (2009). Personal communication with Nandita Gurjar, Group HR Head for Infosys.

Guthridge, M., and Komm, A.B. (2008, May). Why multinationals struggle to manage talent. *McKinsey Quarterly*. Available at: http://www.mckinseyquarterly.com.

Guthrie, J.P. (2001). High-involvement work practices, turnover, and productivity: Evidence from New Zealand. *Academy of Management Journal*, 44, 180–190.

Hall, E.T. (1976). *Beyond Culture*. New York: Doubleday.

Hofstede, G.H. (2001). *Culture's Consequences: Comparing Values, Behaviors, Institutions, and Organizations across Nations* (2nd edition). Thousand Oaks, CA: Sage.

Holland, K. (2008, February 24). Working all corners in a global talent hunt. *The New York Times*. Retrieved from http://www.nytimes.com/2008/02/24/jobs/24mgmt.html

Huselid, M.A. (1995). The impact of human resource management practices on turnover, productivity, and corporate financial performance. *Academy of Management Journal*, 38, 635–672.

Ichniowski, C., and Shaw, K. (1999). The effects of human resource management practices on economic performance: An international comparison of U.S. and Japanese plants. *Management Science*, 45, 704–721.

Jaeger, A.J. (1990). The applicability of Western management techniques in developing countries: A cultural perspective. In A.M. Jaeger, and R.N. Kanungo (Eds.), *Management in Developing Countries* (pp. 131–145). London: Routledge.

Kalra, S.K., and Gupta, R.K. (1999). Some behavioral dimensions of effective managerial style in the Indian context. In H.S.R. Kao, D. Sinha, and B. Wilpert (Eds.), *Management and Cultural Values: The Indigenization of Organizations in Asia* (pp. 287–296). New Delhi: Sage.

Kanungo, R.N., and Jaeger, A.M., (1990). Introduction: The need for indigenous management in developing countries. In A.M. Jaeger, and R.N. Kanungo (Eds.), *Management in Developing Countries* (pp. 1–19). London: Routledge.

Khare, A. (1999). Japanese and Indian work patterns: A study of contrasts. In H.S.R. Kao, D. Sinha, and B. Wilpert (Eds.), *Management and cultural values: The indigenization of organizations in Asia* (pp. 121–136). New Delhi: Sage.

Knowledge@Wharton (2008, September 18). *India's Corporations Race to Train Workers and Avoid being Left in the Dust*. Available at http://knowledge.wharton.upenn/india.

Lado, A.A., and Wilson, M.C. (1994). Human resource systems and sustained competitive advantage: A competency-based perspective. *Academy of Management Review*, 19, 699–727.

Maertz, C.P., and Campion, M.A. (1998). 25 years of voluntary turnover research: A review and critique, in C.L. Cooper and I.T. Robinson (Eds.), *International Review of Industrial and Organizational Psychology* (pp. 49–86). London: John Wiley.

Malkani, D., Pandey, J., and Bhagwati, A.B. (2007). *The High-performance Workforce Study 2007: India*. Mumbai: Accenture.

Margolis, J. D., and Walsh, J. P.(2003). Misery loves companies: Rethinking social initiatives by business. *Administrative Science Quarterly*, 48, 268–305.

Mendonca, M., and Kanungo, R.N. (1990). Performance management in developing countries. In A.M. Jaeger, and R.N. Kanungo (Eds.), *Management in Developing Countries* (pp. 223–251). London: Routledge.

Neal, A., West, M.A., and Patterson, M.G. (2005). Do organizational climate and competitive strategy moderate the relationship between human resource management and productivity? *Journal of Management*, 31, 495–512.

Ng, T.W.H., and Butts, M.M. (2009). Effectiveness of organizational efforts to lower turnover intentions: the moderating role of employee locus of control, *Human Resource Management*, 48 (2), 289–310.

Ngo, H-Y., Lau, C-M., and Foley, S. (2008). Strategic human resource management, firm performance, and employee relations climate in China. *Human Resources Management*, 47, 73–90.

Orlitzky, M., Schmidt, F., and Rynes, S. (2003). Corporate social and financial performance: a meta-analysis. *Organization Studies, 24*: 403–441.

Parker, C.P., Baltes, B.B., Young, S.A., Huff, J.W., Altmann, R.A., Lacost, H.A., *et al.* (2003). Relationships between psychological climate perceptions and work outcomes: A meta-analytic review. *Journal of Organizational Behavior*, 24, 389–416.

Patterson, M., Warr, P., and West, M. (2004). Organizational climate and company productivity: The role of employee affect and employee level. *Journal of Occupational and Organizational Psychology*, 77, 193–216.

Rai, S. (2005, November 2). Outsourcers in India fight for skilled labor. *International Herald Tribune*, 11.

Ready, D.A., Hill, L.A., and Conger, J. A. (2008). Winning the race for talent in emerging markets. *Harvard Business Review*, 86 (11), 62–70.

Riordan, C.M., Gatewood, R.D., and Bill, J.B. (1997). Corporate image: Employee reactions and implications for managing corporate social performance. *Journal of Business Ethics*, 16: 401–412.

Rogg, K.L., Schmidt, D.B., Shull, C., and Schmitt, N. (2001). Human resource practices, organizational climate, and customer satisfaction. *Journal of Management*, 27, 431–449.

Saini, D.S., and Budhwar, P.S. (2007). Human resource management in India. In R. Schuler, and S. Jackson (Eds.), *Strategic Human Resource Management* (pp. 287–312). Oxford: Blackwell.

Saini, D.S., and Budhwar, P.S. (2008). Managing the human resource in Indian SMEs: The role of indigenous realities. *Journal of World Business*, 43, 417–434.

Schuler, R.S. and Jackson, S.E. (1995). Understanding human resource management in the context of organizations and their environment. *Annual Review of Psychology*, 46, 237–264.

Schuler, R.S. and Jackson, S.E. (1999). *Strategic Human Resource Management: A Reader*. London: Blackwell.

Scullion, H., Caligiuri, P., and Collings, D. (2008). Call for papers: Global talent management. *Journal of World Business*, 43: 128–129.

Sen, A. (2007, February 7). *IT and India* [Keynote address at the NASSCOM 2007 India Leadership Forum in Mumbai]. Online edition of *The Hindu*. Available at http://www.hindu.com/nic/itindia.htm.

Singh, K. (2004). Impact of HR practices on perceived performance in India. *Asia Pacific Journal of Human Resources*, 42, 301–317.

Som, A. (2006). Bracing for MNC competition through innovative HRM practices: The way ahead for Indian firms. *Thunderbird International Business Review*, 48, 207–237.

Som, A. (2007). What drives adoption of innovative SHRM practices in Indian organizations? *International Journal of Human Resource Management*, 18, 808–828.

Sparrow, P.R., and Budhwar, P.S. (1997). Competition and change: Mapping the Indian HRM recipe against world-wide patterns. *Journal of World Business*, 32, 224–242.

Steel, R.P. (2002). Turnover theory at the empirical interface: Problems fit and function. *Academy of Management Review*, 27 (3), 346–360.

Steel, R.P., Griffeth R.W., and Hom, P.S. (2002). Practical retention policy for the practical manager. *Academy of Management Executive*, 16 (2), 149–164.

Steers, R.M., and Sanchez-Runde, C. (2001). *Culture, Motivation, and Work Behavior*. In M. Gannon and K. Newman (Eds) *Handbook of Cross-Cultural Management* (pp. 190–215). London: Blackwell.

Towers Perrin (2008). Global workforce study 2007–2008. Available at http://www.towersperrin.com/tp/showhtml.jsp?url=global/publications/gws/index.htmandcountry=global.

Turban D.B., and Greening, D.W. (1996). Corporate social performance and organizational attractiveness to prospective employees. *Academy of Management Journal*, 40 (3), 658–672.

Vandenberghe, C., and Bentein, K. (2009). A closer look at the relationship between affective commitment to supervisors and organizations and turnover. *Journal of Occupational and Organizational Psychology*, 82 (2), 331–348.

Wright, P.M., and McMahan, G.C. (1992). Theoretical perspectives for strategic human resource management. *Journal of Management*, 18, 295–320.

Yeung, A., Warner, M., and Rowley, C. (2008). Guest editors' introduction: Growth and globalization: Evolution of human resource management practices in Asia. *Human Resource Management*, 47, 1–13.

Talent management in China

FANG LEE COOKE

Introduction

The attraction and retention of talent in China has been considered one of the most challenging tasks in human resource management (HRM) due to the severe shortage of talent in the labour market. In their literature review of recent research in global talent management (GTM), Tarique and Schuler (2009) identified three main external drivers of GTM challenge: globalization, demographics, and the demand and supply gap. In the Chinese context, globalization has led to the brain drain of home-grown talent through international migration and from Chinese-owned firms to foreign-owned multinational corporations (MNCs) operating in China. A striking feature of China's economic and social change following its 'Open Door' policy enacted in 1978 has been the growing number of young people participating in higher education. This vast investment in education, however, has not provided the necessary talent pool for the country's rapid development. What may be the institutional failure? In the meantime, globalization and marketization are having an evident impact on the traditional cultural values and socialist ideology that were once held by the nation. What may be the expectations and aspirations of the younger generation of the Chinese workforce in a period of transition?

Moreover, in the light of the talent shortage challenge, GTM literature, which is largely of a prescriptive nature (Collings and Mellahi, 2009; Tarique and Schuler, 2009), has offered a number of strategic HRM interventions with assumed universal utility. This body of literature often cites prestigious MNCs as examples of effective HRM in the global context. Do all MNCs aspire to good HRM practice to gain sustainable competitive advantages? Even if they do, are they able to adopt a global (integrated) HRM strategy without encountering local constraints in the process of transferring best practice and integrating corporate HRM practices? Writers on comparative employment relations (e.g. Rubery and Grimshaw, 2003) have highlighted the fact that the primary motive of MNCs entering host countries may be to take advantage of the local environment for the economic gain of the firm. Dissemination of good practice may take place only as a means to achieving this. This is particularly the case in emerging economies and the least developed countries where labour standards are relatively low and the enforcement of employment regulations remains difficult (Cooke, 2008a). The task of talent management for MNCs is therefore performed in the context of a local labour market and historically-informed employment conditions and social relations that underpin much of the HRM policies and practices. In addition, industrial and organizational factors interact with these institutional and cultural forces in shaping HRM policies and practices (Wright and van de Voorde, 2009).

This chapter contains two main parts in its analysis of talent management in China. First, it examines the national context of and challenges to talent management in China. The chapter then investigates organizational practices by drawing on examples from a number of MNCs operating in a range of sectors in China for illustration. As far as possible, Chinese-owned MNCs are included in the discussion. This is partly because they have not been a focus of study in international HRM, despite being an increasingly important category of firms in the global economy (Luo and Tung, 2007; Cooke, 2008a). These firm level examples reveal the importance of industrial characteristics and the role of senior managers in shaping HRM practices. The intention of the chapter is not to provide best practice case studies of talent management of foreign MNCs operating in China. Rather, it aims to highlight some of the country-specific contexts of talent management in China, the type of HRM practices leading multinational firms in China adopt, and talent management issues firms may encounter. We adopt Lewis and Heckman's (2006: 140) definition of talent management for the purpose of this chapter, in which we see talent management as a 'collection of typical HRM practices, functions or activities'. It is akin to strategic HRM that is aligned with the strategic goals of the organization. Global talent management in this context refers to the management of talent in multinational firms. The chapter focuses on Chinese managers and professionals as the target of talent management.

Talent management in China: context and challenges

Authors on international HRM have stressed the importance of institutional, cultural and industrial/sectoral factors that may influence the configuration of HRM practices in a given country (e.g. Budhwar and Debrah, 2001; Clark and Mallory, 1996; Farndale and Paauwe, 2007; Harzing, 2004; Paauwe and Boselie, 2003; Stahl and Björkman, 2006). In the Chinese context, the legacy of its state-planned economy, the enduring influence of its traditional culture, and the dynamics generated by its economic transformation and the importation of western HRM practices, ideology and culture have created a complex context against which MNCs seek to manage their human resources. In this section, we look at the broad context of, and some of the key challenges to, HRM in China. We focus on a number of key aspects that are essential to talent management, including the extent of skill shortages, the role of higher education in human capital and management development, and the key characteristics of talent management in response to the talent shortage crisis.

Shortage of managerial talent

The shortage of managerial talent in China has been widely observed and regarded as a bottle neck to its economic development (e.g. Björkman and Lu, 1999; Branine, 1996; Bu, 1994; Child, 1994; Dickel and Watkins, 2008; Ralston *et al.*, 1997; Tung, 2007; Walder 1989; Wang *et al.*, 2007; Zhu *et al.*, 2005). This is in spite of the fact that considerable amounts of effort and resources have been invested in the training and development of managerial and professional workers in the last two decades (Cooke, 2005). Not only are state-owned sector organizations short of managers with modern management knowledge and mindsets, but also entrepreneurs in private enterprises suffer from a relatively low level of education. For example, among the 1.52 million managerial employees, only 0.88 per cent had postgraduate degree qualifications and 11.4 per cent had bachelor degree qualifications (*Workers' Daily*, 17 November 2005). In 2007, whilst heads of organizations made up 1.2 per cent of the total workforce, only 14 per cent of them held educational qualification at university degree level (*China Labour Statistical Yearbook 2008*).

The shortage of well trained and experienced managerial talent also has a significant impact on the capability of foreign MNCs to manage their subsidiaries effectively in the Asia region. A study conducted by Manpower in China found that 40 per cent of employers have difficulty in filling senior management positions. Whilst skill shortage for middle managers is slightly less pronounced, this has triggered a wage war (Arkless, 2007). The widely cited McKinsey and Company study conducted in 2005 predicted that Chinese firms seeking global expansion would need 75,000 leaders who can work effectively in global environments in the next 10–15 years. However, the current stock was only 3,000–5,000 (cited in Farrell and Grant, 2005). The same study by McKinsey and Company also reveals that fewer than 10 per cent of the Chinese job candidates were deemed by foreign MNCs operating in China to be qualified for the nine professional occupations including engineers, accounting and finance workers, medical staff and life science researchers. This study highlights one of the main problems in the Chinese education system – the over emphasis on theory at the expense of application and practical solution and team working (cited in Farrell and Grant, 2005). Similarly, Mercer's recent survey on attraction and retention revealed that 72 per cent of MNC respondents believed that the biggest challenge in recruitment was the lack of qualified candidates in the Chinese market (cited in Wilson, 2008).

Human capital development

The shortage of managerial talent in China is partly triggered by the rapid expansion of its economy over the last three decades. However, the higher education and management education system is a major contributing factor to this deficiency. China's higher education sector has expanded dramatically since the mid-1990s, especially since the early 2000s. In 2001, there were a total of 1,225 state-funded regular higher education institutions. By 2007, the number had risen to 1,908. In 2000, over one million full-time students (950,000 graduates and 58,767 postgraduates) graduated from universities; in 2007, 4.79 million (4.48 million graduates and 311,839 postgraduates) graduated (*China Statistical Yearbook 2008*). In the last decade, there has been a sharp rise in those who study management disciplines. For example, in 2001, only 139,943 students majoring in management discipline graduated from universities. In 2007, a total of 1.68 million students studying management qualifications graduated (*China Statistical Yearbook 2008*)[1]. In addition, there has been a significant growth in the number of students seeking postgraduate studies abroad. In 2007, 144,000 students went abroad for postgraduate education, compared to 38,989 students in 2000. In 2007, 44,000 graduates returned to China after their postgraduate education (*China Statistical Yearbook 2008*). Many of them studied business and management subjects.

The rapid expansion of higher education creates a paradoxical situation in the labour market in China. On the one hand, there is mounting pressure for graduate employment. Only about 70 per cent of those who graduated in 2008 found employment within a year (*The Economist* 2009). The unemployment rate in 2009 is likely to be higher due to the global financial crisis. On the other hand, there is an increasingly severe shortage of skilled workers and managerial talent. Worse still, the most highly qualified graduates are lost due to a brain drain to overseas, adding further to the talent shortage problem. It was reported that 80 per cent of the graduates in high-tech related subjects from Tsinghua University have gone to the USA since 1985. A similar proportion (76 per cent) have done the same from Beijing University (Pan and Lou, 2004). Tsinghua and Beijing universities are the two top universities in China. Other premium universities encounter similar trends, albeit to a lesser extent.

The repatriation of thousands of graduates trained abroad has not alleviated the shortage of management talent. A study of Chinese graduates returning from their overseas education revealed that half of them have no formal work experience – a major constraint for their employment opportunity. Only half of the companies are satisfied with the performance of their overseas returnee employees. Employers from industries that require China-specific knowledge, such as real estate, construction, consultancy, legal, finance and banking, and manufacturing are far less satisfied with their returnee employees than employers of other industries. In addition, foreign-invested companies show a lower level of satisfaction (less than 30 per cent were satisfied) of their returnee employees compared with state-invested firms (over 60 per cent were satisfied) (cited in Development and Management of Human Resources, 2008). My interviews with over 40 MNC employers participating in two job fairs in 2008 and 2009 also confirmed that employers felt a significant gap between what they seek and what Chinese graduates trained overseas (as well as home students) possess. A key problem, as noted above, is that the Chinese educational system emphasizes theoretical knowledge and abstract problem solving instead of the development of practical skills and independent and critical thinking. Reproduction of existing knowledge tends to be the mode of study instead of cultivating creative learning. Students who are brought up with this mode of passive learning often find it hard to adapt to the western style of learning and consequently few are able to rise to the challenging opportunity presented by the western MNCs. In addition, it is believed that the one-child policy enacted in the 1980s by the Chinese government to control the explosive growth of population has produced a generation of young people (known as the post-80 generation) who are spoilt by their family, dependent, unwilling to endure hardship but eager to have early success.

Management education and development

Recognizing the pressing needs for developing professional managers with modern management knowledge, the state has been funding management training and education through the development of management development institutes and business schools since the mid-1980s. Broadly speaking, state intervention in management development (MD) can be divided into two stages (see Wang and Wang 2006; Warner and Goodall, 2010 for an overview of MD in China and the role of business schools). The first was from the mid-1980s to the mid-1990s. This was the state's first serious attempt to professionalise state-owned enterprise (SOE) managers and state cadres. The second stage of state intervention in MD started from the mid-1990s till now. It was characterized by the rapid development of business schools and MBA/EMBA and short-term executive management training programmes nation-wide. The globalization of China's economy exposes another significant gap in its human resources – managers who are competent in managing in an international business environment. The demand for up-to-date western management theories and applications surged, resulted in the rapid growth of business schools and MBA/EMBA programmes (see Lau and Roffey, 2002; Wang 1999; Warner and Goodall, 2010). Nevertheless, state involvement remains a defining feature in the second stage of MD. A more recent phenomenon is that the government is taking advantage of foreign MNCs' corporate universities in China by sending senior managers from key SOEs there for training and development (Wang and Wang, 2006).

The effect of leadership/management development through these higher education institutions has not been fully evaluated, nor may it be possible to do so. The intimate involvement of the state in the MBA/EMBA education in contrast to the lack of involvement from the industry/employers, a prominent feature in China's higher education in general, runs the risk that the system may not be producing what the employers need and that management education may be detached from business practice. My interviews with informants from government-sponsored training programmes (38 informants) and EMBA programmes (63 informants) during 2007 and 2008 revealed that while all of them felt that the training is useful on the whole, the benefits of training have not been taken advantage of by their employing organizations. This is due to the lack of post-training evaluation and organizational mechanisms to provide opportunities for them to apply what they have learned to improve organizational effectiveness. Elsewhere, the utility of imported MBA programmes to meet the urgent need for MD has been questioned due to the significant cultural and institutional differences between China and Western societies in both teaching/learning styles and approaches to business management (e.g. Lau and Roffey, 2002; Wang and Wang, 2006).

Nonetheless, MBA/EMBA programmes fill 'the management education gap at all levels and in all sectors' and contribute to the development of powerful management networks nation-wide (Southworth, 1999: 330). Indeed, informants who participated in the EMBA or executive development programmes reported that they were motivated to participate in the training by two main reasons: to learn new knowledge (known as 'to recharge one's batteries' in China) and to develop a wider business network to share ideas/information and provide mutual support. The latter is crucial in the Chinese business environment. This is because *guanxi* (relationships) are important substitutes for formal institutional support. They are often developed to compensate for the absence of the latter (Xin and Pearce, 1996).

The problems revealed above in the development of leadership and management competence suggests that much needs to be done by the stakeholders (i.e. the state, management education providers, employers and individuals) to develop an integrated system in which development needs can be met and developed, and skills and knowledge can be utilized effectively. It also suggests that the most effective way of developing leadership skills may rest outside the existing formal education and executive development forum. More interactive and participant-led fora may be developed for management development purposes.

Challenges to talent management

Given the difficulty in recruiting, developing and retaining managerial and professional talent, many of firms have turned to poaching as a quick fix. Indulged by a tight labour market, individuals are encouraged to look outside their company for better opportunities. They also become less tolerant with their employer when their demands are not met. A study jointly conducted by DDI and Society for Human Resource Management (USA) on talent retention issues in China in 2006–2007 showed that staff turnover rate had increased from 6–8 per cent a few years before to 14–20 per cent in 2007. Linked to this high staff turnover rate is a relatively high annual wage increase rate of 9–14 per cent, compared with that of 2–5 per cent in the USA. In addition, 61 per cent of the employees aged between 25 and 30 were ready to leave their current employer. Worse still, only 8 per cent of the 862 employees surveyed were 'engaged' with their company. In order to attract and retain talent, many firms have reported that they have to offer job candidates job titles, salaries and responsibilities that are well beyond their current capability and level of experience (cited in Zhao, 2008).

For those who intend to leave their employer, the main reasons reported for turnover are: unhappy relationship with the management and failure to fit in with the company culture (cited in Zhao, 2008). These findings echo that from Hui *et al.* (2004) and Chan and Wyatt (2007). Hui *et al.*'s (2004) study observes that Chinese workers value highly a good interpersonal relationship with their supervisors and tend to reciprocate with affective commitment and citizenship behaviour to their supervisor rather than their organization. This reflects the traditional Chinese culture that values interpersonal relationship within a social hierarchical order and suggests that poor relationship with superiors may be a key factor for turnover. Similarly, Chan and Wyatt's (2007: 512) study of the quality of work life of 319 employees in the Shanghai area found that esteem need is the most important factor for life satisfaction and turnover intention, and that managers are more likely to stay with the organization in which 'they feel a greater sense of recognition and appreciation of one's work inside and outside the organization'.

Career advancement is another major reason for the turnover of talented employees, lured by the inflated job titles and salary packages offered by firms desperate to attract talent. A recent study conducted by Manpower in China revealed that two-thirds of respondents make their job move for better career development opportunities. Only 15 per cent of respondents indicated that their main reason for leaving was the prospect of better pay and benefits (Arkless, 2007). However, other research studies revealed that pay is actually far more important in people's job choices and behaviours than we are led to believe and that financial reward is one of the most important factors in retention and motivation in China (e.g. Chiu *et al.*, 2002; Rynes *et al.*, 2004). For example, the Watson Wyatt study 'Work China Employee Attitude Survey' that polled employees from 100 companies in China showed that compensation is by far the most important factor influencing job quit intent. In addition, 'better benefits' is the third most cited reason for turnover (see Figure 8.1, cited in

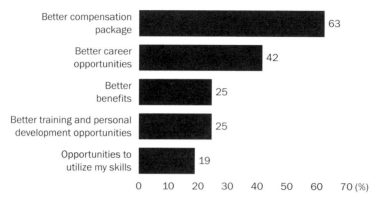

Note: Employees were asked to select their top three reasons, from a list of
20, for leaving the company.

Figure 8.1 Top five reasons employees cite for leaving
Source: Leininger (2007: 28).

Leininger, 2007). This is because earning power is a strong indicator not only of the
individual's ability to work, but also their economic and social status in the newly found
materialistic culture in the country following its 'Open Door' policy in 1978. Nevertheless,
it is important to note that career development opportunities, training programmes,
mentoring and a positive working environment remain crucial to attract and retain talent.

As the competition for talent continues, Chinese firms are reported to have become more
strategic in linking their HRM practices to organizational performance (Law *et al.*, 2003;
Wang *et al.*, 2007; Wei and Lau, 2005; Zhu *et al.*, 2005). Studies by Wei and Lau (2005)
and Wang *et al.* (2007) found that the differences in key HRM practices amongst firms of
different ownership forms in China are diminishing, indicating a trend of convergence in the
HRM practices adopted by foreign-invested and Chinese firms. In addition, Wang *et al.*
(2007: 699) found that 'while foreign-invested companies emphasize humanistic goals
the most, it was private-owned enterprises that linked these goals most tightly with the
high-performance HR practices'. Here, the ability of the private firms to understand and
align their HR strategy with the employees' expectation appears to be a crucial factor in
managing talent effectively. This expectation is shaped by the need for personal growth.
It is also informed by the deeply embedded traditional Chinese cultural value on the one
hand, and the emerging modern value of materialism and social elitism on the other.

Changing values and management mindsets

A number of studies have highlighted the changing expectations of Chinese employees and
values and mindsets of managers in China as a result of its economic and social
transformation over the last three decades (e.g. Bai and Bennington, 2005; Ralston *et al.*,
1995, 1999). For example, Bai and Bennington's (2005) study of SOEs in the coal mining
industry revealed that as a result of increasing pressure from intensified market competition,
SOEs were utilizing modern performance appraisal measures as effective tools to enhance
their management efficiency and productivity. Their study showed that whilst differences

from western performance appraisal practices persist, significant changes were taking place in performance appraisal practices in China that depart from the traditional form. In particular, Chinese cultural values did not seem to impede the implementation of individual performance-related reward schemes.

In some sense, attitudinal changes are more marked amongst workers than managers in the state-owned sector. According to a study conducted by Zhang (2005) who surveyed the managers and workers across the five subsidiaries of a large stock-market listed state-owned enterprise, junior managers appeared to be more conservative and resistant than workers in terms of implementing a new performance management scheme which is aimed to relate performance more closely to financial rewards. By contrast, over half the workers surveyed had a positive attitude towards performance-related pay, and only a small minority of 10–15 per cent felt that competition pressure and distributional variations should be minimized.

Generation gap also appears to be an influential factor in changing outlooks. For example, Ralston *et al.*'s (1999) study on the generational shift in work values amongst the older and younger generations of Chinese managers found that when comparing Chinese managers with western managers, the former are more collective-oriented and Confucianist in their outlook and management style; but when comparing the older and younger generations of the Chinese managers, the latter are more independent and risk-taking in their pursuit of financial gains. This led to Ralston *et al.*'s (1999) conclusion that the younger generation of the Chinese managers may be seen as crossverging their oriental and western influence on the road to modernization.

The pursuit of profit is perhaps boldest in the private sector. A study of 65 Chinese private firms by the author during 2007 and 2008 showed that profit-sharing and stock option schemes were the most widely used and perceived to be the most effective HR mechanism to retain key professional and managerial staff. Then demand for profit-sharing as much as, if not more than, equalled that for training and development opportunities. These findings suggest that the new materialism has overtaken traditional cultural forces that tend to promote egalitarianism and altruism and suppress materialistic desire. Indeed, poaching senior managers with a lucrative remuneration package has been a common tactic deployed by many leading firms in the IT and telecom industry over the last few years in response to intensifying business competition. This has led to worsening wage inflation and instability in the senior management team in a number of firms, both Chinese-owned and foreign MNCs (Cooke, 2008a; Walsh and Zhu, 2007).

The above characteristics and tensions displayed in the context of talent management in China have implications for talent management for MNCs operating in China and Chinese-owned MNCs aspiring to be true global players. In the next section, we investigate existing and emerging practices of talent management adopted by MNC subsidiaries in China, as well as those adopted by leading Chinese-owned MNCs.

Talent management for MNCs: some research evidence

Existing literature on talent management has provided a comprehensive check list to enable firms to manage their talent more effectively, particularly in the international context (e.g.

Heinen and O'Neill, 2004; Scullion and Collings, 2006). Whilst a bundled approach is advocated (e.g. Huselid *et al.*, 1997; Macky and Boxall, 2007) to maximize the effect of HRM practices, emphasis is often placed on the use of non-financial incentives as an effective method of talent retention. These include, for example, providing written performance plans, providing good support in coaching and career development and providing a supportive work environment (Deckop *et al.*, 2006; Lepak and Snell, 1999). A number of studies on the effect of financial incentives on organizational effectiveness also point to the fact that benefit packages help companies to attract, motivate and retain more competent employees and improve service quality (e.g. Baron and Kreps, 1999; Lee *et al.*, 2006; Scullion and Collings, 2006). The effects are more apparent in high-tech firms (Gionfriddo and Dhingra, 1999). Other research evidence also suggests that leading companies are now paying more attention than before to employee growth and welfare (i.e. humanistic goals orientation) in order to retain talent (Levering and Moskowitz, 2004; Wang *et al.*, 2007).

Companies are urged to adopt a total rewards strategy which includes financial benefits, training and career development opportunities and other incentives to retain talent (Malila, 2007). Performance management, mentoring and coaching, diversity management and work–life balance are emerging as some of the key HR initiatives that are considered crucial as well as challenging in the GTM strategy. This is particularly the case when these western developed HR initiatives are applied to significantly different societal contexts such as China. A number of important questions need to be examined here: what HRM practices have MNCs deployed for talent management in China? What challenges do MNCs encounter when they implement these HR initiatives aimed to retain talent? And to what extent have MNCs developed a strategic approach to talent management in China that forms an integral part of their global HR strategy? We explore these issues below, drawing on empirical evidence from a number of foreign MNCs operating in China and Chinese-owned MNCs.

Performance management

Performance management, including appropriate target setting, performance appraisal and reward, is a key element in talent management. Research evidence suggests that MNCs in China are making use of performance appraisal as a key HRM practice. For example, Björkman and Lu's (1999) study of 72 foreign-invested enterprises in China found that nearly half of them had adapted their western performance appraisal system to suit the Chinese culture. Ding *et al.*'s (1997: 611) study of 158 foreign-invested enterprises in southern China showed that 'regular evaluation of individual employee performance and setting employee pay levels based on individual performance have become organizational norms'. They also found that workers were receptive to individual-oriented performance measurement and reward in order to maximize their income. Lindholm's (1999) survey of 604 Chinese managerial and professional employees from MNCs in China found that the respondents were satisfied with the western-style performance management system adopted in their company. They particularly liked the developmental approach in the system and were keen to participate in setting their performance objectives and receiving formal performance feedback. It must be noted that prestigious MNCs in China are attractive to those who have strong career aspirations and desire development opportunities (Cooke, 2005).

Despite employees' receptiveness to western-styled performance management, performance appraisal is perhaps one of the HRM practices that display the most enduring influence of Chinese culture. It has been widely noted that the Chinese culture respects seniority and hierarchy, values social harmony, and adopts an egalitarian approach to distribution (Hofstede, 1991; Takahara, 1992; Yu, 1998). Similarly, egalitarianism has long been recognized as a unique Chinese societal culture and continues to be used by some as a yardstick of fairness and equity in rewards, especially in the distribution of financial incentives. In general, the traditional performance appraisal system in China is reward driven (i.e. focusing on retrospective performance) and tends to focus on the person and behavioural performance (Cooke, 2008b). By contrast, the performance appraisal system promoted in western HRM literature takes a developmental approach (i.e. prospective performance oriented) and focuses on the alignment between individual performance and organizational goals. How to adapt a western approach to performance management to a Chinese workforce proves a challenge to many firms.

Recent evidence from MNCs in China (including Chinese-owned MNCs) points to a diverse range of practices in their performance management. For example, in ZTE and Huawei, the two leading Chinese-owned IT MNCs in which 50 per cent of the workforce are R&D engineers, performance pressure is internalized and employees are expected to be self-motivated. Long working hours and performance-related pay are the norms. As a long-established corporate culture, Huawei's employees have a tradition of bringing their sleeping cushion to the office and work there nearly 18 hours a day, catching only a brief nap underneath the desk when exhausted. The sleeping cushion is seen as a symbol of Huawei's hard-working culture. Aspiring young graduate employees feel the peer pressure to work long hours and achieve results. Huawei's corporate ethos is that those who can endure hardship and are prepared to research hard will get a good return. Each year employees of ZTE and Huawei go through their performance assessment, the bottom 3–5 per cent of performers will be dismissed, a similar proportion of managerial staff who are deemed poor performers will also be demoted or dismissed.

Headquartered in Shenzhen, both firms were established in the 1980s when the IT industry in China was in its embryonic form but was ready to take off. Each firm now has operations and representative offices in more than 100 countries, employing over 40,000 (for ZTE) and 60,000 (Huawei) employees. For both firms, working overtime at short notice is a common staffing measure to meet targets and to provide prompt customer services. Managers interviewed admitted that Chinese expatriates in their overseas subsidiaries have been subject to overtime work more than host country nationals because 'we have more control over our own people and they are more used to the Company's culture [of high performance pressure and excessive overtime]' (Manager, Huawei). Chinese expatriates who are deemed unsuitable for their overseas assignments will be repatriated and repositioned. Some of them would be dismissed if they failed to perform adequately in their new posts. It is common for Chinese firms to request their staff to work overtime, paid or unpaid, at short notice. However, working overtime may be discouraged in some countries for legal, social and cultural/religious reasons. Chinese employees will be requested by their Chinese managers to work the overtime instead. According to the managers, this differential treatment does cause grievances from the Chinese employees who feel a sense of unfairness.

When asked if their corporate HR strategy is adequate in supporting their global business strategy, managers interviewed felt that there is no blue print available to provide guidance for Chinese MNCs in their internationalization process. As such, both firms are adopting a trial and error approach. Managers operating overseas admitted that they have a relatively high level of autonomy in managing their daily activities as long as they conform to the broad regulation of the company and meet their annual performance targets. Many of the HR interventions are designed and implemented at the local level to suit local needs. This is in part because both firms are expanding rapidly and their headquarters cannot cope with all the queries and demands from local operations. In comparison, Huawei managers seem to have slightly more autonomy than their ZTE counterparts, the latter being state-owned.

Interestingly, not all western MNCs take a developmental approach to manage their managers in China, as is evidenced in ServiceCo (pseudonym), a French-owned subsidiary in Shanghai that provides cleaning, catering, security and facilities maintenance services to industrial parks and commercial centres/shopping malls. ServiceCo has been encountering serious staff turnover problems amongst its low grade staff (approximately 1,800 employees). Poor people management skills of the line managers have been identified as the main cause of the company's retention problem. In order to address the problem, ServiceCo introduced employee retention rate as one of the key performance indicators for its line managers. This proves to have had some positive effects. In addition, managerial staff are given a selection of company benefits, flexible working time, holidays, pay rise, performance-related pay, and company sponsored training. However, there are limited management development activities in place to help managers improve their people management skills. According to the HR Director, the HR department plays mainly an administrative role, with no strategic input in the business. None of the staff, including the HR Director, working in the HR department have HR qualifications or came from an HR background. There is no formal HR policy in ServiceCo. This is partly a result of the high staff turnover of HR officers. As the HR director said:

> 'Ironically, it is the HR department that has the highest staff turnover rate amongst all the departments that have professional and administrative staff. HR skills are highly transferable and there is a short supply of HR professionals in the market. They can walk into a job very easily.'

Although the French-owned operation has been established for over ten years, there is no sense of identification from the Chinese employees that they are working for a foreign MNC. Most of the staff are Chinese, with only a few French expatriates heading up the senior management positions. All HRM practices are developed locally without any influence from the French headquarters. Little attempt has been made to cultivate a French culture in ServiceCo. On the contrary,

> 'The French are even more Chinese than the Chinese. The General Manager has been here for a long time and is very familiar with the labour regulations and knows exactly how to take advantage of it, including how to avoid paying social security premium and overtime for the staff'

(HR Director, ServiceCo)

Employee development

Talent shortage and poaching has made many Chinese firms cautious in allocating resources for human resource development (HRD) for fear of loss of trained staff. This has resulted in insufficient provision of training and development for employees. For example, Yang and Li's (2008) study found that a significant proportion of university graduate employees in the Beijing area had never received any training from their employer due to the latter's lack of concern about employee retention. Only a small number of firms in China have a graduate management trainee programme in place to develop their managers in-house. Some use this as an HR technique to attract talented candidates for recruitment. Others require their new recruits to go through a period of training and development before they can assume their position. These are primarily well-known MNCs, particularly those operating in the knowledge intensive sector.

For example, Huawei established its Huawei University in 2005 to provide tailored training courses to its employees and customers. New employees receive one to six months induction training at the University on corporate culture, product knowledge, marketing and sales techniques, and product development standards, etc. The university is responsible for training and developing workers, technicians, managers and future leaders of Huawei. Employees and managers from overseas subsidiaries are selected and sent to Huawei headquarters for training and development in order for them to better understand Huawei's product and marketing strategy. They are expected to internalize Huawei's corporate culture and business process and disseminate it back home. Chinese employees are also sent abroad for assignments to gain wider experience of the product and to understand local customers' needs and technical environment. Cross-functional teamworking between design and application is encouraged to help R&D engineers to understand the field situation.

Though less well versed than Huawei in its corporate statements on HRD, ZTE also stresses the importance of employee career development and benefits. A training and development academy is in place in the headquarters to deliver most of the activities. As the majority of its employees are university graduates and are engaged in high-tech production activities, induction training and continuous training are key features, though technical skill acquisition remains the key component of training. Similar to the employee development paths offered by Huawei, ZTE employees are given 'Three Career Development Paths' from which they can choose to follow a technology, service or management career. Like Huawei, Chinese employees may be sent abroad to broaden their knowledge and experience, and host country national employees may be selected for technical training and management development in ZTE (China). It is clear that ambition to become a major global player in the IT and telecom industry and the nature of the business have encouraged both Huawei and ZTE to invest heavily in training and developing their professional and managerial staff. Both firms employ prestigious international consultancy firms to help them design management processes and systems, including some of the HRM programmes. The HRM programmes and policy statements of Huawei and ZTE show a relatively high level of resemblance to that of prestigious foreign MNCs, although the substance still bears many Chinese characteristics, notably the corporate culture and work ethics.

In comparison, prestigious western-owned MNCs generally have a much more sophisticated MD programme than Chinese firms. It has been reported (e.g. Lane and Pollner, 2008) that firms like P&G and Motorola have developed highly effective localized MD programmes to nurture Chinese talent. In addition, foreign MNCs tend to pay more attention to developing the soft skills, such as leadership skills, problem-solving and communication. By contrast, Chinese MNCs emphasize more the grasp of technical skills, system knowledge and the internalization of corporate culture.

Mentoring as a new HR technique

Mentoring is being adopted by MNCs and leading Chinese firms as a formal HRM scheme for employee development, often as part of the MD programme. The mentoring system is different from the traditional apprentice system adopted in China, particularly in the SOEs during the state-planned economy era. The apprentice system focuses on the development of craft/technical skills and behavioural conduct/personality of the protégé within the moral framework defined by the socialist state. By contrast, the mentoring system that is promoted in the western HR literature and adopted by a small, albeit increasing, number of firms in China has a broader focus. In principle, the mentor is not only responsible for inducting the mentee into the system of the organization, but also instrumental in guiding the career development of the mentee. The emphasis is on both the professional development and personal growth of the mentee and the alignment of their needs with those of the organization. Here, the mentor plays an important role in sharing his or her knowledge about the organization with the mentee, hence re-enforcing the organizational culture. For example, mentoring forms an important part of the training and development system for junior professional employees in Huawei. Mentoring is an integral part of the supervisor/mentor's job and their performance in this role forms part of the formal assessment in their performance appraisal (Cooke, 2010a).

While mentoring has long existed in China as an informal organizational practice, sometimes without the awareness of either the mentor or the mentee, it is the formal mentoring system developed in the western HRM literature that is being promoted in China. Despite the fact that many foreign MNCs and Chinese MNCs have introduced a mentoring system, a common problem is its patchy implementation contingent upon individual mentors' competence, willingness and preference in their role. For example, an informant from KPMG (China) revealed that some mentors (known as counsellors) meet with their mentee regularly and provide counselling support beyond what the company specifies, whereas some mentees rarely have opportunities to meet with their mentors other than their annual meeting to fill in their annual appraisal form as a formality. More revealingly, the majority of mentors are female senior colleagues as it is believed that women are more suited to the role.

Talent retention in post-acquisition integration

Joint ventures (JV) and acquisitions have been a major route for foreign MNCs to enter the Chinese market (Child *et al.*, 2001; Cooke, 2008a; Luo, 2000). In 2006, inbound acquisitions of Chinese companies by foreign firms were reported to be in the vicinity of US$20 billion, accounting for nearly one-third of the total foreign investment in China (People's Daily Online, 2007). It is believed that a growing number of global MNCs are buying a stake of Chinese firms as part of their strategic development in China (Cooke, 2008a; Wang *et al.*, 2004). Post-acquisition integrations are notoriously difficult, particularly in the cross-country context (e.g. Dameron and Joffre, 2007). Appropriate reward and incentive plans (e.g. stock options and retention bonus) have been recognized as important HR interventions for attracting and retaining key talent in acquisitions (Cartwright and Cooper, 2000; Child *et al.*, 2001; Schuler and Jackson, 2001). It is a short-term strategy for the acquiring firm to 'buy in' the commitment and loyalty of the acquired employees, particularly in an unfamiliar recruitment market (Cartwright and Cooper, 2001). Importantly, the retention of the top management team of the acquired firm has been found to be both challenging and crucial in maintaining the post-acquisition performance of the acquired firm (Kiessling and Harvey, 2006; Krug and Hegarty, 2001; Tarique and Schuler, 2009).

In the cross-border acquisitions of Chinese private firms in the IT/telecom industry, financial incentives and promotion have been two main mechanisms deployed by the US-based acquiring firms to retain key managers to facilitate post-acquisition integration and subsequent business development in the Chinese market (Huang and Cooke, 2010). An in-depth case study (Huang and Cooke, 2010) of four pairs of US-Sino firms reveals that the Chinese private firms in the IT industry held significant bargaining power over their US acquirers due to the former's large market share and strong business relationship with the state-owned telecom client firms. Retaining the founding owner managers of the Chinese-acquired firms was considered crucial for the US acquirers because their departure would not only lead to the loss of key business relationships but also trigger a domino effect of turnover of junior managers and R&D engineers. As a result, key managers of the Chinese acquired firms were provided with share options, owner CEOs were promoted to be general managers of the new MNC subsidiaries and were given more power and autonomy in decision-making than other business unit managers of the same rank in the MNC. Some of them were further promoted within the MNC, reporting directly to the CEO. Business decisions that required headquarters approval were 'fast-tracked'.

This autonomy proved crucial to winning trust from the acquired staff and provided a stable environment for them to carry out business development in both products and markets. In addition to securing the top management team's commitment, significant concessions were made in order to retain key engineers and professional staff from the acquired firms. For example, the reward packages of the acquired employees were ring-fenced, and they had a higher salary level than staff from other operations of the acquiring firms in China. More interestingly, one of the acquiring MNCs actually abandoned its original consultant-designed performance management system and adopted the one used by its Chinese-acquired firm as it had proved to be more effective in linking employees' performance with the organizational objectives.

Nevertheless, changes have been made over time in harmonizing and standardizing the performance management procedures for managers in two of the MNCs in order to provide comparable information to aid decisions on management development and promotion. In fact, performance management and reward for managerial staff are deemed strategic elements and receive direct intervention from the foreign acquirers. This is because managers of the acquired firms bring critical resources to the acquiring firms. Following the retention of key managers, maintaining and enhancing their motivation becomes essential to harnessing their contribution to the new parent (Cartwright and Cooper, 2000; Schuler and Jackson, 2001). This requires continuous investment from the foreign acquirers in management appraisal and reward.

However, how to design a performance-related reward system that is seen as fair by employees and affordable by the company remains a key challenge. Another challenge is to develop line managers' interest and competence in performance management as they are the key to people management. Research evidence suggests that performance management has not been fully accepted by managers as an effective tool in managing human resources (also see Cooke, 2008b). Here, the US-owned acquiring firms have learned that it is necessary to adopt a gradual approach in applying a western performance management model to their Chinese staff, despite the need to make changes to bring the acquired firms' HR systems in line with those of the new owner firms. As such, the performance management system evolved in the post-acquisition new subsidiaries is very much a hybrid rather than a standardized system of the MNC. It incorporates the US-owned MNCs' emphasis on training and development on the one hand, but retains the heavy focus on financial reward to reflect current Chinese labour market characteristics on the other. In some ways, Huang and Cooke's (2010) study supports the arguments made by Chen and Wilson (2003) and Wilson *et al.* (2006). That is, it is difficult for the foreign firm to implement a standardized global HR system if managers of the local partner question the value and utility of the system for the local context. This is particularly the case when the local partner possesses strong bargaining power, because market pressures feature prominently in how the firm chooses to operate 'in the period after an international M&A' (Rees and Edwards, 2009: 26).

Diversity management

The concept of diversity management (DM), popularized in the USA in the 1990s, is increasingly promoted as a strategic people management technique that will enhance organizational competitiveness (Cooke, 2010b). Some US-owned MNCs also roll out their domestic-designed DM programmes to their global operations (Nishii and Özbigin, 2007). The intention of promoting DM in global operations is to address the talent shortage problem and to enhance employees' engagement by accommodating the diverse needs of individuals and social groups. Existing studies have revealed unique societal contexts in which diversity issues are embedded, and as such, diversity may be manifested in different meanings and substantive issues across national boundaries (Cooke and Saini, 2010). For example, in the US and UK, workforce diversity may include: gender, race, ethnicity, religion, age, disability, immigration status, social class, political association, marital status, parental status, sexual orientation, ex-offenders and so on. Many of these differences are accepted by the society concerned, protected by law and accommodated in company policy. However, some of these diversity characteristics may not be acceptable legally and/or socially in oriental countries like China, where age, gender, disability, and place of origin (e.g. rural v. urban) are the main causes of social inequality (Cooke, 2010b). These societal differences undoubtedly present significant challenges to MNCs that wish to design and implement a global DM programme to retain and harness talent.

Research evidence shows that many Chinese managers (interviewed by the author) have not heard of or thought about the concept of 'diversity management'. Few Chinese firms have a formal HR policy or affirmative action plan to promote gender equality or DM. A search on company websites of a number of leading Chinese firms also reveals the limited publicity of such a policy, indicating that such a policy is either not available or exists only in brief. Leading Chinese-owned MNCs such as Huawei, ZTE and Lenovo are among the few exceptions. Even with these leading firms, awareness of the notion of diversity management remains limited amongst managers and employees. There are few HR initiatives in place to accommodate the diverse needs of employees and to harness their diverse talent. Instead, line managers often devise their own 'policy' on an *ad hoc* basis to deal with individual issues as and when situations arise. Managers typically talk about the need to manage diversity from the perspective of conflict avoidance rather than value-addition to the business. As far as possible, they prefer to adopt an egalitarian approach to deal with all employees to avoid resentment of differentiated treatments. This is despite the fact that nepotism remains a key feature in organizational life in many Chinese firms.

Given the low level of awareness of the concept of and the needs for managing diversity in China, western MNCs seeking to enhance their recruitment and retention outcome by promoting DM initiatives in their Chinese operations may face significant hurdles. For example, a regional HR director of a highly reputable MNC revealed that the recruitment agency firm they deployed in China systematically screened out female graduate job candidates, even though their quality was as high as, and in some cases higher than, that of their male counterparts. The MNC has a global corporate policy of equal opportunity and imposes a gender ratio in the recruitment target. As a result, the Chinese subsidiary's gender ratio statistics consistently fell below those of the corporate target. When this intervention of the recruitment agency firm was discovered, the HR director drew the attention of staff from the agency firm to the corporate policy and requested them not to discriminate against female candidates. This request was brushed aside by the Chinese recruitment staff, who tried to convince the HR director that this is a common practice in China as women employees are deemed less productive due to their family commitment.

Work–life balance

Work–life balance is one of the key components in western DM literature. Work–life/family-friendly initiatives such as flexible working arrangements are being promoted as good HRM practices to attract and retain talent. However, work–life conflicts in China derive from a range of sources that may be different from those manifested in western societies and require different HR initiatives in the Chinese context (Cooke, 2010a). Whilst family commitment remains a key source of work–life conflicts, work intensity, including long working hours, appears to be the main HR issue amongst managers and professionals in MNCs and private firms in China. This is largely due to heightened market competition and the fast growth of firms, particularly those in fast-growing industries such as telecommunication, IT, consultancy, finance and real estate industries. Work intensification has led to health problems, retention issues and labour disputes.

For example, PricewaterhouseCoopers (China) (hereafter PwC China) experienced a serious labour dispute incident in 2004. Employees in several major cities went on strike in protest at unbearable working hours and the unacceptably low level of overtime pay. At the time of the strike, the average working time for an employee was seven days per week and with no more than five sleeping hours every day. After the dispute was settled, PwC China introduced a dedicated employee care programme, called 'We Care', to look after its employees. Activities of the programme include: free movie tickets, discount tickets to concerts and musicals, Yoga and Tai Chi classes in offices, numerous sports and fun days such as 'PwC China Cup', family day, stress management seminars, health talks, free influenza vaccination programme and Focus group meetings to identify areas for improvements (PwC website, accessed in 2008). Other foreign MNCs have similar programmes in place to address work–life conflict problems.

It needs to be noted that organizing and sponsoring social life for employees and their families has long been a workplace welfare provision in SOEs and to a lesser extent in private firms as part of the Chinese paternalistic culture. Unlike the western culture that is of an individualistic nature where work–life balance means, amongst other things, giving employees more time to spend with their family in private, involving family members in company-sponsored events is an important part of the work–life balance initiatives in China. However, work–life balance alone may not be sufficient to retain talent. Well educated Chinese young workers are ambitious and eager to fulfill their career potential. They not only expect lucrative financial packages, but also demand early promotion and (overseas) career development opportunities from their employers. Where these demands are not met or when there are better offers elsewhere, they are ready to switch employers. It is also worth pointing out that Chinese managers, at least those interviewed by the author, may not be receptive to the idea of having a formal HR policy on flexible work arrangements for employees. They prefer to deal with it informally on a case-by-case basis rather than institutionalizing the arrangement which may be taken advantage of by misbehaving employees. They believe that it is important they retain the power to exercise their discretion to reward employees who are deemed loyal and well-behaved (Cooke, 2010b).

Conclusions

This chapter has analysed some of the tensions in and challenges to talent management in China in a period of economic and social transformation. It has revealed some of the HRM practices adopted by MNCs in their endeavour to attract, retain and motivate talent. Some of these initiatives, such as diversity management and work–life balance, are relatively new to China, where HR issues may be manifested in different ways to those found elsewhere. China appears to western countries perhaps institutionally and culturally one of the most distanced societies. As such, many HR interventions that have been successfully adopted in other parts of the world may not be effective in China without adaptation. It can be argued, therefore, that enduring cultural and institutional factors are likely to make it difficult for MNCs to implement a global TGM system.

As we have seen in this chapter, the main challenge to talent management in China is the shortage of managerial and professional talent. Given the deficiency in the educational institutions and the reluctance of firms to invest in training and development, poaching is a widely adopted method for firms to acquire talent. In addition, performance-related reward is commonly used as a motivational mechanism to incentivize higher performance. In other words, firms are focusing on employees' current performance rather than their future productivity. With the exception of a few prestigious MNCs, HRM practices in the majority of firms in China are neither systematic nor human goals-oriented as prescribed in western strategic HRM literature. The 2008 global financial crisis has to some extent reduced the problem of talent retention for many firms due to the temporary economic downturn in certain sectors. But this has exposed some firms to another challenge – how to manage outplacement and minimize its negative impact on remaining employees.

Existing studies on HRM in China often differentiate organizations by their ownership, classifying foreign MNCs as one category in order to highlight how their organizational practices differ from those of domestic firms. In general, foreign MNCs are considered to be more strategic in their HRM. They invest more in training and development; adopt a more development oriented performance management system; and have a fair approach to reward based on competence and performance. By contrast, domestic Chinese firms are seen to adopt an *ad hoc* approach to HRM with a high level of managerial prerogative. Training opportunities are limited and nepotism remains common in recruitment and reward. Whilst ownership forms are an important source that explains variations in HRM practices, research evidence reported in this chapter shows that there is a level of convergence amongst firms of different ownership forms, as was noted by a number of studies (e.g. Wei and Lau, 2005; Wang *et al.*, 2007). More importantly, the HRM practices of MNCs are diverse. Therefore, to discuss MNCs as one category would be an over-simplification that conceals variations derived from their country-of-origin and importantly sectoral orientation. Research evidence shows that, compared with their counterparts operating in the labour intensive sector, MNCs in the high-tech sector in China are far more proactive and developed with their HRM initiatives to manage their talent. However, these interventions are high-performance oriented and are often underpinned by financial reward. The emphasis on financial incentive and performance-related pay reflects the high-growth nature of these businesses on the one hand and the expectation of employees to share organizational gains on the other.

In addition, the internal environment, such as the role of the HR managers and the HR department, plays an important part in determining HRM practices (Tarique and Schuler, 2009). As Björkman *et al.*'s (2008) study revealed, the use of expatriates and the background of the HR managers are important determinants of subsidiary HRM. Nevertheless, we cannot readily assume that expatriates are committed to transferring parent country practices, as is shown in the ServiceCo case. Research evidence also suggests that western MNCs operating in China have largely relied on host country managers to manage their operations and that many MNCs adopt a pragmatic instead of a strategic approach to managing their managerial talent. These findings have further implications for the global strategy of MNCs, as actions and behaviours of host country nationals may diverge from the corporate intent as a result of individual personal preference and interpretation of the operational environment.

Finally, the characteristics of HRM practices in China as revealed in this chapter have implications for theories in strategic international HRM. They challenge the primarily prescriptive nature of the global talent management literature. It is important to note that MNCs are neither necessarily active disseminators of good practice, nor are they passive recipients of host country constraints. Instead, they co-shape the environment (Child and Tsai, 2005), and in some cases reinforce undesirable local practices, particularly when the environment is not effectively regulated by laws or business norms. The findings of HRM practices and challenges in China also have implications for talent management in other Asian countries which may share similar labour force characteristics and relatively high economic growth on the one hand, and encounter similar problems of skill shortage, performance management and talent retention on the other.

Note

1   Qualifications include PhD, Masters, bachelors, diplomas and certificates, and study modes include full-time and part-time, on-site and distance learning.

References

Arkless, D. (2007) 'The China talent paradox', *China–Britain Business Review*, June: 14–15.

Bai, X. and Bennington, L. (2005) 'Performance appraisal in the Chinese state-owned coal industry', *International Journal of Business Performance Management*, 7, 3: 275–287.

Baron, J.N. and Kreps, D.M. (1999) *Strategic Human Resource Management: Framework for General Managers*, New York: John Wiley and Sons, Inc.

Björkman, I. and Lu, Y. (1999) 'The management of human resources in Chinese-western joint ventures', *Journal of World Business*, 34, 3: 306–324.

Björkman, I., Budhwar, P., Smale, A. and Sumelius, J. (2008) 'Human resource management in foreign-owned subsidiaries: China versus India', *International Journal of Human Resource Management*, 19, 5: 964–978.

Branine, M. (1996) 'Observations on training and management development in the People's Republic of China', *Personnel Review*, 25, 1: 25–39.

Bu, N. (1994) 'Red cadres and specialists as modern managers: An empirical assessment of managerial competencies in China', *International Journal of Human Resource Management*, 5, 2: 357–383.

Budhwar, P. and Debrah, Y (eds) (2001) *HRM in Developing Countries*, London: Routledge.

Cartwright, S. and Cooper, L. C. (2000) *HR Know-how in Mergers and Acquisitions*, London: IPD.

Chan, K.W. and Wyatt, T. (2007) 'Quality of work life: A study of employees in Shanghai, China', *Asia Pacific Business Review*, 13, 4: 501–517.

Chen, S. and Wilson, M. (2003) 'Standardization and localization in Chinese joint ventures', *Asia Pacific Journal of Management*, 20: 397–408.

Child, J. (1994) *Management in China during the Age of Reform*, Cambridge: Cambridge University Press.

Child, J., Faulkner, D. and Pitkethly, R. (2001) *The Management of International Acquisitions*, Oxford: Oxford University Press.

Child, J. and Tsai, T. (2005) 'The dynamic between firms' environmental strategies and institutional constraints in emerging economies: Evidence from China and Taiwan', *Journal of Management Studies*, 42, 1: 95–125.

China Labour Statistical Yearbook 2008, Beijing: China Statistics Press.

China Statistical Yearbook 2008, Beijing: China Statistics Publishing House.

Chiu, R., Luk, W. and Tang, T. (2002) 'Retaining and motivating employees: Compensation preferences in Hong Kong and China', *Personnel Review*, 31, 4: 402–431.

Clark, T. and Mallory, G. (1996) 'The cultural relativity of human resource management: Is there a universal model?' in T. Clark (ed.), *European Human Resource Management*, Oxford: Blackwell, 1–33.

Collings, D. and Mellahi, K. (2009) 'Strategic talent management: A review and research agenda', *Human Resource Management Review*, doi. 10.1016/j.hrmr.2009.04.001.

Cooke, F. L. (2005) *HRM, Work and Employment in China*, London: Routledge.

Cooke, F. L. (2008a) *Competition, Strategy and Management in China*, Basingstoke: Palgrave Macmillan.

Cooke, F. L. (2008b) 'Performance management systems in China', in Varma, A. and Budhwar, P. (eds), *Performance Management Systems around the Globe*, London: Routledge, pp.193–209.

Cooke, F. L. (2010a) 'The changing face of human resource management in China', in Rowley, C. and Cooke, F. L. (eds), *The Changing Face of Chinese Management*, the Routledge 'Working in Asia' series, London: Routledge pp. 28–51.

Cooke, F. L. (2010b) 'Social responsibility, sustainability and diversity of human resources', in Harzing, A. and Pinnington, A. (eds), *International Human Resource Management*, 3rd edition, London: Sage.

Cooke, F. L. and Saini, D. S. (2010) 'Diversity management in India: A study of organizations in different ownership forms and industrial sectors', *Human Resource Management* 49, 3: 477–500.

Dameron, S. and Joffre, O. (2007) 'The good and the bad: the impact of diversity management on co-operative relationships', *International Journal of Human Resource Management*, 18, 11: 2037–2056.

Deckop, J., Konrad, A., Perlmutter, F. and Freely, J. (2006) 'The effect of human resource management practices on the job retention of former welfare clients', *Human Resource Management*, 45, 4: 539–559.

Development and Management of Human Resources (2008) 'Review', *Development and Management of Human Resources*, 10: 4.

Dickel, T. and Watkins, C. (2008) 'To remain competitive in China's tight labour market, companies must prioritize talent management – and track compensation trends', *China Business Review*, July–August: 20–3.

Ding, D., Field, D. and Akhtar, S. (1997) 'An empirical study of human resource management policies and practices in foreign-invested enterprises in China: The case of Shenzhen Special Economic Zone', *International Journal of Human Resource Management*, 8, 5: 595–613.

The Economist (8 April 2009) 'Chinese unemployment: Where will all the students go'? Internet source: http://www.economist.com/world/asia/displaystory.cfm?story_id=13446878, accessed on 12 May 2009.

Farndale, E. and Paauwe, J. (2007) 'Uncovering competitive and institutional drivers for HRM practices in multinational corporations', *Human Resource Management Journal*, 17, 4: 355–375.

Farrell, D. and Grant, A. (2005) 'China's looming talent shortage', *The McKinsey Quarterly*, 4, http://www.mckinseyquarterly.com/article_page.aspx?ar=1685, accessed on 3 March 2007.

Gionfriddo, J. and Dhingra, L. (1999) 'Retaining high-tech talent: NIIT case study', *Compensation and Benefits Review*, 31, 5: 31–35.

Harzing, A. (2004) 'Strategy and structure of multinational companies', in A. Harzing and J. Ruysseveldt (eds), *International Human Resource Management*, London: Sage, pp. 33–64.

Heinen, S. J. and O'Neill, C. (2004) 'Managing talent to maximize performance', *Employment Relations Today*, 31: 67–82.

Hofstede, G. (1991) *Cultures and Organizations, Software of the Mind*, New York: McGraw-Hill.

Huang, K. and Cooke, F. L. (2010) 'Cross-border acquisitions and business dynamics in the IT and telecom industry', in Rowley, C. and Cooke, F. L. (eds), *The Changing Face of Chinese Management*, the Routledge 'Working in Asia' Series, London: Routledge.

Hui, C., Lee, C. and Rousseau, D. (2004) 'Employment relationships in China: Do workers relate to the organization or to people'? *Organization Science*, 15, 2: 232–240.

Huselid, M.A., Jackson, S.E. and Schuler, R.S. (1997) 'Technical and strategic human resource management effectiveness as determinants of firm performance', *Academy of Management Journal*, 40: 171–188.

Kiessling, T. and Harvey, M. (2006) 'The human resource management issues during an acquisition: the target firm's top management team and key managers', *International Journal of Human Resource Management*, 17: 1307–1320.

Krug, J., and Hegarty, W. (2001) 'Predicting who stays and leaves after an acquisition: A study of top managers in multinational firms', *Strategic Management Journal*, 22, 2: 185–196.

Lane, K. and Pollner, F. (2008) *How to address China's growing talent shortage*, McKinsey Quarterly, 3: 33–40.

Lau, A. and Roffey, B. (2002) 'Management education and development in China: A research note', *Labour and Management in Development Journal*, 2, 10: 1–18.

Law, K., Tse, D.K. and Zhou, N. (2003) 'Does human resource management matter in a transitional economy? China as an example', *Journal of International Business Studies*, 34, 3: 255–265.

Lee, C., Hsu, M. and Lien, N. (2006) 'The impacts of benefit plans on employee turnover: A firm-level analysis approach on Taiwanese manufacturing industry', *International Journal of Human Resource Management*, 17, 11: 1951–1975.

Leininger, J. (2007) 'Recent compensation and benefit trends in China', *The China Business Review*, 34, 4: 28–30.

Lepak, D.P. and Snell, S. A. (1999) 'The human resource architecture: Toward a theory of human capital allocation and development', *Academy of Management Review*, 24: 31–48.

Levering, R. and Moskowitz, M. (2004) 'Fortune 100 best companies to work for', *Fortune*, 149, 1: 56–83.

Lewis, R. and Heckman, R. (2006) 'Talent management: A critical review', *Human Resource Management Review*, 16: 139–154.

Lindholm, N. (1999) 'Performance management in MNC subsidiaries in China: A study of host-country managers and professionals', *Asia Pacific Journal of Human Resources*, 37, 3: 18–35.

Luo, Y. (2000) *Partnering with Chinese Firms: Lessons for International Managers*, Aldershot: Ashgate Publishing Ltd.

Luo Y. D. and Tung, R. (2007). 'International expansion of emerging market enterprises: a springboard perspective', *Journal of International Business Studies*, 38, 481–498.

Macky, K. and Boxall, P. (2007) 'The relationship between "high performance work practices" and employee attitudes: An investigation of additive and interaction effects', *International Journal of Human Resource Management*, 18, 4: 537–567.

Malila, J. (2007) 'The great look forward: China's HR evolution', *China Business Review*, 34, 4: 16–19.

Nishii, L. and Özbilgin, F. (2007) 'Global diversity management: Towards a conceptual framework', *International Journal of Human Resource Management*, 18, 11: 1883–1894.

Paauwe J. and Boselie P. (2003) 'Challenging "strategic HRM" and the relevance of the institutional setting', *Human Resource Management Journal*, 13, 3: 56–70.

Pan, C. G. and Lou, W. (2004) 'Study on situation and development environment for Chinese talents', in C. G. Pan and L. Wang (eds), *The Report on the Development of Chinese Talents*, No.1, Beijing: Social Sciences Academic Press, pp.1–46.

People's Daily Online, 'Foreign firms turn to M&As for expansion', 27 April 2007, Internet source: http://english.peopledaily.com.cn/200704/27/eng20070427_370339.html, accessed on 21 February 2009.

PricewaterhouseCoopers, 'Work–life Balance', PwC careers, Internet source: http://www.pwccn.com/home/eng/graduate_worklife.html, accessed on 3 January 2008.

Ralston, D., Gustafson, D., Terpstra, R. and Holt, D. (1995) 'Pre-post Tiananmen Square: Changing values of Chinese managers', *Asia Pacific Journal of Management*, 12, 1: 1–20.

Ralston, D., Holt, D., Terpstra, R. and Cheng, Y. K. (1997) 'The impact of national culture and economic ideology on managerial work values: A study of the United States, Russia, Japan and China', *Journal of International Business Studies*, 28(1): 177–207.

Ralston, D., Egri, C., Stewart, S., Terpstra, R. and Yu, K.C. (1999) 'Doing business in the 21st Century with the new generation of Chinese managers: A study of generational shifts in work values in China. *Journal of International Business Studies* 30(2): 415–428.

Rees, T. and Edwards, T. (2009) 'Management strategy and HR in international mergers: choice, constraint and pragmatism', *Human Resource Management Journal*, 19, 1: 24–39.

Rubery, J. and Grimshaw, D. (2003) *The Organization of Employment: An International Perspective*, Basingstoke: Palgrave Macmillan.

Rynes, S., Gerhart, B. and Minette, K. (2004) 'The importance of pay in employee motivation: Discrepancies between what people say and what they do', *Human Resource Management*, 43, 4: 381–394.

Schuler, R. S., and Jackson, S. E. (2001) 'HR issues and activities in mergers and acquisitions', *European Journal of Management*, 19, 3: 239–253.

Scullion, H. and Collings, D. (2006) 'International talent management', in Scullion, H. and Collings, D. (eds) *Global Staffing*, London: Routledge, pp. 87–115.

Southworth, D. (1999) 'Building a business school in China: The case of the China Europe International Business School (CEIBS)', *Education and Training*, 41, 6/7: 325–330.

Stahl, G. and Björkman, I. (eds) (2006) *Handbook of Research in International Human Resource Management*, Cheltenham: Edward Elgar Publishing.

Takahara, A. (1992) *The Politics of Wage Policy in Post-Revolutionary China*, London: Macmillan.

Tarique, I. and Schuler, R. (2009) 'Global talent management: Literature review, integrative framework, and suggestions for further research', *Journal of World Business*.

Tung, R. (2007) 'The human resource challenge to outward foreign direct investment aspirations from emerging economies: The case of China', *International Journal of Human Resource Management*, 18(5): 868–889.

Walder, A. (1989) 'Factory and managers in the era of reform', *China Quarterly*, 118: 22–43.

Walsh, J. and Zhu, Y. (2007) 'Local complexities and global uncertainties: A study of foreign ownership and human resource management in China', *International Journal of Human Resource Management* 18, 2: 249–267.

Wang, Z. M. (1999) 'Current models and innovative strategies in management education in China', *Education and Training*, 41, 6/7: 312–318.

Wang, J. and Wang, G. (2006) 'Exploring national human resource development: A case of China management development in a transitioning context', *Human Resource Development Review*, 5, 2: 176–201

Wang, X., Bruning, N. and Peng, S. Q. (2007) 'Western high performance HR practices in China: A comparison among public-owned, private and foreign-invested enterprises', *International Journal of Human Resource Management*, 18, 4: 684–701.

Wang, W., Zhang, J. J. and Li, B. (eds) (2004) *China Mergers and Acquisitions Yearbook*, Beijing: Posts and Telecom Press.

Warner, M. and Goodall, K. (eds) (2010) *Management Training and Development in China*. London: Routledge.

Wei, L. and Lau, C.M. (2005) 'Market orientation, HRM importance and competency: Determinants of strategic HRM in Chinese firms', *International Journal of Human Resource Management*, 16, 10: 1901–18.

Wilson, M., Chen, S. and Erakovic, L. (2006) 'Dynamics of decision power in the localization process: comparative case studies of China–Western IJVs', *International Journal of Human Resource Management*, 17, 9: 1547–71.

Wilson, B. (2008) 'Hidden dragons', *People Management Magazine Online*, http://www.people management.co.uk/pm/articles/2008/08/hidden-dragons.htm, accessed on 4 September 2008.

Workers' Daily, 17 November 2005.

Wright, P. and van de Voorde, K. (2009) 'Multilevel issues in IHRM: Mean differences, explained variance, and moderated relationships', in Sparrow, P. (ed.), *Handbook of International Human Resource Management*, Chichester: John Wiley, pp.29–40.

Xin, K. and Pearce, J. L. (1996) 'Guanxi: Connections as substitutes for formal institutional support', *Academy of Management Journal*, 39, 6: 1641–58.

Yang, H.Q. and Li, J. (2008) 'An empirical study of the employment quality of university graduates', *Labor Economy and Labor Relations*, 2: 87–90.

Yu, K. C. (1998) 'Chinese employees' perceptions of distributive fairness', in Francesco, A. M. and Gold, B. A. (eds), *International Organisational Behavior*, New Jersey: Prentice Hall, pp.302–13.

Zhang, L. H. (2005) 'A case study analysis of the remuneration change strategy of a state-owned enterprise', *Development and Management of Human Resources*, 11, 1: 47–9.

Zhao, G. (2008) 'What to do when employees are not engaged with the company'? *Development and Management of Human Resources*, 2: 35–40.

Zhu, C., Cooper, B., De Cieri, H. and Dowling, P. (2005) 'A problematic transition to a strategic role: Human resource management in industrial enterprises in China', *International Journal of Human Resource Management*, 16, 4: 513–31.

Talent management in the Middle East

ABBAS J. ALI

Introduction

Endowed with abundant energy reserves, geographically situated in a globally strategic place, and with an enthusiastic workforce, the Middle East has become an arena where rival world powers and multinational corporations (MNCs) vigorously compete for influence and domination. Since the early 1970s, the region has witnessed rapid economic change coupled with rising expectations, political instability, and undelivered promises. The unity of contradiction or, more precisely, the coexistence of economic progress and setbacks, wealth and poverty, should be viewed as a notable hallmark of the region's landscape and a definite proof that nothing is certain except change in this vital part of the world. Indeed, these opposing forces appear to complement each other and may become instrumental for profound and all-encompassing change.

The region's intriguing culture, expanding wealth, and ever-emerging business opportunities have added a new value for business engagement in the Middle East. In fact, for years, managers of MNCs have underscored the region's potential and its market capacity to evolve. Both are attractive aspects which set it apart from other neighboring regions. Additionally, the prevailing prudent financial policies and the presence of substantial currency reserves, especially among the oil-producing countries, allow the region to minimize the economic impact of the 2008 financial crisis. In fact, the IMF (2009) reported that the region is likely to fare better than countries in other regions of the world. In terms of the job market, a slight upturn was experienced in the second quarter of 2009 (Ghosh, 2009).

Nevertheless, to analysts and business people the speed and unpredictability of unfolding political events in the region have been a major concern. These events and unfamiliarity with the nature of the Middle East conflict may induce these observers to reach pessimistic business conclusions. In a globalized world, such business decisions might be regarded as illogical, impractical, and certainly inconsistent with the globalization imperative. In fact, political instability should not be a determining reason for forsaking business opportunities and market engagements. In a speech to the World Economic Forum, George W. Bush (2008) argued that most technological and economic changes had taken place in the second half of the 20th century and suggested that for the Middle East the first half of the 21st century could be the time when similar advances were realized, stating that "This region is home to energetic people, a powerful spirit of enterprise, and tremendous resources. It is capable of a very bright future—a future in which the Middle East is a place of innovation and discovery, driven by free men and women."

Probably, affective managing of human capital is the most pressing challenge in the region. Indeed, talent management (TM) is strategically situated to play a vital role in the region's economic progress. For years it was neglected by both corporations and governments. In recent years, however, it has taken on an added value as economic development programs have generally failed to produce tangible improvement in the wellbeing of the people in the region. There are various drivers of TM which make it essential to face the mounting complex challenges that countries in the region confront. Specifically, the major drivers include: huge investments by governments in infrastructure, rapid integration in the world economy, MNCs' increasing demand for qualified personnel, phenomenal growth in higher education institutions, and shortage in leadership and certain competencies essential for sound development.

Aguirre, Post, and Hewlett (2009) indicated that currently only 4 percent of the global talent pool comes from the Middle East (including North Africa). They stated, however, that the region has an above-average economic growth and is likely to be a strong source of global talent. This chapter has several key aims: to survey the economic, social, and political environment; examine the capacity to nurture and absorb talent; identify major trends which have taken place in the field of human capital, including types of structural changes, diversities, turnovers, and shortages in professional and skilled labor; highlight factors which sustain or impede human capital formation; suggest steps to alleviate talent shortages; and specify ways to unlock human talent and unleash resources to optimize resource utilization and lift performance.

In particular, this chapter addresses several questions regarding talent management. Does the region have the capacity and the necessary environment for nurturing talent? Does the region have reasonable opportunities to absorb existing talent? What are the new trends in talent management in competitive markets? What are the existing factors which sustain or impede human capital formation and development? Do countries in the region, individually or collectively, have talent strategies? How capable are business and government institutions of facing the mounting global need for talent to effectively compete in the 21st century and beyond?

The region has the potential to be a formidable international economic player. This is especially true as the region accounts for more than 61 percent of world's oil reserves, experiences a rapid growth in higher education, and, over the last few years, has accumulated a considerably large sum of sovereign wealth funds (SWFs). These factors have enabled the region to embark on new mega economic projects and invest heavily in human capital. In 2007, A.T. Kearney reported that countries in the Middle East were newcomers to the offshoring industry, but had many attributes that could make them attractive locations for shared services. Its 2009 report, however, has noted that the region is emerging as a hot offshoring destination for the world. Furthermore, A.T. Kearney (2010) reported that the Middle East/North Africa region is clearly the world's most attractive region for retail expansion. In addition, strong European investment in the region, consumer familiarity with modern retail concepts, and petrodollar wealth are the primary factors making the region a fertile market for retail expansion. The report estimated that more than $9 trillion will flow into the region by 2020, making growth in retailing and consumption an eventual trend in the next decade.

The chapter is structured into the following sections: An overview of regional aspects, talent capacity, trends in TM, factors sustaining or impeding human capital formation and development, confronting talent shortages, coping with mounting challenges, and conclusion.

Overview of the Middle East

The term "Middle East" is here used to denote what is politically called Middle East and North Africa. The region is home to Arab countries, Iran, Israel, and Turkey. Despite its popular use, it implies an area of more restrictive geographic scope than is accurate, and suggests a degree of internal uniformity that is unjustified by reality. Countries such as Turkey, Iran, Israel, Egypt, Tunisia, Morocco, and Yemen are lumped together under this convenient political umbrella. Despite its political risk and seemingly formidable challenges, the region was and remains culturally intriguing and economically valuable for any global economic player.

The region is home to more than 490 million people scattered in an area that exceeds 16 million sq. km. Among the most prosperous countries in the region in terms of market sophistication, are Israel, Iran, Saudi Arabia, United Arab Emirates (UAE), and Turkey. Israel is technologically a power center with world-class human skills, while Iran is rich in natural resources and has the largest and most mature middle class in the region. Its entrepreneurs have traditionally been active in the global markets and show domination in nearby markets such as UAE, Bahrain, Afghanistan, etc. Nevertheless, since the Islamic revolution in 1979, Iran has suffered from "autocratic" management orientations (Amirshahi, 1998). Turkey, an emerging market, is the bridge between the West and East. Unlike Iran, both Turkey and Israel have recently accelerated market reform and economic revitalization, invested heavily in high-tech, and have a genuine interest in integration in the world economy.

Saudi Arabia and UAE are the most dynamic and largest markets in the Arabic speaking part of the region and primarily rely on expatriates to carry out major economic activities. These two countries have huge SWFs and have initiated profound economic reforms to ease their global economic integration. Like the rest of the Arab countries, however, they have adopted a form of Sheiko-Capitalism (Ali, 1995). In this system, the fate of the market economy is contingent on the ruler's wishes. That is, Sheiko-Capitalism is characterized by personal rather than by institutional procedures. The government is always ready to interfere and to manage the market mechanism when political considerations dictate.

The Arab part of the region is either resource-based (oil) (Algeria, Iraq, Libya, Kuwait, Oman, Qatar, Saudi Arabia, and UAE) or lacks oil and inadequately utilizes their other natural resources (Djibouti, Egypt, Jordan, Lebanon, Mauritania, Morocco, Sudan, Tunisia). In recent years, most of the countries in the region have experienced a growth in the middle class due to privatization, educational achievements, and the increasing presence of business opportunities in various sectors, especially in banking, insurance, real estate, and retailing.

Nevertheless, invariably, all countries in the region have a large public sector and in some countries like Egypt, Iraq, Algeria, and Saudi Arabia, the public sector is a major source of employment. General economic indicators are provided in Table 9.1. It appears that only Israel, Lebanon, Tunisia, and Turkey, among non oil producers, have a per capita income which exceeds $7,000. In addition, all the non oil-producing countries are import dependent. Fourteen of the twenty-three countries in the region have achieved $5,000 or more per capita. With the exception of Djibouti, Mauritania, Sudan, and Yemen, the rest have either high per capita income (e.g., Qatar, UAE, Saudi Arabia, Bahrain, Israel, Kuwait, etc.) or a reasonable one (e.g., Turkey, Algeria, Syria, Lebanon, etc.). The 2009 UN Human Development Index that measures the average achievements in a country based on three dimensions of human development (longevity, knowledge, and an appropriate standard of living) provides a more realistic and promising picture of the situation in the region. Nine countries (see UNDP, 2009) ranked among the highest or high nations (Bahrain, Israel, UAE, Kuwait, Libya, Oman, Qatar, Saudi Arabia and Turkey). The rest of the countries ranked at the medium category (ranging between .50 and .79). This indicates that citizens have opportunities to realize their potential, increase their choices, and enjoy the freedom to lead lives they value (UNDP, 2009). Accordingly, the region is considered to be a fruitful place for human capital formation and nurturing talent.

In terms of FDI, the region has witnessed a rise for the sixth consecutive year (UNCTD, 2009). The lion's share of inflow is dominated by a few countries (Saudi Arabia, Turkey, UAE, and Egypt). Nevertheless, the majority of the countries rank above average on the Globalization Index (See Table 9.2). Lebanon, Jordan, Israel, Bahrain, and UAE top the list. Four countries in the region (Qatar, UAE, Israel, and Saudi Arabia) are among the first thirty nations on the 2009 Global Competitiveness Index. Likewise, on the 2008 Ease of Doing Business Index, three countries in the region (Saudi Arabia, Bahrain, and Israel) ranked at the top thirty. On the 2009, Economic Freedom Index, five countries (UAE, Bahrain, Jordan, Kuwait, and Oman) were ranked at the top forty countries in the world.

Regional talent capacity

The above discussion, while highlighting general economic and human resource conditions, suggests that the Middle East has the potential to unlock its resources and establish a sound foundation for economic growth and development. Nevertheless, the region, in general, faces formidable challenges in effectively meeting the rising expectations of its population. In fact, there are pressing concerns regarding the region's ability to nurture and absorb talent. In particular, there are two issues essential for talent management: share of the youth in the region and the unemployment rate among the young and general population. Both issues constitute a major hurdle that must be confronted. The large presence of youth in the workforce and their high unemployment rate represent a major challenge to both government and business corporations. The Youth usually have different orientations and some of them, despite their formal education, are often under-qualified. The Arab Human Capital Challenge (2009) reported that regional growth has not been "youth employment friendly" as the region has failed in effectively creating jobs for the youth. The CEOs in the report argued that there was an insufficient supply of qualified national labor. Neither the

Table 9.1 Major economic indicators

Country	GDP ($ billion)	GDP (per capita $) ppp	Population (million)	Labor force (million)	Unemployment rate %	FDI inward flows ($ million)	Human Development Index
Iran	382.3	12,800	66.4	24.35	12.5	1,492	0.777
Israel	188.7	28,200	7.2	2.96	6.1	9,639	0.930
Turkey	798.9	12,000	76.8	24.06	10.7	18,198	0.798
Algeria	171.3	7,000	34.8	9.46	12.5	2,646	0.748
Bahrain	19.7	37,200	0.73	0.56	15	1,794	0.902
Djibouti	0.97	3,700	0.52	0.35	59	234	0.513
Egypt	158.3	5,400	83.1	24.60	8.4	9,495	0.716
Jordan	19.1	5,000	6.3	1.62	12.6	1,954	0.769
Iraq	93.8	4,000	28.9	7.74	18.2	–	–
Kuwait	159.7	57,400	2.7	2.08	2.2	56	0.912
Lebanon	28.0	11,100	4.1	1.48	9.2	3,606	0.796
Libya	108.5	14,400	6.3	1.64	30	4,111	0.840
Mauritania	3.6	2,100	3.1	1.31	30	103	0.557
Morocco	90.5	4,000	34.9	11.29	10	2,388	0.646
Oman	56.3	20,200	3.4	0.97	15	2,928	0.839
Qatar	116.9	103,500	0.83	1.12	0.4	6,700	0.899
Saudi Arabia	467.7	20,700	28.6	6.74	11.8	38,223	0.835
Sudan	62.3	2,200	41.1	11.92	18.7	2,601	0.526
Syria	44.5	4,800	20.2	5.59	8.6	2,116	0.736
Tunisia	41.8	7,900	10.5	3.66	14.1	2,761	0.762
UAE	270.0	40,000	4.8	3.27	2.4	13,700	0.903
Yemen	27.6	2,400	23.8	6.45	35	463	0.567

Source: Based on *Factbook*, CIA Publications, U.S. Government Documents, 2009; *World Investment Report 2009*, UNCTD, UN: New York, Human Development Reports, UN Publications, 2009.

Table 9.2 Regional competitiveness index

Country	Global competitive index rank	Ease of doing business rank	Economic freedom rating index	Globalization index 2009
Iran	–	137	112	41.49
Israel	27	29	78	74.69
Turkey	61	73	88	66.42
Algeria	83	136	131	54.75
Bahrain	38	20	20	72.89
Djibouti	–	163	–	–
Egypt	70	106	79	62.20
Jordan	50	100	34	75.51
Iraq	–	153	–	–
Kuwait	39	61	30	68.02
Lebanon	–	108	–	78.56
Libya	88	–	–	–
Mauritania	127	166	109	51.55
Morocco	73	128	104	62.64
Oman	41	65	36	63.30
Qatar	22	39	–	65.51
Saudi Arabia	28	13	–	62.87
Sudan	–	154	–	38.86
Syria	94	143	124	50.58
Tunisia	40	69	90	65.12
UAE	23	33	19	69.26
Yemen	–	99	–	41.82

Source: Based on *The Global Competitiveness Index 2009–2010* rankings, World Economic Forum, 2009; *Economic Rankings*, The World Bank Group, June 2008–May 2009; Economic Freedom of the World 2009 Annual Report, The Fraser Institute, 2009; KOF Globalization Index 2009.

existing educational system nor the political climate allows new graduates to take initiatives or assume leadership roles. Nevertheless, because of their energy, enthusiasm, and the sheer number in the workforce, the youth segment may serve as an instrument for labor and economic reform.

The percentage of youth in the region's population is considerably high. About 60 percent in the region are less than 30 years old. The youth (defined as those between the ages of 15 and 24) numbered about 90 million in 2005. This number is expected to exceed 95 million in 2025. The youth segment constituted 34 percent of the workforce in 2005 and experienced an unemployment rate of 23 and 33 percent for males and females, respectively (Assaad and Roudi-Fahimi, 2007). The aggregate unemployment rate for youth is about 25 percent, well above the world average of 14 percent (Middle East Youth Initiative, 2009). Though the regional aggregate unemployment rate declined from around 11 percent in 1998 to about 9.4 percent in 2008, the unemployment rate still remains one of the highest in the world (Behrendt, Haq, and Kamal, 2009). The unemployment rate, however, differs among countries with Djibouti having about 59 percent and Qatar, a country with a similar population size but rich in resources, having .04 percent. In general, relative to other states, unemployment in the Gulf Cooperation Council (GCC) (Bahrain, Kuwait, Qatar, Oman, Saudi Arabia, and UAE) is low (see Table 9.1). Since the early 1970s, the GCC states have relied on expatriates to carry out essential economic activities and these countries, due to increasing oil revenues, have experienced remarkable economic growth.

Certainly, unemployment in the region calls into question whether or not the region has the economic capacity to absorb existing talent. Can the region generate enough jobs and opportunities to utilize the existing energy and skill? About 100 million new jobs have to be created in the region for the next decade (World Economic Forum, 2009). On average, the region has done well in terms of GDP and economic growth. In fact, the region experienced high growth between 2002 and 2008 and according to the World Bank (2009) the GDP, despite the global economic downturn, is expected to increase by 3.8 percent in 2010 and 4.6 percent by 2011. Nevertheless, the region appears to squander its wealth and has not met the rising expectations of its population (Dhillon, 2009). In the *Middle East Youth Initiative* (2009), it was noted that despite six years of relatively high growth in the Middle East (2002 and 2008) the transition to adulthood for many young citizens "has remained stalled and, in some ways, outcomes have worsened. Young people continue to struggle in attaining job-relevant skills and high quality education."

However, the region is home to about 490 million people and many countries have embarked on ambitious economic development plans. In particular, the six GCC countries have invested heavily in infrastructure, energy, and real-estate. Likewise, countries such as Israel, Iran, and Turkey have revitalized their economy with an emphasis on technologies and export-oriented industries.

The World Bank (2009) classified the region into three categories based on the degree of availability of natural resources, mainly oil and labor abundance. These are:

Resource-poor, labor abundant These countries include Djibouti, Egypt, Jordan, Lebanon, Morocco, Tunisia, and West Bank and Gaza. Most of these countries have no oil and are the source for exporting labor to the oil-rich countries. In particular, Egypt, Lebanon, and West Bank and Gaza have traditionally provided the Arab Gulf area with needed labor. These countries have educated and skilled personnel who have been instrumental in building the GCC economy and public institutions.

Resource-rich, labor abundant This category includes Algeria, Iraq, Iran, Syria, and Yemen. The first four countries have been a source for skilled labor. In addition, most of these countries are where oil and other natural resources are found. These countries have untapped resources and under certain political environments could be vital economic players.

Resource-rich, labor importing These include Bahrain, Kuwait, Libya, Oman, Qatar, Saudi Arabia, and the UAE. Relative to the other two categories, these countries have, for the last six decades, been importing labor from various countries to meet demand for a variety of jobs ranging from house servants and engineers, to doctors and university professors. The percentage of expatriates in the workforce range between 79 percent to over 90 percent in the UAE. The dependency of these countries on foreign labor is perpetuated by the existence of a welfare state and the primary role that their governments play in the economy.

For the foreseeable future, Israel, Turkey, and the resource-rich countries are more likely to generate both wealth and jobs for their population. The Hay Group (2009) reported that there is a high probability for unleashing performance in the region stating,

Most organizations in the Middle East have registered exceptional financial performance over the last few years and the combination of public and private sector reforms in the region have led to significant improvements in efficiency. However, Hay Group research has found that Middle Eastern organizations are sitting on substantial reserves of efficiency and productivity that they have yet to set free from their employees.

In a survey of 13,376 employees across the region, bayt.com (2009), a Middle East job site, found that most participants were motivated and that 94 percent feel that the work they do is significant to their respective corporations and that they utilize their skills and abilities in doing their work. The study indicated that banking/finance, energy and petrochemicals, and IT and communication industries are the top-paying industries. In particular, the study pointed out that most participants were willing to recommend private sector organizations and foreign MNCs as employers. This demonstrates that there is a recognition that privately-owned domestic organizations and MNCs are playing a significant role in the economy and in creating jobs. That is, the public sector is no longer seen as the engine for generating jobs. The region is home for a large sum of sovereign wealth funds. The GCC countries alone are expected to invest around $3 trillion in the region by 2020 (Böhme, Chiarella, and Lemerle, 2008). This infusion of capital and the gradual increase in FDI inflows are expected to create ample economic opportunities and, thus, ease unemployment pressure.

Trends in talent management

Like many other regions in the world, the Middle East has experienced structural change in its workforce, and organizations have confronted issues ranging from diversity, turnover, and shortages in professional and skilled labor. Given the fact that the region is relying on trade with other regions and several of its countries are highly dependent on oil export, talent nurturing and management in today's economy will be a decisive factor in shaping the region's economic future and role in the global market. This may explain why, in the last few years, governments and business organizations alike have given careful consideration to talent management. The first Middle East Talent Management Summit was organized in 2007 in Dubai and was followed by a second one in 2008. These events, along with others, underscore the seriousness of the challenges that organizations confront and highlight important trends which have taken place in the field of human capital. These are outlined below:

1 *Fair Access to Career Growth and Influence.* The increasing share of youth in the population may indicate that a growing number of Middle Easterners are joining the talent marketplace. While this phenomenon contributes to economic growth— Demographic Dividend—(Aguirre *et al.*, 2009) it forces corporations to change their recruiting and training methods. This is especially true in countries which have dynamic business environments (e.g., UAE, Bahrain, Saudi Arabia, Turkey, etc.). Indeed, companies have to nurture this talent, and naturally these young recruits are inclined to see others like them in positions of power (Ready, Hill, and Conger, 2008). Thus, there has been a steady increase in young personnel assuming senior management positions. Bayt.com (2009) found that many employees are motivated by long-term career growth

and development opportunities. Furthermore, a large number of women are graduating from colleges and, in many cases, the number of female graduates exceeds males. The International Labor Organization (2007) reported that, while the Middle East and North Africa may still have the lowest share of women in non-agricultural paid employment at 28.2 percent, the increase in this variable for the region has been strongest compared to all other regions, rising 3.7 percent over the past decade. The report indicated that women's employment in good quality jobs in legislative, senior official, or managerial positions has notably increased reaching an absolute percentage increase of almost 2 percent; a level of 11 percent in 2004.

2 *Diversification.* In many parts of the region, there has been an increasing diversity in terms of ethnicity, geography, educational achievement, in addition to gender and age. Even though this development is highly feasible in the GCC countries, manual work and related jobs are performed by Asian workers, especially from the Indian subcontinent. Highly skilled jobs in marketing, strategic planning, R&D, and human resource planning are occupied by Westerners, Lebanese, and Palestinians while engineering and teaching jobs are dominated by expatriates from India and other Arab states.

3 *Focusing on talent.* Traditionally, most jobs are filled with little regard to qualifications. In growth economies like those of the oil-producing countries and especially the GCC, citizens were given jobs based on considerations irrelevant to tasks or job requirements. Foreign workers were selected based on availability and lower wages. In recent years, three developments (MNCs recruiting practices, participation in the global economy, and an uncertain economic future) have induced firms to rethink their talent needs. Corporations, especially those which operate globally, have developed plans to recruit talent from all over the world. For example, Alghanim Industries, a Private Kuwaiti-based conglomerate, hired Andrew Finch, to lead its talent management department. The Company was the recipient of the Hewitt Associates' "Best Employer in Middle East 2009" award. Its recruitment program states that the company is interested in hiring productive individuals who are fully comfortable with the corporate world and are acclimated to working with the diverse work force of 49 different nationalities within the company. Likewise, Hay Group (2008) reported that senior managers in the Middle East continue to get salary increases of between 15 to 20 percent and that the demand for management talent far outstrips supply.

4 *Recruiting.* An increasing number of firms are using online recruiting. While traditional methods like newspapers and TV, employment agencies, recruitment agencies, colleges, and word-of-mouth are used across the region, the online recruiting and specialized online agencies are becoming the favorite choice. Recruiting agencies like mihnati.com and bayt.com have a thriving business. Specialized recruiting for senior executives and highly skilled personnel is increasingly utilized by firms which engage globally.

5 *Discrimination.* Though the ILO (2007) noticed an increasing participation of women in the workforce and an easier access for women to managerial positions and fair compensation, the organization indicated that women still face discrimination. Furthermore, in most cases, Westerners and citizens are given a higher pay scale than those from developing countries. In recent years, high performance corporations have moved away from high basic salaries (Mercer, 2008a) and toward incentive packages linked to performance and business objectives (Business Intelligence Middle East, 2009). Likewise, governments, due to pressures exercised by international and local civic rights

organizations, have introduced new laws that are intended to provide protection and ensure the dignity of employees, be they expatriates or citizens. This trend inaugurates a new practice in human resources and a nurturing of talent, away from the outdated discriminatory practices.

6 *Succession planning.* Until recently, in both government and private sectors, the issue of succession was not discussed. In government, this was usually a political decision made arbitrarily by those in higher positions. In the private sector, where family business is the norm, succession is problematic and mostly left to political maneuvering among members of the extended family after the passing of the patriarch. In recent years, western practices have gradually taken root and more companies have begun to treat succession issues as a leadership development matter.

7 *Training and development.* There has been a shift in training and development for employees away from structured, classroom learning to e-learning and participation in group activities and observation where the focus is on work and work-related activities. While classroom learning is still common, many organizations are sending their employees abroad, having retreats, and enrolling them in distance learning courses. Furthermore, many countries in the region have invited western trainers and thinkers to conduct seminars to their senior staff, both to broaden their perspectives and to adapt to newly adopted technologies. In fact, an increasing number of corporations are utilizing technology to facilitate learning and professional growth.

8 *Retention.* This is a pivotal issue in the years ahead as turnover in the private sector appears to be increasing in recent years. The Bayt.com (2009) found that there was an overall "unrest" in the job market as many employees are either planning to leave their current jobs or are actively looking for other jobs. This is a new trend in the region. Five major forces have contributed to the emergence of this event: the economic downturn, an accelerating trend to diversify the economy which opens new opportunities, mobility of the workforce, a steady shortage in skilled labor as many skilled expatriates are either moving back to their home country or looking for emerging opportunities elsewhere (Mercer, 2008b), and countries which have sponsorship systems have recently relaxed regulations giving employees in certain industries the right to switch employers without the approval of their current employer. Therefore, retention of skilled and professional employees is becoming the most critical issue facing corporations in the region.

9 *Performance-related pay.* Privatization and liberalization have made it possible to move away from the traditional system of offering citizens jobs and benefits without regard to accountability and performance. In the public sector, however, this trend has not taken root.

Certainly, the demographic shift in population in favor of the youth segment, coupled with substantial growth in higher education institutions, translates into a large portion of the workforce which is young and educated. This fact along with a shortage of skilled labor to meet economic booms in some parts of the region, will intensify and strengthen the trend toward more sophisticated practices necessary for talent nurturing and retention.

Factors sustaining or impeding human capital formation and development

Whether or not the aforesaid above trends are sustainable is a matter for debate. This is primarily because the region is shaped by a unity of contradiction which can be either an obstacle or a facilitator for talent management. Indeed, regional political instability and economic vulnerability stemming from reliance on global market conditions have a significant impact on economic growth and, subsequently, the labor market. While political instability has become a hallmark of the regional landscape, vulnerability to global trade is an emerging and alarming factor. This is because Middle Eastern countries, being substantially open economies, are affected, during times of international economic crisis, by the brunt of rising protectionism across the world and consequently their global trade will be affected by restrictive measures undertaken by the rest of the world (Pradhan, 2009).

The region, however, enjoys three promising and relevant developments: economic expansion and growth, highest levels of labor force growth, and youngest labor force (World Bank, 2007). These developments can be strengthened if regional levels of violence subside and outstanding political problems are addressed objectively and seriously, leading to a permanent peace. Political instability has been a detrimental factor for human capital formation as it fuels anxiety and uncertainty surrounding the future and economic welfare, and frustrates and distracts people from engaging in productive economic activities and participating fully in economically vital projects. Consequently, talent may flow to other countries and TM personnel may find it difficult to recruit and retain needed competencies (e.g., instability in Iraq since 1980 has led to mass migration of Iraqis to other countries leaving Iraq in a shattered economic situation). In the Arab Human Capital Challenge (2009), a comprehensive survey of the region's most influential CEOs, 587 CEOs perceived domestic political instability and global terrorism to be the most serious threat to the business environment and to regional growth and development. Moreover, it diverts scarce resources for unproductive engagements (e.g., UAE has a deal with Lockheed alone for $7 billion in 2009; Saudi Arabia signed military contracts with both the U.S. and France totaling more than $30 billion in 2008).

Under normal conditions, growth in population, especially the youth segment, coupled with an abundance of natural resources leads to ample market opportunities. How these resources are deployed may prove to be a decisive factor in shaping the future and the nature of talent. Effective deployment, however, depends on several factors including: economic reforms, privatization, stock markets, regional integration, better governance, higher education, training and development institutions, competitive labor laws, and the gradual participation of the private sector in economic planning. These developments are briefly discussed below.

Economic reforms Faced with both internal and external pressures, almost all governments in the regions have embarked on economic reforms. These reforms have made it possible for local entrepreneurs to unleash capabilities and for MNCs to invest in attractive and untapped economic sectors (e.g., insurance, banking, petrochemicals, IT and communications, and education). These have contributed to opening opportunities and increasing competition for recruiting and retaining workforce. The World Bank (2009) reported that governments in the region are now reforming at a rate similar to those in Eastern Europe and Central Asia.

Privatization This development accelerated after the collapse of the Soviet Union. Governments in the region gradually decided to dismantle many of their state enterprises. Though the degree of privatization varies across the region, the trend is expected to encourage entrepreneurship and the spirit of innovation. Furthermore, it may create a competitive environment and competition for qualified personnel.

Formation of stock markets Since 1995, the number of companies in each country that are registered on the stock exchange has increased dramatically. This is more notable in Saudi Arabia, Kuwait, Egypt, Morocco, Tunisia, UAE, Oman, Jordan, and Bahrain. More cooperation among countries in the region regarding stock markets and financial reform is needed to increase investors' confidence and economic stability. In the region, there is a large amount of liquidity that could be invested in productive sectors thereby creating more opportunities for employment and career development.

Proliferation of regional and bilateral trade agreements The GCC countries have one of the most successful agreements in the region on trade, investment, and travel. The Mugreb countries, or the Arab West, have also agreements among and between themselves, such as the one between Morocco and Tunisia, Algeria and Libya, etc. There is also the Greater Arab Free Trade Agreement. Nevertheless, interregional merchandise exports among members of the region is still very low relative to total regional exports (World Bank, 2007). The Arab countries and Iran, also, have bilateral agreements with nations outside the region such as the one with the European Union and the U.S. For example, the U.S. has separate free trade agreements with Jordan, Oman, Tunisia, and Morocco. Furthermore, as of 2006, ten countries (Bahrain, Egypt, Jordan, Kuwait, Morocco, Oman, Qatar, Saudi Arabia, UAE, and Tunisia) have joined the World Trade Organization (WTO) and six others have applied for membership. These agreements, along with membership in the WTO, encourage competition and eventually will lead to more open trade regimes and liberalization of the economy.

Improving governance the increasing scrutiny of public practices and fraud exercised by local civic organizations, international agencies, and media outlets has forced governments in the region to introduce measured reforms in public enterprises. For no less than four decades, governments in the region tolerated corruption and bribery and ignored essential public services. In recent years, governments, however, have enacted several policies and laws to reform public administration and oblige public officers and bureaucrats to show transparency and accountability. According to the World Bank (2007), in terms of reform, the region as a whole ranked on average in the 64th percentile, which is the highest worldwide and ranked in the 67th on improving the mechanism for government accountability, making the quality of public administration relatively high, ranking above East Asia, Latin America, South Asia, and Sub-Saharan Africa.

Educated labor force The growing numbers of technical and higher education institutions have contributed significantly to increasing rates of skilled and professional personnel. This is particularly true in Egypt, Algeria, Iraq, Syria, Iran, Libya, Morocco, and Saudi Arabia. The World Bank (2007) reported that, on average, enrollment rates in higher education increased by two-thirds between 1990 and 2000, and continued to increase between 2000 and 2003 in all but Kuwait, Qatar, and Yemen. Governments in the region spent an average of 5 percent of GDP on education, whereas most East Asian and Latin American countries spent closer to 3 percent (Middle East Youth Initiative, 2009). Many educated people, however, because of the lack of suitable jobs in the local markets tend to migrate to other countries, especially within the region. MNCs operating in the region may find it easier and useful to hire host countries' nationals.

Training and development institutions Since the 1980s, there has been a phenomenal increase in the number of training and consulting institutions. In addition, almost all major corporations in the region have their own training and development centers (e.g., National Bank of Kuwait, Sabic, etc.). In recent years, foreign groups have established their own offices in the region (e.g., Hay Group, Mercer, Hewitt, Accenture, etc). More importantly, many governments in the region have recognized the importance of education and the allocation of talent. While Israel, and to a degree Turkey, and Iran have been pioneers in moving toward creating high tech and knowledge creation, Saudi Arabia, in particular, has allocated billions of dollar in establishing knowledge cities. These are expected to enhance skills in the region and contribute to human capital formation, productivity, and innovation.

Competitive labor laws GCC countries and others in North Africa have in recent years changed their labor laws to meet the global challenge. These new laws are aimed at protecting employees' rights, providing them with needed security, and enhancing their career prospects.

Private sector Without exception, the region, in recent years, has experienced a significant increase in the role of the private sector in the economy. Governments, invariably, have initiated market openness and privatization programs thereby enlarging the economic space of the private sector. In fact, liberalization of investment laws and encouragement to national and foreign investors have been instrumental in creating new enterprises. In the GCC area, for example, governments enacted several laws that make it easy for the private sector to compete in open markets and encourage investors to actively pursue a wide range of activities which, until recently, were monopolized by public enterprises or strictly regulated.

Improvement in labor productivity The UN's *Millennium Development Goals Report 2009* indicated that the region experienced an increase in labor productivity relative to other developing regions. Furthermore, in its report, *Global Employment Trends*, the International Labor Organization (2009) reported that output per worker in the region far exceeds that of the world average. While, labor productivity does not guarantee the creation of new jobs, it does demonstrate an improvement in skills and organizational disciplines.

Despite the positive developments mentioned above, the region still experiences certain deficiencies in addition to lack of freedom, political unrest, and foreign military interventions. These deficiencies may slow economic growth and adversely impact talent management. These deficiencies are briefly discussed below:

Obstructive work climate Senior managers and leaders apply a coercive style in dealing with subordinates; thus, they fail to unleash untapped efficiency and productivity (Hay Group, 2009). Leaders contribute significantly to cultivating and retaining competent employees. In fact, in the developed world, engaging and inspiring talent has increasingly become an essential leadership task. In a survey conducted by *McKinsey Quarterly* (see Dewhurst, Guthridge, and Mohr, 2009) it was found that leadership attention to employees is important in retaining top talent. This is not the case in the region where most business leaders appear not to value the pivotal role that employees play in productivity and growth. For example, Boer and Turner (2007) argued that, in the GCC, business leaders search "the world for the cheapest sources of labor rather than investing in building the skills of the national workforce and increasing that country's labor productivity." Certainly, this state of affairs will make it difficult to attract competent and loyal employees and may increase, too, the rate of turnover for skilled jobs. Likewise, discrimination at the workplace despite notable decrease is still common (International Labor Organization, 2007). This very fact constitutes an obstacle for human capital formation and may induce turnover.

Low female participation in the workforce In the last four decades, the number of women graduating from secondary and higher education institutions has increased dramatically. Subsequently, the rate of female participation in the labor force has jumped from, for example, 24 percent in 1990 to 31 percent in 2005. This improvement, however, is still not in line with developments in other parts of the world. In fact, the rate of participation is still the lowest among developing regions (World Bank, 2007).

Weak legal institutions and institutional arrangements Because of the nature of a political system where power is concentrated in the ruling families, the legal system and other institutions, especially economic, have been either weak or marginalized. Indeed, weak legal and economic institutions in the region are considered the greatest obstacle to economic growth and accountability and transparency (Ali, 2008). The *Arab Human Development Report 2009* warned of weak legal protection and institutions. It is estimated that in the Arab part of the region, the private business sector loses about $20 billion a year due to lack of qualified legal personnel and the vagueness and contradictions of legislations within each country (Shrieh, 2009).

Weak private sector Despite privatization and market reform, the public sector is still dominant. Entrepreneurs, with a few exceptions, are reluctant to take major initiatives independent of government approval and support. Furthermore, the public sector employs more than a third of the workforce and the private sector has weak job-generating capacity (*Arab Human Development Report 2009*). The private sector's influence on skill development is weakened in two ways (Middle East Youth Initiative, 2009): the public sector offers graduates higher pay than the private sector and often better job security, and the wage scale and high costs of layoffs prevent private enterprises from underscoring the rewards for productivity and a wider skill set.

Weak structural foundations of the economy While Israel, Turkey, Syria, and Iran appear to have a balanced growth strategy, the rest have not been able to provide the needed foundations for sound economic progress. The *Arab Human Development Report 2009* asserted that many Arab countries are turning into increasingly import-oriented and service-based economies. It stated that "The types of services found in most Arab countries fall at the low end of the value adding chain, contribute little to local knowledge development and lock countries into inferior positions in global markets."

Low quality of education Israel has a first-class educational system and relatively strong educational culture with an emphasis on discovery and transforming the country into a high-tech empire. The rest of the region, however, does not exhibit the same. The Middle East Youth Initiative (2009) and the *Arab Human Development Report 2009* have both emphasized the poor quality of education and lack of linking skills to market needs. Generally this type of education does not give priority to needed technical or vocational skills. Indeed, the first reported, "the lack of skills among workers as a major constraint on business growth." Table 9.3 shows that in higher education, those who specialized in science and engineering constitute on average about 22.6 of total enrolled students while China and South Korea have 46.8 and 41.1 percent respectively. The emphasis on social sciences and humanities is clearer in Egypt and Saudi Arabia where the share is 76 and 75.6 percent.

Table 9.3 Distribution of university students by field

Country	Year	Education and humanities	Social Science	Medicine	Scientific, Technical, and Engineering	Other
Algeria	2003	16.4	38.2	7.0	18.0	20.2
Bahrain	2002	10.0	50.0	7.1	21.0	12.0
Djibouti	2003	20.0	51.0	0.0	22.0	7.0
Egypt	1995	35.0	41.2	7.4	10.2	6.1
Iran	2003	17.6	27.5	7.3	38.2	9.3
Iraq	2003	30.8	21.3	8.1	24.1	15.8
Jordan	2002	30.0	21.3	10.0	30.0	4.0
Lebanon	2003	21.2	38.8	8.5	25.7	5.8
Libya	1999	30.3	18.3	17.0	30.8	3.6
Morocco	2003	27.6	47.8	3.9	18.3	2.3
Oman	2003	54.2	21.1	2.8	14.0	7.9
Qatar	2003	19.1	48.3	3.9	19.1	9.5
Saudi Arabia	2003	60.7	15.1	4.6	13.6	6.1
Syrian Arab Republic	1994	29.2	28.2	11.5	25.3	5.8
Tunisia	2002	22.0	27.0	7.0	31.0	13.0
UAE	1996	57.8	13.6	1.7	24.1	2.8
West Bank and Gaza	2003	42.4	33.4	5.6	18.1	0.4
MEAN		**30.8**	**32.2**	**6.7**	**22.6**	**7.7**
China	1994	22.8	9.4	8.9	46.8	12.1
Korea	2002	23.4	20.4	7.3	41.1	7.9
Chile	2002	20.0	35.0	9.0	32.0	5.0
Mexico	2002	15.0	42.0	8.0	32.0	4.3

Source: Mena Development Report, 2007, The World Bank.

Confronting talent shortages

Generally and until recently, countries in the region did not seem to give priority to talent formation. There is an exception, however, as Israel, since its inception, has been determined to be a global high-tech center. In 1959, the Israel Defense Forces established an elite computer unit called Mamram. Along with other defense units such as Rafael and Intelligence Corps, these units have been responsible for channeling private business with highly skilled workers and for producing thousands of business-related patents each year. Since its early years, the state in Israel has developed a coherent policy for passing on scientific knowledge, nurtured in military-based institutions, to industry. This policy has served Israel well and has eased the transformation of the country into a scientific superpower. The Israel high-tech industry is responsible for 48 percent of all of Israel's industrial exports (See Griml, 2008). In terms of U.S. patents granted in 2008, Israel had 1,166 while the rest of the region had only 89 patents. The largest economy in the region in terms of GDP, Turkey, had only 16 while Egypt, the largest in terms of population, had 2 granted patents in the same year (See Table 9.4). The accumulated granted patents for 1995–2008, Israel had 16,805 while the rest (18 countries) had 1,110 patents.

Table 9.4 Number of U.S. patents granted as distributed by year of patent grant

Country	Patents granted 2008	Accumulated patents (1995–2008)
Bahrain	0	4
Egypt	2	113
Jordan	0	21
Kuwait	15	103
Oman	5	7
Saudi Arabia	30	310
Syria	0	20
UAE	9	57
Yemen	0	3
Turkey	16	207
Iran	2	75
Iraq	1	10
Israel	1,166	16,805
Qatar	1	4
Tunisia	2	23
Lebanon	2	70
Morocco	4	70
Algeria	0	13
Djibouti	0	0
Total	**1255**	**17915**

Source: U.S. Patent and Trademark Office. Last Modified: 03/26/2009.

Over several decades, the government in Turkey has encouraged its entrepreneurs and cultivated friendly relationships with the business communities. In Iran, during the Shah era, the government ignored, for political reasons, the business associations and especially the traditionally independent merchant groups. This is exactly what Shambayati (1994) found in 1970s. He indicated that in Turkey there were strong and independent business associations, and some sectors of society were financially and organizationally strong enough to make demands upon the state outside the corporatist structure. Therefore, the state had to be responsive to the demands of entrepreneurs and the established industrial class. In Iran, the state relied primarily on oil revenues, which it completely controls. The entrepreneurs were clients of the state and had no reason to challenge it. In contrast, the traditional merchants (well-established bourgeoisie) were suspicious of the state and the latter had neither the economic incentive nor the administrative capacity to control them. Therefore, the state never bothered to establish links with domestic businesses and was not responsive to their demands. In recent years, both countries have purposely encouraged entrepreneurship, and Iran, in particular, has invested heavily in defense-related industries. However, it is not known yet, whether or not Iran will successfully emulate the Israeli example of using government facilities and funds to shore up technology entrepreneurs and transfer its economy into a high-tech hub. Turkey's industrial policy, however, focuses on small business, export-oriented industry, and on niche industrial strategies (e.g., yacht, fashion, leather, and textile industries).

In the Arab states, governments have relied primarily on state enterprises and until recently entrepreneurs were left on their own. The *Arab Human Development Report 2009* indicated that for about "two and half decades after 1980, the region witnessed hardly any economic growth." The report asserts that Arab economic problems are mainly political as "All Arab heads of state wield absolute authority, answering to none," and thus have produced an unhealthy environment termed, "un-freedom." There are signs, however, that talent consideration appears to top the list of official priorities of most governments in the region. MNCs' presence in the region, rising entrepreneurs, recommendations by international organizations (e.g. IMF, World Bank, UN agencies) along with mounting pressures from recent economic crisis, activists, and human rights groups have sensitized governments to rethink their human capital policies and approaches. Lately, Saudi Arabia and the UAE have started knowledge cities and mega science projects. Other governments, especially oil-based countries, have also initiated various programs to sustain their economic vitality and cope with growing human capital challenges.

The world financial crisis, however, has sent a wave of fear across the region after Dubai experienced difficulty in meeting its debt obligation in November 2009. The appearance of overall regional resilience is suddenly shattered demonstrating that openness to the world market and unregulated economic growth have their price. This in fact has far-reaching implications for talent management. There will be pressure to undertake fundamental reform in the labor market especially in the GCC countries. This reform has to be strategically linked to talent creation and the role of workforce in economic development. While expatriates will be needed for years to come, the exodus of expatriates, for example from the UAE during the current crisis, calls for rethinking the role of nationals in the labor market and the necessity for granting expatriates with needed competencies either citizenship or residency with a citizenship option. As Boer and Turner (2007, p. 15) argue, young talent may seek to change employment norms in the region and reject the "idea that the only private-sector jobs in fast-growing economies are designed for expatriates, with salaries that don't meet local standards." While non-financial motivators have been widely practiced in the region, the depth of financial crisis may offer business owners and executives an opportunity to recognize talented employees and enhance their commitment by underscoring their contributions and their vitality to the organization and society. The crisis, too, may induce a critical reassessment of the ongoing relationship between the state and the dominant family houses in the private sector and ease the emergence of entrepreneurs.

In 2008, Bayt.com surveyed 2,927 employees across the region. It found (see Table 9.5) that top industries attracting talent are: banking/finance, telecommunications, energy and petrochemicals, airline, and construction. The sectors which experience shortages in skilled labor are found to be healthcare and medical service, education, aerospace, and agriculture. The industries that lack domestic talent are government/ civil service, aerospace, education/academia, and healthcare/medical services. Most of the industries that are successful in attracting talent globally are the same as those which generally attract talent. Interestingly, the survey found that jobs that were sought more by jobseekers and employers alike are almost identical (e.g., information technology, banking/finance, engineering/automotive/construction/oil and gas, sales/marketing). The results indicate that the region experiences shortages not only in emerging (e.g., telecommunication, banking, aerospace, healthcare, etc.) but also in traditional industries (agriculture, construction, education, etc.).

Table 9.5 The state of talent in the regions

State of talent	Ranking order
1. Top talent-attracting industries	Banking/Finance, Information Technology, Telecommunications, Oil, Gas and Petrochemicals, Airline, Construction
2. Top sectors with shortage of skilled labor	Healthcare/Medical services, Education/Academia, Aerospace, Agriculture/Forestry
3. Top industries lacking domestic talent	Government/ Civil Service, Aerospace, Education/Academia, Healthcare/Medical services
4. Top sectors sourcing talent internationally	Information Technology, Education/Academia, Oil, Gas and Petrochemicals, Telecommunications, Banking/Finance
5. Top industries successfully attracting global talent	Banking/Finance, Oil, Gas, and Petrochemicals, Information Technology, Construction
6. Top industries unsuccessful in attracting global talent	Market Research, Pharmaceuticals, Charity/Voluntary sector, Transport/Travel, Government/Civil service
7. Most sought-after positions by jobseekers	Information Technology, Banking/Finance, Engineering/ Automotive/Construction/Oil and Gas, Sales/Marketing, Architect/Interior Design
8. Most sought-after positions by employers	Information Technology, Banking/Finance, Engineering/ Automotive/Construction/Oil and Gas, Sales/Marketing, HR/Training

Source: www.bayt.com, 2008. Top industries in the Middle East.

No doubt, most governments in the region invest significant amounts of their resources in developing and managing human talent. In fact, countries in the region, individually and collectively, realize that developing, energizing, and effectively deploying and utilizing their workforce, is the only vital strategy to transferring their economies into a global player. The fact remains that countries in the region differ in their strategies and capacities to develop and deploy human capital. Furthermore, almost all of them, especially in the Arab world, face formidable hurdles in coping with global challenges and the need to diversify their economies and provide sound economic foundations for future generations. These hurdles make utilizing or improving existing talent difficult. They are:

Trapped talent The public sector employs a large share of the workforce. This sector is generally characterized by bureaucracy and inefficiency. There is little concern, if any, for productivity, performance, and active participation in the organization's processes. Young employees who join the sector may initially exhibit enthusiasm and ambition. Due to the prevailing organizational culture and influence of their senior peers (socialization), their aspirations may not see fruition. Because of job security, relatively high salaries, and a work culture that sanctions indifference, the new talent is never utilized. That is, talented employees are there in body but not in spirit as their ambition fades.

Underutilized talent Unlike young nationals, expatriates face high insecurity in their employment. In many countries, expatriates are never granted citizenship and changing jobs is highly restricted by the sponsorship program; employees are not allowed to switch employers unless the original employer agrees. Likewise, in many cases these employees can be deported in a short time irrespective of their years of service or residency. This creates a situation where expatriates may not work up to their full potential and their talent is never fully utilized.

Low R&D budget The region ranks low relative to other regions in terms of scientific discovery and about .05 percent of its GDP is spent on R&D (World Economic Forum, 2009).

Lack of employee and employment protection under the law Compensation, for example, is not linked to performance and there is no uniformity or articulation of policy, even within the same firm, as different compensation packages are offered to employees depending on nationality and other non-work related factors (Mercer, 2008a).

The first two elements may indicate that there is no purposeful utilization and engagement of existing talent, while the last two obstruct the development and retention of talent. More importantly, the presence of these elements manifests not only a lack of articulated talent policy at the macro level, but also an absence of an understanding of the centrality of human capital in national and economic development and the necessity for integrating talent management in national and firm strategic planning. Ultimately, this exacerbates talent shortages and obstructs a competitive and entrepreneurial spirit.

Coping with mounting challenges

Both the *Arab Human Development Report 2009* (AHDR) and Middle East Youth Initiative underscore the urgency to utilize and engage human talent in order to compete globally and build sound economic foundations for the future. They highlight the fact that there is an inseparable relationship between quality of life and the development and nurturing of human talent. Without effective management and engagement of talent, the prospect for development becomes a distant reality. This is because mismanagement of talent leads not only to limited but also missed opportunities and a deepening general sense of insecurity and vulnerability.

Certainly, under the current conditions, the region's capacity to create wealth and jobs for its people is significantly curtailed. The AHDR reported that some 60 percent of the population is under 25 years of age, making the region one of the most youthful regions in the world and, simultaneously, it has the highest rate of unemployment in the world. This fact, coupled with weak private sectors and dependent entrepreneurs, demands a profound change in development outlook and priorities. Specifically, in terms of human capital, there is an urgent need to unlock human talent and unleash resources to optimize resource utilization and lift performance. Among the most pressing and feasible steps are:

1 *Reinvigorating talent multiplication.* Cheese, Thomas, and Craig (2007) argue that there is a valuable pool of workforce that is often ignored and must be discovered, developed, and deployed to create value for society and ensure competitiveness. In the Middle East, both the trapped and underutilized talent of employees, be they nationals or expatriates, must be recognized, motivated, and deployed to achieve important goals and effectively apply existing resources.

2 *Engage private sector and entrepreneurs.* Given access and opportunities to contribute freely to economic development and to compete globally will unleash talent and create the jobs essential for reducing unemployment.

3 *End the interlocking relationship between the state and family businesses.* Sager (2007) argues that the market in the region is dominated by state enterprises and family business groups. The latter depend on the government for contracts and business and tend to support government policies. He states, "The private sector is also dominated by family businesses that have a close relationship to the state, and it is this relationship which prescribes their attitude toward political reform." This relationship not only obstructs market functions but also tends to limit and constrain the emergence of entrepreneurs. Furthermore, due to their dependence on the state, family business groups have a tendency to engage in service activities, avoid innovative approaches, and oppose reforms in labor laws and regulations.

4 *Introduce compensation packages compatible with global trends.* Applying best practice in recruiting, developing, motivating, and retention is essential for deploying talent and minimizing turnover and chronic unemployment. There is a need to institutionalize assessment in recruiting and in linking rewards to performance.

5 *Invest in R&D.* Discovery and innovation is impossible without coherent policies for establishing an environment conducive to creative and critical thinking. The concept of championing new ideas and sponsoring competition projects should be promoted in all sectors, especially the private sector.

6 *Grant citizenship to expatriates with needed skills and knowledge.* Those expatriates who contribute to human capital formation and quality of life should be rewarded and be offered a citizenship option.

7 *Move away from state security towards human security.* Obsession with the power and security of the state often blinds governments from improving the general quality of life and prioritizing development issues. Freedom and peaceful resolutions to chronic political problems in the region may not only ease economic growth and regional integration but also contribute to the efficient utilization of existing resources and building of sound institutions.

8 *Diversify the economy and invest in knowledge-creation institutions.* This transformation is essential for job and wealth creation. It certainly enhances the ability of member countries to compete in the global marketplace, facilitates regional economic integration, and enlarges the labor market.

9 *Facilitate the emergence and growth of independent business and civic organizations.* In many cases, existing business organizations are an extension of the government. Having independent business organizations not only eases state and family business domination but also encourages market and labor reforms.

10 *Design growth strategies.* Policymakers and regional institutions should focus on devising investment and labor policies that ease domestic investment and integration. Building legal and market institutions that enable national entrepreneurs to mobilize resources and optimize access to domestic capital contributes to talent growth and sound development. Likewise, government and corporations alike should monitor trends in human capital and identify potential talent gaps.

11 *Build sound vocational and science and engineering institutions.* This should be done in cooperation with the private sector and labor and professional organizations. Having

these institutions may contribute to connecting learning to the job market and its evolving needs.

Conclusion

Certainly, talent management in the region is in its infancy stage. Neither companies nor countries appear to have even thought of talent strategy. At best, talent management is left to trial and error. This should not be a surprise as even in the United States talent management practices are still dysfunctional (Cappelli, 2008). Nevertheless, given the global economic downturn, increasing competition for talent workforce, and generally moderate economic growth coupled with a fast growth in the population in the region, an absence of a well formulated talent strategy at national and company level is a cause for concern. Indeed, the development and deployment of talent is impossible without first recognizing existing human capital and identifying potential talent gaps.

Unlike other developing regions, the Middle East has plenty of natural resources and untapped talent. These, along with its locational advantage, can enable the region to overcome difficulties and embark on the strategies necessary for unleashing the potential of its population. In fact, there has been an increasing interest in utilizing human capital and a growing belief within the region that the strength of any organization and nation stems primarily from its workforce. This development, as manifested in the establishment of knowledge cities and knowledge-creation institutions, inaugurates a departure from the traditional mode of thinking which has left development issues to state bureaucracy and politicians.

Researchers may find it interesting to tackle issues related to the role of expatriates in knowledge transfer and in sensitizing nationals to best practice. Furthermore, while impediments to effective talent cultivation in the region are widely covered, researchers should focus on talent retention and why certain qualities are needed more than others. In addition, social aspects in the region can facilitate and ease interaction and recognition, and researchers may think of ways to utilize existing social norms and informality in talent recognition, cultivation, deployment and retention.

In conclusion, the subject of TM in the region is of growing importance and in future it is expected to be one of the most important challenges the region faces. The question is not whether policymakers and senior business executives appreciate the importance of talent. Rather, the question is: Can the region, individually and collectively, focus its resources and efforts on moving ahead by engaging and deploying its human capital through designing and executing sound talent management models? The evidence and the arguments presented in this chapter provide a mixed picture. However, there is a strong possibility that the growing talent in the region will not be wasted and an opportunity for economic prosperity will not be missed.

Acknowledgment The author wishes to thank Professor Helen Bailie for her comments on an earlier version of this chapter.

References

Aguirre, DeAnne, Post, Laird, and Hewlett, Sylvia (2009). The Talent Innovation Imperative. *Strategy and Business*, Autumn (56), 38–41.

Ali, Abbas J. (1995). Management in a Sheiko-Capitalism. *International Studies of Management and Organization*, 25 (3), 3–6.

Ali, Abbas J. (2008). *Business and Management Environment in Saudi Arabia: Challenges and Opportunities for Multinational Corporations*. New York: Routledge.

Amirshahi, M. (1998). Empirical study of managerial value systems and decision making styles among the managers in Iran. Unpublished Ph.D. dissertation. Curtin University, Perth, Western Australia.

Arab Human Capital Challenge (2009). Mohammed Bin Rasheed Al Maktoum Foundation. Dubai, UAE.

Assaad, Ragui, and Roudi-Fahimi, Farzaneh (2007). *Youth in the Middle East and North Africa: Demographic opportunity or challenge?* Population Reference Bureau. Washington, D.C.

A.T. Kearney (2007). The shifting geography of offshoring—the 2009 global services location index. Chicago.

A.T. Kearney (2009). *Building the Optimal Global Footprint*. Chicago.

A.T. Kearney (2010) *Global Expansion: A Must for Retailers*. A.T. Kearney Study. Chicago.

Bayt.com (2009). *Employee Motivation Study*. Available at: www.http://www.bayt.com/

Behrendt, Christina, Haq, Tariq, and Kamal, Noura (2009). *The impact of the financial and economic crisis on Arab states: Considerations on employment and social protection policy response*. Beirut, Lebanon: *International Labor Organization*.

Boer, Kito and Turner, John (2007). Beyond oil: Reappraising the Gulf States. *McKinsey Quarterly*. (Special edition), pp. 7–17.

Böhme, Markus, Chiarella, Daniele, and Lemerle, Matthieu (2008). The growing opportunity for investment banks in emerging markets. *McKinsey Quarterly*, 7, 3–9.

Bush, George W. (2008, May 18). Speech at world economic forum. Available at: http://georgew bush-whitehouse.archives.gov/news/releases/2008/05/print/20080518-6.html.

Business Intelligence Middle East (2009, June 11). Gulf companies view talent management as more important since economic crisis. Available at: http://www.bi-me.com/doc_print.php?id=37769.

Cappelli, Peter (2008). Talent management for the twenty-first century. *Harvard Business Review*, 86 (3), 74–81.

Cheese, Peter, Thomas, Robert, and Craig, Elizabeth (2007). *The Talent Powered Organization*. Philadelphia: Kogan Page.

Dewhurst, Martin, Guthridge, Matthew and Mohr, Elizabeth (2009, November). Motivating people: Getting beyond money. *McKinsey Quarterly*, 1–5.

Dhillon, Navtej (2009). *The Middle East in a Post-Oil Boom Era?*. Brookings Institute, Washington D.C.

Ghosh, D. (2009, August 16). Mideast job market feels buoyant. *Times of Oman*. Available at: www.timesofoman.com.

Griml, Guy (2008, May 9). We hereby declare the establishment of a high-tech empire. *Haaretz*. Available at: http://www.haaretz.co.il/hasen/spages/981415.html.

Hay Group (2008). *World Pay Report*. Singapore.

Hay Group (2009). *Lift off: Unleashing Performance in the Middle East*. Hay Group: Dubai, UAE.

International Labor Organization (2007). Discrimination at work in the Middle East and North Africa. Available at: http://www.ilo.org/declaration/info/factsheets/lang—en/docNameWCMS_DECL_FS_92_EN/index.htm

International Labor Organization (2009). *Global Employment Trends*. International Labour Office, Geneva.

IMF (2009, May 10). Middle East, North Africa weathering global crisis. Available at: http://www.imf.org/external/pubs/ft/survey/so/2009/car051009a.htm.

KOF (2009). Globalization index. Available at: http://globalization.kof.ethz.ch/

Mercer (2008a, April 21). Middle East survey–increase in expatriate population fuels growth in western-style pay and benefit. Available at: http://www.mercer.com/print.htm?indContentType=100&id Content=1304160&indBodyType=D&reference=

Mercer (2008b). Spoken word: Total rewards challenges in the emerging markets of the Middle East. Available at: http://www.mercer.com/print.htm?indContentType=100&idContent=1301090&indBodyType=D&reference=true

Middle East Youth Initiative (2009). *Missed by the boom, hurt by the bust: Making markets work for young people in the Middle East*. Brookings Institute: Washington, D.C.

Pradhan, Samir (2009). Global protectionism threatens Middle East's world trade. Available at: www.grc.ae.

Ready, Douglas, Hill, Linda, and Conger, Jay (2008). Winning the race. *Harvard Business Review*, 87(3), 63–70.

Sager, Abdulaziz (2007). The private sector in the Arab World—road map towards reform. In *Arab Reform Initiative*, 10 December 2007. [http://arab-reform.net/IMG/pdf/ARB19_Gulf_Sager_ENG.pdf].

Shambayati, Hootan (1994). The rentier state, interest groups, and the paradox of autonomy: State and business in Turkey and Iran. *Comparative Politics*, 26 (3), 307–331.

Shrieh, Ali (2009, September 12). Lack of qualified legal experts costs the Arab World $20 b a year. *Asharq Al-Awsat*, No. 11246. Available: www.aawsat.com.

UN (2009). *Human Development Report 2009*. Available at: http://hdr.undp.org/en/reports/global/hdr2009/

UN (2009). *The Millennium Development Goals*. Available at: http://www.un.org/millenniumgoals/pdf/MDGReport_2009_ENG.pdf

UNCTD (2009). World Investment Report 2009. New York: UN.

UNDP (2009). *Arab Human Development Report 2009*. New York: UN.

World Bank (2007). *Middle East and North Africa 2007: Economic development and prospects*. Washington D.C.: The World Bank.

World Bank (2009). *Global Economic Prospects 2009: Commodities at the Crossroads*. Washington D.C.: The World Bank.

World Economic Forum (2009). World economic forum in the Middle East: Roadmap for participants. Available at: http://www.weforum.org/pdf/Middle_East/MERoadmap2009.pdf

Talent management in Central and Eastern Europe

VLAD VAIMAN AND NIGEL HOLDEN

'On the mental map which people carry in their heads Western and Eastern Europe are not just determined by points of the compass. They are terms of orientation in a shifting intellectual landscape, where all bearings are relative and paradoxes abound'.

Norman Davies (2007)

Introduction

In this chapter we address the issue of talent management (TM) in the countries of Central and Eastern Europe (CEE). We will argue that the CEE countries are beset with considerable contextual complexities, both culture-related and institutional in character, and that these complexities combine to make the TM landscape unusually challenging to apprehend both in theory and practice. The scene will be set with reference to the contentious issue of region's socialist legacy. From here the discussion will move forward to a commentary on the labour market as well as leadership issues and performance management as a prelude to a section reviewing the status of TM in the CEE countries. This section, built around our telephone interviews in summer 2009 with three HR managers with specific responsibility for their companies' HR practices, including TM, throughout the CEE countries. Their companies are a US-based MNC, an Austrian automotive components supplier and a Danish industrial enterprise.

We highlight five aspects of their concerns, which help to frame the TM landscape in the CEE region:

- identification of talent
- expatriation issues
- English-language competence
- CEE as a TM learning context
- local perceptions of foreign firms as employers.

The key objective of this chapter is to outline the essential complexities of social, cultural and institutional influences on TM as a philosophy and practice in CEE countries. Particular attention will be paid to (a) human factors that give individual countries and the region a distinctive character from a TM perspective, and (b) three foreign firms, whose contrasting experiences of – and diversity of reactions to – their CEE employees and potential recruits highlights, on the one hand, enlightenment and, on the other, startling parochialism.

Talent management in CEE countries: the tricky issue of the socialist legacy

It is no longer contested that HR assumptions and practices differ significantly from one country to another (for an overview, see: Brewster, Mayrhofer, and Morley, 2004). It surely follows that talent management must vary too. We see this very clearly in the CEE region – 'that zone of hard experience' (Davies, 2007) – where country-specific factors reveal distinctive and in some cases possibly unique 'embeddings' which influence perceptions of talent and its management. It is some 20 years since the CEE countries rid themselves of their Moscow-oriented socialist regimes. All have espoused the concept of the market economy, but modern business practices – from Frankfurt an der Oder on the western periphery of the socialist world to Vladivostok at its eastern extremity – are still influenced by the socialist attitudes and assumptions. For that reason, and despite the fact that many former socialist CEE countries are now members of the EU, the region was characterized as creating a kind of capitalist system without capitalists (Eyal, Szelényi, and Townsley, 1998).

We contend that this description still has force. After all, there is no commentator on the CEE economies and management systems who has declared one country – let alone the entire region – to have completed the transition to the market economy. Yet few people, and in that we include the citizens of the CEE countries, would disagree with Zupan and Kase (2005) that the region is endowed with a well-educated, knowledgeable, and skilled workforce. It is against this background that we need to understand TM in this region where:

- 'In living memory *millions* have been victims of forced migrations, interethnic violence, religious intolerance, political persecution, genocidal war; have seen their countries disappear, their borders change.
- History is ever-present and memories are long.
- The communist experiment still conditions mentalities and even creates nostalgia'

(Holden, 2002).

To these points we can usefully add that 'the differences of languages and culture between the peoples and cultures of the region . . . seem just as striking as any alleged similarities' (Lord, 2000). In short, we are concerned with a group of countries that not only defy tricky classification among themselves, but are also not well understood in Western Europe, let alone farther afield (Crampton, 2004). Overall, we agree with Hollinshead (2010: 174) that 'in the post-communist era, the activities of personnel management cannot be isolated from broader societal issues'. This chapter reflects this perspective rather than one that rests on certain assumptions about talent management, which in our view cannot be easily mapped on to the CEE countries (for an overview of current issues in talent management see Tarique and Schuler, forthcoming; Schoemaker and Jonker, 2005).

Management scholars love to cluster regions on the basis of a narrow group of features of shared identity (Sebestyen, 2009). In the case of the countries of Central and Eastern Europe this is an especially fraught issue whether from historical, geographical, political, economic, cultural and even *emotional* perspectives. To underline the geographical complexities: if readers care to put the terms 'map of Central and Eastern Europe' into a search engine, they will find that there is no agreement even among geographers as to what countries – specifically those closest to Mother Russia – to include. Hollinshead (2010: 173) has noted that definitions of the CEE region 'may vary but typically include the Czech Republic, Slovakia, Hungary, Poland, Albania, Bulgaria, Romania and the countries constituting the former Yugoslavia, as well as the former German Democratic Republic'. Consistent with that we shall in this chapter take a pragmatic line. Our purview does not embrace Russia, but includes the countries which were coercively created on the Soviet model after the Second World War, which today are held to be 'former socialist countries', 'transitional economies' and even 'emerging markets', and some of which are EU members. But these labels are but flags of convenience, as it were.

By this stage it is clear that the CEE countries constitute a TM landscape of cultural, geopolitical and institutional features of exceptional complexity. Certainly, the region is not to be approached by the normal route: namely the imposition of standard Western frameworks, which make no allowance for local mood and tone and definitely not for historical legacy (Hofstede, 2007). For his part Hollinshead (2010: 173–174) notes that regarding HR issues in general 'a number of trajectories can currently be discerned':

- HR issues are directly associated with the transition.
- There is a greater interest in the micro-level: 'the socially embedded behaviours of managerial and other actors at the workplace level'.
- Interest in the issue of 'convergence of employment practices in eastern and western enterprises': convergence, though inconsistent across the region, being connected to EU equal opportunities legislation.
- Through joint ventures (JVs), 'attention has been given to international staff mobility and knowledge diffusion' (p. 174).

In addition, there is a trend, not so obvious to the outside world, in which 'the position of female employees has become more precarious', which is a nominal reversal of socialist employment concepts that encouraged gender equality. In case, incidentally, there should be readers who consider that we are placing too much emphasis on the potency of the socialist legacy, we quote this finding from a 2008 article about management in East Germany.
A survey of entrepreneurs and managing directors of companies with 50 to 1,000 employees established that 'East German top management is to an astonishing extent influenced by the *past*, thanks to the reproduction of economic elites who already held responsible positions before 1989' (Martens, 2008; original emphasis). Neither in former GDR nor in other transition countries is the *ancien régime* yet dead and buried (see Davies, 2007; Hroch, 2000); its effects and behaviours are still in evidence, as we shall find. We now begin our quest of TM as a concept and practice in the CEE countries by highlighting the labour market.

Labor market in CEE

Since the early 1990s there has been de-regulation, privatization and the move from an economic system with highly centralized control (and massive inefficiencies) to the market-economy system. The transition has been arduous, painful and for many unjust.

There are now marked differences in wage levels and the wage distribution. On the top of the list of the countries with the most unequal wage distribution stands Azerbaijan, followed by Russia, Armenia, Estonia and Moldova. Surprisingly, in Macedonia wage distribution has been identified as being most equal of the CEE countries (Heinegg, Melzig, and Sprout, 2007). Regarding wages, most of the CEE countries have not yet reached the real wage level before transition, although they have been rising in the last years throughout the region. In 2007, the Bulgarian and Macedonian real wages were about 55 per cent of their respective real wages in 1989. Moreover, the Czech Republic, Poland and Hungary have already exceeded 1989 levels (Heinegg *et al.*, 2007).

As the state has receded from being the sole employer to one of several types, the region's entrepreneurs have become very significant employers. Nowadays, small and medium-sized enterprises (SMEs) represent a sizeable share of employment in Central and Eastern Europe. For instance in Poland, Latvia, Slovenia and Macedonia, SME employment rates account for more than 60 per cent of total employment. In contrast to SME employment trends, self-employment is at a very low level. In 2005, a United Nations Economic Commission for Europe study evaluated self-employment rates of 1 per cent in Belarus, 9 per cent in Bulgaria and 17 per cent in Poland (Heinegg *et al.*, 2007).

Not surprisingly employment rates vary widely in the region of Central and Eastern Europe. In 2005, countries that have witnessed low but rising unemployment rates were Slovenia (6.3 per cent), Moldova (7.3 per cent), Romania (7.7 per cent) and the Czech Republic (7.9 per cent). Bosnia-Herzegovina (46.6 per cent) and Macedonia (37.3 per cent) had the highest unemployment rates, which were expected to rise even further. Other countries with worrying and growing unemployment rates close to 20 per cent were Poland, Slovakia as well as Serbia and Montenegro (Heinegg *et al.*, 2007). Particularly, young persons under 25, elderly, and long-time unemployed were still are affected by unemployment to the highest degree (Glazer, n.d.).

In Bosnia-Herzegovina, almost 46 per cent of the total unemployed people are between 15 and 24 years of age. Approximately 40 per cent of people aged 15 to 24 are unemployed in Poland and Slovakia, and a staggering 50 per cent in Macedonia and Serbia and Montenegro. The situation looks a bit better in the Czech Republic and Slovenia with 16 per cent of the aforementioned age group being unemployed. In such circumstances many young people try and study hard to secure opportunities to get placements at universities and business schools abroad, and notably at those in 'old' EU countries.

Central and Eastern Europe has seen significant labour migration especially since EU enlargement in 2004 (*The Economist*, 2009; International Labour Organization, 2007). Taking the example of Poland, the CEE country with the most perturbing unemployment situation about 7 years ago – employment figures have started recovering in the last 4 years, but labour migration of more than one million Polish nationals is having an enormous impact on these figures (International Labour Organization, 2007). For a majority of the CEE countries, including those which joined the European Union in 2004 and 2007, barriers to international mobility are mostly removed. While most move across Europe to get seasonal work in the agricultural sector or obtain low-paid jobs in factories as well as in still fairly labour-intensive sectors such as railways and health service, there is also a brain drain of mainly young people seeking research and teaching opportunities in universities or offering special knowledge to technology businesses. From a TM perspective, there are strong grounds for suggesting that the key feature of the CEE labour market is that it generally fails to make itself attractive to a sizeable proportion of the young and talented.

In concluding this section, we should note a very obvious and still in a sense new feature of the labour market. In socialist times millions of people in CEE countries were compelled to learn Russian. Since the beginning of the transformation countless numbers – especially younger people – have enthusiastically learnt English to enhance their opportunities for study and even (permanent) residence abroad or to work for a foreign-owned company in their own country. They see this as enhancing their talents. Given that so few expatriate managers learn any language of the CEE region, foreign firms are *very dependent* on the English language skills and/or German language skills of their local employees. We will come back to this point in one of our subsequent sections.

Leadership in CEE

The concept of leadership in post-socialist Europe is a problematical one. For decades the word connoted exclusive rule and control by the Communist Party or nominal equivalent (i.e., Socialist Unity Party in the GDR, the Polish Workers' Party in Poland, etc.) and subservience by the rest of the population. The Communist Party operated in effect as a country's personnel department. Any concept of talent was subordinated to political requirements in that loyalty to the Party transcended other considerations: in other words, the most important talent or set of talents was the one that could further the aims of the socialist state. Talent, we might say, had to be seen to be literally 'politically correct'. Those with the politically correct attitudes and commitment formed the *nomenklatura*,[1] the exclusive talent pool which served as 'a magic circle of top bosses' (Davies, 1984).

The *nomenklatura* system is the socialist correlate of talent management as succession 'of the right people'. Other talents – for instance, for producing scurrilous (i.e. 'anti-socialist') literature or films – could easily be construed as 'deviant', and lead to unpleasant interviews with the secret police, incarceration or worse. Such forbidding circumstances meant that 'everyone suspected everyone else, and the mistrust this bred was the foundation of social existence' (Funder, 2004). An outcome was that people in general had to develop a special talent for survival in a socialist country: this was a talent for playing the system (Fink, Holden, and Lehmann, 2007).

The upshot was that the socialist system produced a workforce that was in general bored, uncommitted and cynical. Except for those who wielded considerable power, the workforce – whether in factories, coalmines or government offices – performed their jobs with a minimum of information and deprived of the opportunity to make any decision or take any kind of initiative. When the socialist countries collapsed at the end of the 1980s followed by the once mighty Soviet Union in 1991, there was wide-spread belief in the West that the populations, being exposed to the 'joys' of the market-economy system, would soon abandon the mental habits and attitudes acquired under totalitarianism.

But already in 1994 a Harvard Business School working paper argued that the principles of four business areas were especially problematical for the former socialist countries of CEE to absorb and apply: financial management, business strategy, marketing know-how and HRM (Aguilar, Loveman, and Vlachoutsicos, 1994). Ten years later a study of HRM development in the Czech Republic would reveal confusions about the distinction among terms like labour relations, employment relations and industrial relations (Koubek and Vlachtova, 2004); and two years after that a survey of Poland, whilst noting that that country's 'prospects are bright and its problems solvable', pinpointed weaknesses of skills in so-called 'soft management' (*The Economist*, 2006).

This same survey, incidentally, cited a foreign observer who characterized the Polish idea of being a boss as 'still sitting in a big office being rude to people' (*The Economist*, 2006). This is pure unreconstructed socialist management. So it is today when the difference between salaries of managers and employees remains relatively small, the power differentials are still quite high. Leadership in this context is about the exercise of power and has little to do with delegation on the one hand, or coaching and team-building on the other. Management development, therefore, is definitely not a priority for CEE managers nor do they seem inclined to recruit first-class managers externally. According to a survey conducted by Preveden (2003), while 52 per cent of EU managers are recruited externally on a regular basis, only 20 per cent of the CEE managers state that they are often using external recruiting. This suggests that there is a marked preference for talent as a potentially less threatening internal resource.

From Romania comes a revealing observation by a local management educator: 'A problem for Romanians is that we don't have models of good democratic leadership. Leaders are always presented as tough and strong by the media, but these may be the wrong values . . . and there's the problem that leaders are generally seen as crooks because all of that's going on since Communism' (Dalton and Kennedy, 2007). And who is to say that Western values as to the nature of business leadership are necessarily correct in the CEE countries?

Performance management in CEE

To date, a number of performance management systems have been implemented in a variety of private organizations throughout Central and Eastern Europe. A recent study by the Amrop Hever Group indicates that almost half of the leading investors operating in CEE perceive performance management as important, and more than 40 per cent as a critical competency that can increase organizational performance in the region. Additional findings showed that the majority of organizations in the area already possess this key competency, but its full potential has not been realized in many cases. The current economic downturn, therefore, should be seen as an incentive to invest in performance management to ensure long-term success (Touiller, 2009).

The importance of these arrangements is that they expose employees to procedures for increasing organizational performance, including regular talent reviews and well-structured retention plans which identify the key contributors to the company's performance, such as top talents, best performers and high potentials, whilst fostering promotion and job enrichment. But most CEE organizations are as yet a long way from a situation in which it is a standard practice for the existence of procedures aimed at aligning individual achievement goals with corporate strategy.

There is also an interesting twist in all this. It is not by any means the case that expatriate managers (e.g., of foreign-owned companies) are necessarily seen as desirable role models. Their way of entering and taking over businesses in the virtually defunct communist countries was seen as a form of 'colonialism' (Martens, 2008). In this vein in Poland expatriate managers have been perceived to be aloof, authoritarian and arrogant (Allen, 2003). It would be naïve to think that such attitudes were strictly confined to Poland among the former socialist countries. Thus, expatriate managers can encounter resistance to 'real' Western management years after the collapse of the communist system (Hurt and Hurt, 2005).

HRM and talent management in CEE countries today: an overview

Talent management, as it is commonly identified, in Central and Eastern Europe is a somewhat new concept both to scholars and practitioners (Knez and Ruse, 2004). Most extant academic work concentrates on either case studies of Western MNC subsidiaries or general descriptions of HRM and HR practices in specific CEE countries, sometimes just briefly mentioning talent management issues (see Kiriazov *et al.*, 2000; Zupan, 1998; May *et al.*, 1998; Soulsby and Clark, 1998; Shekshnia, 1998; Crow, 1998; Tung and Havlovic, 1996; Koubek and Brewster, 1995; Brewster, 1995; Bangert and Poor, 1993; Puffer, 1993). This is to be expected for reasons which are by now obvious – it is largely foreign-owned firms that grasp the nature of TM as good managerial practice.

In reality, a commonly accepted importance given in the West to the issues of strategic HRM in general and talent management in particular has not entirely penetrated thick barriers of traditionalism in CEE organizations, especially those owned by their respective states. Such organizations used to have a highly standardized and bureaucratic attitude towards personnel issues (Weinsten and Obloj, 2002). This sort of approach can be explained by the CEE legacy of the central planning system on the one hand and by a full integration of the personnel function with the firm-level Communist party structures on the other (Sarapata, 1992; Vlachoutsicos and Lawrence, 1990).

One of the major challenges that face companies in CEE countries nowadays is their attempts to transform traditional personnel (administrative) activities to those of a strategic nature that add value to the organization (Weinsten and Obloj, 2002). And although the need to move from purely administrative to more strategic HRM (and talent management issues) has already emerged, there is still little evidence that this shift has actually materialized. In the past ten years, not many positive changes in this regard have been recorded – there is still significant lack of consistency in HR strategies, HR managers are often not members of top management teams, and HR policies and practices that support business needs are not efficiently implemented (Zupan, 1998; Brewster *et al.*, 2000; Zupan and Kase, 2005).

More meaningful and effective transformation of the HR function (and as a consequence, HR policies and procedures related to talent management) could be observed in CEE-based subsidiaries of foreign MNCs, which tend to bring their own HRM models to host organizations (Mills, 1998; Zupan and Kase, 2005). The first important steps taken by foreign MNCs include transformation of selection procedures, compensation, performance management system, and other policies and practices necessary for successful integration of the host organization into the MNC. According to Taylor and Walley (2002), these models are usually accepted by host organizations on either an 'as is' basis with no local modification or after a period of strong resistance. These variations do result in significant differences in how these models are adopted and utilized in various industries within a country, as well as between CEE countries (Zupan and Kase, 2005).

As just mentioned, the approaches to talent management in CEE are as diverse as the countries themselves. For example, comparing Slovenia and Estonia, Alas and Svetlik (2004) notice that there are significant differences in such important HR policies and practices as recruitment, training and development, flexible work arrangements, professionalization of personnel and HR functions, and retention. In addition, it is important to remember that organizations in some CEE countries (such as Poland, Slovenia, and the Czech Republic) have started implementing major changes in their HRM policies a bit earlier than organizations in other parts of CEE (Estonia, Latvia, Lithuania), and therefore, the level of advancement in these policies is also quite different. All in all, however, most CEE companies with a majority of domestic ownership still employ mainly centralized and administrative HR practices, thereby disregarding or neglecting strategic issues of talent management.

Despite visible differences between the CEE countries in terms of their approaches to what in the West is referred to as talent management efforts, there are two factors that distinguish nearly all CEE organizations from their Western counterparts. The first issue concerns both the perceived importance of HRM and the subsequent level of investment in human resources, which is significantly higher in the West (Alas and Svetlik, 2004; Zupan and Kase, 2005). On an individual level, it is possible to notice that job security seems to be a common theme for Eastern European employees in general, and they seem to value it significantly higher than most of their Western colleagues (Fey, Björkman, and Pavlovskaya, 2000).

The second issue is of vital importance to local employers as well as foreign firms making significant investments in CEE countries. Retaining young people, who – unlike their parents and grandparents – have been partially educated in other countries, notably in Western Europe and to a lesser extent in North America, represents a serious challenge. These young people speak and write good English and do not want to remain in their native countries. They want to seek a new life elsewhere and plan their careers accordingly. For this reason, to cite an Austrian economics body,[2] referring to a consultancy survey about talent management in the CEE countries, the pool of high potentials is dropping across the region in general and so is loyalty to employers. Hence there is much job-hopping. Not surprisingly, the issues of human capital, and particularly talent management, in CEE organizations will become more and more crucial as years go by (Svejnar, 2002).

Three TM perspectives

It was against this somewhat perturbing background that we invited three HR managers of foreign concerns to share their impressions of talent management in CEE countries. The interviews, conducted by telephone, took place between June and August 2009. Of the three

HR managers, only one was willing for his company to be identified. This company, hereafter Company A, happens to be the Austrian arm of IBM (an organization well known for imposing its own systems on local employees). The second company is a major Austrian concern in the automotive sector, and the third is a major Danish industrial corporation. All these companies have substantial worldwide operations and have HR managers responsible for CEE employees. None of three managers is resident in any CEE country, but all make frequent visits to the region.

Having established this preliminary information, we asked each of the three informants questions to elicit comments on five issues with respect to talent management in the CEE countries:

- identification of talent
- expatriation issues
- English language competence
- CEE as a TM learning context
- local perceptions of foreign firms as employers.

The questions elicited both company-specific answers as well as some impressionistic responses. As we shall see, our very small sample of respondents by no means gave uniform answers.

Identification of talent

There was no uniformity among our informant companies. Company A uses instruments, including individual development plans, which are based on the concept of MBO and on performance, which focus on employees' potential. The aim is to identify high-potential employees. Anyone who emerges as having 'top talent' will be earmarked for prioritized development. It is not necessarily the case that such top talent will find their career limited to the CEE economic-linguistic zone. In a not dissimilar way Company B identifies employees with talent in companies that it has taken over in CEE countries. These employees will be considered to be 'the best locally available' and as such will be groomed for future management responsibility in the region and not always in their own country. Such people will eventually take over from expatriate managers from the company's headquarters in Austria.

So, both Company A and Company B are adopting HR strategies that are concerned with pinpointing an inevitably small number of employees who have been identified with talent for regional or even international management responsibilities. The TM strategy of Company C is rooted in quite different concerns which are CEE-specific and which make TM 'more complicated and more challenging than in Western Europe'. Company C has recognized that young people, in particular, want a career path with a strong international component and, as a long-term goal, the opportunity to work 'in the West' – in other words, to seek a new life in a new country where life's prospects are seen to be better. For this reason there is a high degree of job-hopping among ambitious local staff working for international companies (such people are not interested in working for local companies).

This leads to the situation of companies losing good staff in whom there has been a certain amount of investment (e.g., through development initiatives in the local country as well as in Denmark), to companies who offer an improved salary and possibly more international engagement. In this sense the company finds that TM in CEE means that HR initiatives designed for other countries or regions *must* be modified for CEE countries, where the ultimate career aim is not so much to get to the top of the company as to leave the home country. One initiative of Company C, which is strongly committed to the notion of employer branding, is to organize various recruitment events in CEE cities which will allow it to build up a database of potential employees, who may be amenable to approach in the future.

Expatriation issues

Company C does not send managers to CEE countries on an expatriate basis, so we can only supply the views of the two companies in our small sample. Company A has years of experience of expatriation, whereby managers from major centres, including corporate headquarters, are assigned to given countries for a few years. But within this globally integrated concern expatriation is in decline. The reason for this is that the company is creating major regional hubs and placing functions where the competencies are. For instance, HR hub may be located in country X, while the operations hub is in country Y. This development has led to less expatriation in its traditional sense but to more opportunities for virtual expatriation. In other words, CEE employees, identified as talented, may therefore find themselves attached to a hub which is geographically remote from their country (or city) of residence.

Company B also has a tradition of sending expatriate managers all over the world, including Russia, Hungary, Germany, the USA, etc. At present there are about 130 people (out of a total workforce of 5,800) working abroad on their expatriate assignments. Expatriation is underpinned by two important objectives:

- to roll out their expertise to other places of the world from the headquarters – through knowledge and technology transfer, and
- to support projects through coaching, leadership, communication, etc.

English-language competence

All foreign companies operating in CEE countries are overwhelmingly dependent on local employees with a reasonably good to excellent command of English. Both companies A and B claimed though that competence in English was not a central issue in TM. Company A even maintained that 'sometimes people get to commanding roles without good English', although it is frankly hard to imagine this. A not dissimilar position is held by Company B, according to which, 'while knowledge of English is important, it is not our first consideration. In general, all we require is basic English – for us, as an engineering company, technical expertise is more important'. Against that, the company concedes that in CEE countries 'even basic English may be a problem'. Therefore, it does in fact seek to recruit 'people with above-average English qualifications'. But while finding these people is important, it is claimed, it is not the main concern: 'being there for our customer is our first priority, independently of location'. All this suggests not only inconsistency in policy, but also highlights a serious problem for Company B: how to source the kind of talented people for their CEE business operations who do in fact have a good command of English.

Once again the point of departure for Company C is rather different. English is the working language of the company, so all locally recruited staff must have some competence in English. It has emerged, however, that many of the better salesmen are less proficient in English. Whilst this may not affect their job performance *per se*, it handicaps the people concerned because they cannot take part in training programmes in Denmark – even for one which is in English for sales and negotiation – or other cross-border initiatives. So far the company has not found a workable solution to the problem. Unlike other classes of employees, such as those in managerial positions and most of the young graduates, the salesmen have limited English and restricted international experience, if any.

CEE as a TM learning context

Company A's most significant deduction about CEE countries is that there are 'very few people' in CEE with the potential to 'become executives in other world markets . . . since both their talent and potential for growth may be far below those of their Western European counterparts'. Here we are talking about a huge company with highly standardized HRM procedures from recruitment to personnel development. It must be concluded that these procedures are not readily adjustable to suit potential – indeed actual – employees from CEE countries. So it is not entirely surprising to discover that CEE people are less rigorously screened than their counterparts in, say, Western Europe. Hence, the company's approach is to base its TM policies on 'the immediate business needs' in the region.

Company B, for its part, prides itself on having a system for talent management recognition and development that would be acceptable worldwide. Yet, as with company A, it is conscious of a general qualitative difference in TM in the CEE region. For the way it runs its business in this part of the world the priority is to find talent in the form of proven technical expertise and experience. Managerial talent, according to the company, is in short supply: 'Sometimes people there are surprised when asked for their opinion or asked to participate in the managerial decision making'.

Company C's main discovery is that young graduates, educated abroad to some extent and speaking good English, are much focused on their own careers, whereby the attraction of joining a foreign company is that it is a stepping stone rather than an end in itself. In this sense the job market in CEE countries has a built-in 'distortion'. The major practical lesson for the company has been to develop initiatives which motivate young recruits so that they identity their career aspirations with the company. The company offers *ab initio* the prospect of a career with international opportunities. Thus, the young recruits take part in various kinds of corporate activities (e.g., development programmes in Denmark or elsewhere where they get to see the company and colleagues from other countries from new perspectives). But, in the words of the company, 'it is a slow process'.

Another key learning point concerns securing the trust of employees. The company has found that the notion of an appraisal as a confidential discussion for the benefit of the individual is still largely alien. For older staff, brought up in a socialist regime, the prospect of a confidential discussion with one in authority would not suggest a constructive experience. So, the company conducts 'development interviews' instead, designing them to be motivating.

Local perceptions of foreign firms as employers

Both Company B and Company C are aware that foreign firms are sometimes viewed as exploiters. Company C does not really recognize this, suggesting that local perceptions are directly related to the degree of progress towards the market-economy system. Poland, Hungary, Czech Republic and Slovenia are cited as the most advanced countries by Company A: countries where 'there is less need for patronizing and closely supervising those [local employees]'. Company B is aware that there exist negative local perceptions, but they are of no major concern. The company believes that it does a good job in the CEE countries as far as TM is concerned; one aspect of which is to have a hands-off approach as much as possible. This broadly reflects the view of Company C, aware of concrete cases among other companies who have earned a reputation for heavy-handed management approaches to its CEE employees. But these cases 'apply especially in countries where progress to the market economy has been less smooth'.

Discussion

Let us now use the testimonies of our three informant companies to reflect on the TM landscape in CEE. Whilst they constitute a very small sample, we are nevertheless able to draw some important conclusions about their behaviours, practices and attitudes. First we may take it as read that TM is a new concept in these countries; it is a part of the managerial package coming with foreign – notably Western – employers. They bring with them the alien notion that their local employees can be viewed as talent not for the state, not for some political entity, but for a foreign company headquartered in a distant country. But Company A and Company B make it plain that they do not consider the CEE countries to be a particularly good source of talented people. Indeed Company A as much as admitted that in those countries whose progress towards the market economy has been slower it is necessary to be 'patronizing'.

It comes as no surprise that Company A finds it so difficult to source people in the CEE countries – for them perhaps *the most important talent is that which predestines individuals to be able to adapt to the company's tried and tested procedures*. No wonder that it does not see the CEE as a significant talent pool for managerial succession, and that it is even prepared to compromise its normal standards. Company B, which prided itself on a world-wide TM system, was also not much different in attitude, finding that CEE is a poor hunting ground for managerial talent. The company in addition encountered retrenched attitudes that had not vanished from the socialist past ('people are surprised when asked for their opinion, or asked to participate in the managerial decision making').

What is also striking about Company A and Company B is the way in which they discussed their actual and potential CEE employees – not only somewhat dismissively, but almost exclusively in terms of the needs of company procedures, on the one hand, and business needs, on the other. Neither company gave the impression that it was close to its CEE workforce or indeed wanted to be so. A clue as to their detachment from their own employees arose in their vague and even contradictory attitudes about the desirable English-language competence of their CEE employees. This detachment is the metaphor of non-listening organizations. The fact too that it occurred neither to Company A nor to Company B that they might be perceived as indifferent or arrogant employers confirms their strong sense of untouchability. It is indeed difficult not to draw the conclusion that neither Company A nor Company B has learnt anything of practical significance in the CEE's TM landscape. All this stands in marked contrast to the Danish concern, Company C.

Of the three informant companies, only Company C gives the clear impression of being close to its CEE employees. It is the only one that appears to be with a key element of the *Zeitgeist*, whereby young people – in reality in their hundreds of thousands throughout the region – have a view of career development that is linked to working for foreign firms, which they view as catalysts to an international career and better life in general. Recognition of this fact made Company C introduce initiatives to make itself an employer that could to some extent appeal to these aspirations.

Compare this to Company A and Company B, which persuading themselves that CEE is low on talent, do not take any special initiatives, but compromise their own ideals. Company A, to use its own words, has introduced 'slack' into its TM practices, whilst Company B has opted for a 'hands-off' management approach. Both companies give the impression that CEE employees are overall not a good investment. What they may not have realized is that their attitudes of disdain will communicate themselves to their local employees. Company C with its commitment to employer branding can be said to have limited scope for negative perceptions based on sheer arrogance; no doubt Company A and Company B think that company branding is too sophisticated a concept for the benighted masses of former socialist countries to grasp.

We summarize our findings as follows. Company A is dominated by procedures, which have to be compromised because of the inferiority of local talent. Company B does not quite trust local talent, whilst Company C – by far the smallest of the three organisations – is the only one that attempts to accept local conditions as they are. This company builds its TM approach around younger people, trying to offer interesting careers to secure their loyalty. Thus of the three companies, Company C is the only one that takes a pragmatic, even experimental approach (which is a hallmark of Danish management, as it happens).

Conclusions

We were at pains at the beginning of this chapter to prepare the ground by discussing at some length the context of the TM landscape in Central and Eastern Europe. We touched albeit briefly on the legacy of the region's terrible twentieth century, the complex cultural and linguistic diversity as well as the thorny issue of governance structures. Beyond that, we alerted readers to what might be called 'the dark side' of TM in the CEE region: namely, an insidious arrogance on the part of foreign employers towards their locally recruited staff. Two of the three companies who feature in this chapter proved to be exponents of such prejudice; their dismissiveness was an unmistakable element of this discourse. Those same two companies did not appear to be aware of their negative attitudes. The attitude – and corrective practices – of Company C revealed that this company was sensitive to powerful socio-cultural undercurrents which the other two appeared not to discern.

Our modest case material therefore highlights some significant HR messages for foreign corporations operating in CEE countries:

- An arrogant or dismissive attitude to local employers can blind outsider firms to important underlying trends which are products of complex motivations.
- HR procedures, no matter how well tested in other countries, may need to be bolstered with region-specific initiatives for embracing *inalienable* local aspirations.
- Firms that pride themselves on their strong corporate image without a modified approach to employer branding restrict their chances of understanding – and therefore tapping into – talent pools of special, developable skills.

Finally, we state our conviction that a TM policy that does not or cannot identify worthwhile talent in a potential workforce of millions of well-educated people does not have the right to call itself by that name.

Notes

1　A Russian dictionary from the Soviet period defines 'nomenklatura cadres' as 'workers [*rabotniki*], personally appointed by the highest authorities' (Ozhegov, 1984), which in the Soviet context would be unambiguous in its connotations.
2　http://www.wdf.at/content/site/home/newsstudien/article/258.html

References

Aguilar, F., Loveman, C. and Vlachoutsicos, C. (1994). *The Managerial Challenge in Central and Eastern Europe*. Boston, Mass.: Harvard Business School working paper, 95–141.

Alas, R. and Svetlik, I. (2004). Estonia and Slovenia: Building Modern HRM Using a Dualist Approach. In Brewster, C., Mayrhofer, W., and Morley, M. *Human Resource Management in Europe: Evidence of Convergence?*. Oxford: Elsevier Butterworth-Heinemann, pp. 353–384.

Allen, G. (2003). Rethinking Hofstede: Intercultural Management in Poland. *Transformations in Business and Economics*, Vol. 2, No. 2 (4).

Bangert, D. and Poor, J. (1993). Foreign involvement in the Hungarian economy: its impact on human resource management, *International Journal of Human Resource Management*, 4(4): 817–40.

Brewster, C., Mayrhofer, W. and Morley, M. (2000). *New Challenges for European Human Resource Management*. London: Macmillan.

Brewster, C., Mayrhofer, W. and Morley, M. (2004). *Human Resource Management in Europe: Evidence of Convergence?* Oxford: Elsevier Butterworth-Heinemann.

Brewster, C. (1995). Towards a 'European' model of human resource management. *Journal of International Business Studies*, 26(1): 1–21.

Briscoe, D. (2008). Talent management and the global learning organization. In Vaiman, V. and Vance, C.M. (eds.) *Smart Talent Management: Building Knowledge Assets for Competitive Advantage*. Cheltenham: Edward Elgar Publishing Limited.

Crampton, R.J. (2004) *Eastern Europe in the Twentieth Century*. London: Routledge.

Crow, M. (1998). Personnel in transition: The case of Polish women personnel managers. *Personnel Review*, 27(3): 243–61.

Dalton, K. and Kennedy, L. (2007). Management culture in Romania: Patterns of change and resistance. *Journal for East European Management Studies*. Vol.12, No. 3, pp. 232–259.

Davies, N. (1984). *God's Playground: A History of Poland*. Oxford: Oxford University Press.

Davies, N. (2007). *Europe East and West*. London: Pimlico.

The Economist (2006). Survey of Poland. 12–9 May.

The Economist (2009). Central and Eastern Europe: No panic, just gloom. 14 May.

Eyal, G., Szelényi, I. and Townsley, E. (1998). *Making Capitalism without Capitalists: Class Formation and Elite Struggles in Post-communist Central Europe*. New York: Verso.

Fey, C.C., Björkman, I. and Pavlovskaya, A. (2000). The effect of human resource management practices on firm performance in Russia. *International Journal of Human Resource Management*, 11, 1, 1–18.

Fink, G., Holden, N.J. and Lehmann, M. (2007). Survival by subversion in former socialist economies. In Hutchings, K. and Mohannak, K. (eds). *Knowledge Management in Developing Countries: A Cross-cultural and Institutional Approach*. Cheltenham: Edward Elgar, pp. 35–51.

Funder, A. (2004). *Stasiland: Stories from Behind the Berlin Wall*. London: Granta Books.

Glazer, J. (n.d.). *Trends in Eastern Europe Public Employment Services Concerning New Services*. Retrieved 1 December, 2009, from http://www.ess.gov.si/eng/CurrentNews/25–5–01govor.htm.

Heinegg, A., Melzig, R., and Sprout, R. (2007). *Labor Markets in Eastern Europe and Eurasia*. USAID Working Paper series on the transition countries, No. 6. Washington D.C.: USAID.

Hofstede, G. (2007). Culture: organizations, personalities and nations. *European Journal of International Management*, Vol. 1, Nos. 1/2, pp.14–22.

Holden, N.J. (2002). Central Europe: A precarious playground of business cultures. Keynote address at CEI (Central Europe Initiative) Summit Economic Forum, Skopje, November.

Hollinshead, G. (2010). *International and Comparative Human Resource Management*. London: McGraw-Hill.

Hroch, M. (2000). Central Europe – The rise and fall of an historical region. In Lord, *Central Europe: Core or Periphery?* Copenhagen: Copenhagen Business School Press, pp. 21–34.

Hurt, M. and Hurt, S. (2005). Transfer of managerial practices by French retail food retailers to operations in Poland. *Academy of Management Executive*. Special issue on the global transfer of management knowledge, pp. 36–48.

International Labour Organization (2007). *Labour Markets in Central and South Eastern Europe: Positive Trends, Persisting Problems and New Challenges*. Retrieved 1 December, 2009, from http://www.ilo.org/global/About_the_ILO/Media_and_public_information/Press_releases/langen/WCMS_082184/index.htm.

Kiriazov, D., Sullivan, S.E. and Tu, H.S. (2000). Business success in Eastern Europe: understanding and customizing HRM, *Business Horizons*, 43(1): 39–43.

Knez, M. and Ruse, D. H. (2004). Optimizing your investment in your employees. In Berger, L.A. and Berger, D.R. (eds) *The Talent Management Handbook*, New York: McGraw-Hill.

Koubek, J. and Brewster, C. (1995). Human resource management in turbulent times: HRM in Czech Republic, *International Journal of Human Resource Management*, 6(2): 223–47.

Koubek, J. and Vlachtova, E. (2004). HRM in Bulgaria and Czech Republic. In Brewster, C., Mayrhofer, W. and Morley, M. *Human Resource Management in Europe: Evidence of Convergence?* Amsterdam: Elsevier.

Lord, C. (2000). Editor's note in Lord, C. *Central Europe: Core or Periphery?* Copenhagen: Copenhagen Business School Press.

Martens, B. (2008). East German economic elites and their companies two decades after the transformation ('Wende'): Still following the patterns of the 1990s. *Journal for East European Management Studies*. Vol. 13, No. 4, pp. 305–326.

May, R., Young, C.B. and Ledgerwood, D. (1998). Lessons from Russian human resource management experience. *European Management Journal*, 16(4): 447–60.

Mills, A. (1998). Contextual influences on human resource management in the Czech Republic. *Personnel Review*, 27(3): 177–99.

Ozhegov, S. I. (ed.) (1984). *Slovar' russkogo yazyka*. Moscow: Russkii Yazyk.

Preveden, V. (2003). *Perspectives of Leadership in CEE: Summary of Results of the Leadership Study*. Zagreb: Roland Berger Strategy Consultants.

Puffer, S.M. (1993). Three factors affecting reward allocations in the former USSR. *Research in Personnel and Human Resources Management*, 3: 279–98.

Sarapata, A. (1992). Society and Bureaucracy. In Connor, W.D. and Ploszajski P. (eds) *Escape from Socialism*. Warsaw: IFIS Publishers.

Sebestyen, V. (2009). *Revolution 1989: The Fall of the Soviet Empire*. London: Wiedenfeld and Nicolson.

Shekshnia, S. (1998). Western Multinationals' Human Resource Practices in Russia. *European Management Journal*, 16(4): 460–5.

Schoemaker, M. and Jonker, J. (2005). Managing intangible assets: An essay on organizing contemporary organizations based upon identity, competencies and networks. *The Journal of Management Development*, 24(5/6): 506–518.

Soulsby, A. and Clark, E. (1998). Controlling personnel: management and motive in the transformation of the Czech enterprise. *International Journal of Human Resource Management*, 9(1): 79–98.

Svejnar, J. (2002). Transition economies: Performance and challenges. *The Journal of Economic Perspectives*, 16(2): 3–28.

Tarique, I. and Schuler, R. (forthcoming) Global talent management: literature review, integrative framework, and suggestions for further research. *Journal of World Business*.

Taylor, D. and Walley, E.L. (2002). Hijacking the holy grail? Emerging HR practices in Croatia. *European Business Review*, 14(4): 294–303.

Touiller, J. (2009). *The Human Resources Agenda for CEE and CIS: Trends, Challenges, and Opportunities, 2009–2014*. The Amrop Hever Group.

Tung, R.L. and Havlovic, S.J. (1996). Human resource management in transitional economies: The case of Poland and the Czech Republic. *International Journal of Human Resource Management*, 7(1): 1–19.

Vlachoutsicos C. and Lawrence, P. (1990). What we don't know about Soviet management. *Harvard Business Review*, November–December: 50–63.

Weinstein, M. and Obloj, K. (2002). Strategic and environmental determinants of HRM innovations in post-socialist Poland. *International Journal of Human Resource Management*, 13 (4): 642–659.

Zupan, N. and Kase, R. (2005). Strategic human resource management in European transition economies: building a conceptual model on the case of Slovenia. *The International Journal of Human Resource Management*, 16 (6): 882–906.

Zupan, N. (1998). Human resource management in Slovenia. *Journal of Human Resource Management*, 1(1): 13–32.

Index